Rethinking Biblical Literacy

Rethinking Biblical Literacy

Edited by
Katie Edwards

Bloomsbury Academic
An imprint of Bloomsbury Publishing Plc

B L O O M S B U R Y
LONDON • NEW DELHI • NEW YORK • SYDNEY

Bloomsbury T&T Clark

An imprint of Bloomsbury Publishing Plc

Imprint previously known as T&T Clark

50 Bedford Square
London
WC1B 3DP
UK

1385 Broadway
New York
NY 10018
USA

www.bloomsbury.com

BLOOMSBURY, T&T CLARK and the Diana logo are trademarks of Bloomsbury Publishing Plc

First published 2015

© Katie Edwards with contributors, 2015

British Library Cataloguing-in-Publication Data

A catalogue record for this book is available from the British Library.

ISBN: HB: 978-0-56740-321-6
PB: 978-0-56705-098-4
ePUB: 978-0-56752-108-8
ePDF: 978-0-56765-751-0

Library of Congress Cataloging-in-Publication Data

Rethinking biblical literacy / edited by Katie Edwards.
pages cm
ISBN 978-0-567-40321-6 (hbk)– ISBN 978-0-567-05098-4 (pbk)– ISBN 978-0-567-52108-8 (epub)– ISBN 978-0-567-65751-0 (epdf) 1. Bible–Criticism, interpretation, etc. I. Edwards, Katie, 1974- editor.
BS511.3.R4685 2015
220.09'051–dc23
2014038151

Typeset by Fakenham Prepress Solutions, Fakenham, Norfolk NR21 8NN
Printed and bound in India

DISCLAIMER

Every effort has been made to trace copyright holders and to obtain their permission for the use of copyright material. The publisher apologizes for any errors or omissions there may be and would be grateful if notified of any corrections that should be incorporated in future editions of this book.

CONTENTS

Introduction ix

Part 1   Located Literacies

1   Biblical Literacy: The Irish Situation   Máire Byrne (Milltown Institute) 3

2   What the Bible Really Means: Biblical Literacy in English Political Discourse   James G. Crossley (University of Sheffield) 23

3   The Quest for Biblical Literacy: Curricula, Culture and Case Studies   Iona Hine (University of Sheffield) 47

Part 2   Visual Literacies

4   Loss of the Bible and the Bible in *Lost*: Biblical Literacy and Mainstream Television   Matthew A. Collins (University of Chester) 71

5   Streetwise About the Bible: Unexpected Allusions (to the Text) in Unusual Places   Amanda Dillon (Mater Dei Institute) 95

6   Mary, Mary, Quite Contrary: Eve as Redemptrix in Madonna's 'Girl Gone Wild'   Alan W. Hooker (University of Exeter) 119

7   Biblical Literacy and *The Simpsons*   Robert J. Myles
    (University of Auckland) 143

Part 3   Popular Literacies

8   Lisbeth and Leviticus: Biblical Literacy and *The Girl
    with the Dragon Tattoo*   Caroline Blyth (University of
    Auckland) 165

9   A Big Room for Poo: Eddie Izzard's Bible and the Literacy
    of Laughter   Christopher Meredith (University of
    Winchester) 187

Index 213

INTRODUCTION

At the time of publication it seems we are experiencing renewed attention to the Bible in the media. The year 2014 saw the much-hyped release of Noah and Ridley Scott's *Exodus: Gods and Kings* to a deluge of media surrounding their 'accuracy' as a biblical films. Not content with a big-budget Hollywood epic, the UK TV channel ITV began work on a series based on the biblical flood story, and in the run up to Easter 2014 UK Prime Minister David Cameron outed himself as 'evangelical' in flurry of seasonal messages and claimed that 'Jesus invented the Big Society 2,000 years ago'. The American Bible Society also released its annual State of the Bible report to the press, this year distinguishing between 'Bible lovers and sceptics', with the lovers defined as those 'engaged with the Bible' who 'Believe the Bible is the actual or Inspired Word of God with no factual errors, or believe the Bible is the Inspired Word of God with some factual errors. Bible lovers, the society explains, read the book at least four times per week. Bible sceptics, on the other hand: 'Selected the most negative or non-sacred view ... saying they believe the Bible is just another book of teachings written by men, containing stories and advice'. The report warns, 'now there are just as many Americans sceptical of the Bible as there are engaged with the Bible' and that '50% of all adults believe the Bible has too little influence in society'. The UK-based Bible Society also released its latest research on biblical literacy to the press in early 2014. It warned that knowledge of the Bible is in decline – alarmingly so – and urged us to 'use it or lose it' to stem the tide of biblical ignorance and illiteracy. The Bible Society's Pass it On campaign to address this fall in levels of biblical literacy encourages parents and grandparents to read Bible stories to children, including via a Bible Bedtime App.

This is a contradictory picture.

Popular culture, then, is in a constant state of retelling, reinterpreting and re-appropriating biblical stories, characters and figures, and yet annual reports from Christian organizations repeatedly warn us of a steep decline in biblical literacy. Could the situation be more complex than the quantitative research has reported to date? After all, despite the findings of the Bible societies, biblical stories are woven into the very fabric of contemporary culture, and despite regular lively debates about levels of biblical literacy, the fundamental question remains: what is 'biblical literacy' and is it possible to measure it? Biblical literacy, it seems, is a contested concept that is used frequently and agreed on rarely. Each interest group has a different definition of what they mean by 'biblically literate', but what they all share in common is a lamentation of its dismaying decline.

This volume intends to complicate and problematize the biblical literacy debate so far. Specialists in the Bible and culture are brought together to discuss the ubiquity of the Bible in popular culture and its impact on biblical literacy. There is no overriding thesis here; the aim of the volume is not to offer a simple counter claim to the prevalent 'biblical literacy in decline' argument but to offer multiple perspectives on the biblical literacies evidenced in popular culture.

PART ONE

Located Literacies

1

Biblical Literacy: The Irish Situation

Máire Byrne (Milltown Institute)

This work seeks to address the current situation of biblical literacy in the Republic of Ireland by looking at the shift from historical world-renowned biblical literacy to a society that although still largely Catholic is, for the most part, quite biblically illiterate.

The historical situation will be briefly laid out, focusing on the early use of biblical texts in Irish society and the early Christian church. Ireland has traditionally been known as the 'Island of Saints and Scholars' (a phrase that originated in the fourth to the tenth centuries) due to the proliferation of missionaries that emanated from the country during this time. The period also saw the production of many illustrated copies of the gospels, such as the Book of Kells.

The modern situation will be examined in light of the dominance of the Catholic church over education (especially at primary and secondary levels) and the attitudes of the hierarchy towards the Bible and biblical studies, particularly in relation to how Catholic religious education at primary and second level addresses the Bible in syllabi and guidelines.

Introduction

There has been very little research conducted into the use and knowledge of the Bible in Ireland. This work will hopefully go some way in setting out a path for future research, especially when it is situated in a book that attempts to delve into alternative ways of looking at literacy in the United Kingdom. Oftentimes, self-examination begins with comparing yourself to the standards set by others, and it is to be hoped that by taking heed of how other countries view and indeed address biblical literacy Ireland may start to embrace the cultural and religious heritage that the Bible and biblical texts have brought.

My impetus for research in this piece is my occupation as a teacher of Religious Education in second-level schools and as a contract lecturer in Biblical Studies and Sacred Scripture in adult and third-level education. Due to the lack of research and data available, it is difficult to avoid anecdotal evidence of the lack of biblical literacy among the Irish. When one examines the influence that the Bible has had on the history and culture of countries such as the United States, the situation in Ireland appears stark.[1]

In most other countries, it would appear a mammoth task to discuss the attitudes of all Christian denominations that may contribute to the biblical literacy of the population of that country. However, in Ireland, any study of biblical literacy must concentrate for the most part on the attitudes and literacy scales of Irish Catholics. It is impossible to quantify the influence that religion has on Irish culture and Irish identity. As a nation, we are defined by others as a Catholic country. In fact, our long and deep-rooted association with Roman Catholicism has become so a part of culture that it is often only when someone who is not familiar with this points out how Catholicism (and religion in general) permeates every part of our day-to-day lives that we take notice. For example, some of the peculiarities that Irish people often pay no attention to are the daily playing of the Angelus bells (a Christian devotion in memory of the Incarnation) on the national radio station and television stations at midday and six o'clock and the banning of the sale of alcohol on Good Friday. Newsreaders on morning news shows often use phrases such as 'God help us' or 'our prayers are with the family'.[2] Despite this unfailing reliance on religious language in everyday life, Ireland has never embraced the Bible as an integral part of our cultural identity, through popular culture or through religion. While membership of the Catholic Church is on the decline and public debate centres on the influence of the church in the wake of recent child abuse scandals, Ireland remains an overwhelmingly Catholic country. According to results from the most recent census of the population, taken in April 2011, 84.2 per cent of people in the Republic of Ireland (or 3.86 million people) described themselves as Roman Catholic.[3] This figure admittedly represents a drop from the 86.8 per cent of the population who did so in the

---

[1]For a comprehensive view of the biblical presence in American culture, see Claudia Setzer and David A. Shefferman (eds), *The Bible and American Culture: A Sourcebook*, London: Routledge, 2011. The book examines various cultural reference points from political speeches to popular songs to illuminate the varied uses of the Bible in American life.

[2]Máire Byrne, 'Rethinking Irish Catholic Identity', in *Studying Faith, Practicing Peace*, Irish Peace Centres), 2010, p. 26.

[3]Central Statistics Office, Ireland, *Profile 7: Religion, Ethnicity and Irish Travellers*, Dublin: Stationery Office, 2012, p. 6.

2006 census but, in actual terms, the 2011 figure is an increase of 179,889, or 4.9 per cent, on the 2006 figure.[4] It stands to reason, therefore, that any examination of biblical literacy needs to start with Irish Roman Catholics' attitudes to the Bible.

Defining biblical literacy

For the purposes of this work and taking into account the lack of any quantitative or qualitative research into biblical literacy in Ireland, I have chosen to take the definition offered by the Bible Literacy Project in the United States.[5] This group is a non-profit organization, founded in 2001, which sees its aims as encouraging and facilitating the academic study of the Bible in public schools. While this is far removed from the Irish situation, a survey conducted in conjunction with the Bible Literacy Project in 2005[6] was mainly educational in its focus in that it addressed teachers and students and spoke about biblical literacy in an educational context, using educational terms. As this is the context where I would see my own work being located, it seemed obvious for the purposes of comparison to use the Bible Literacy Project's definition of biblical literacy or 'Bible Literacy' as a starting point. It is also important for this work that although my research is based on Roman Catholic attitudes to the Bible, the definition of being biblically literate would be Roman Catholic in context. In its qualitative research, the Bible Literacy Project interviewed 41 high school teachers, all of whom were American, but who came from different cultures, religions and educational backgrounds.

In the results of the survey, 40 of the 41 interviewees defined a high school student's biblical literacy in terms of practical Bible knowledge, as referenced in both speech and writing. The teachers defined biblical literacy as basically consisting of four components:

1 Knowing the Bible
2 Being familiar with popular Bible characters
3 Being able to recognize common biblical phrases
4 Being able to connect the knowledge to references in literature.[7]

---

[4]This anomaly, of an increase in numbers and percentage but a drop overall, is because the general population of the Republic increased by 348,404, to 4.58 million between 2006 and 2011.

[5]www.bibleliteracy.org [accessed 8 January 2013].

[6]M. Wachlin, B. R. Johnson and the Biblical Literacy Project, 'Bible Literacy Report: What Do American Teens Need to Know and What Do They Know?', Front Royal, VA: Biblical Literacy Project, 2005, p. 8.

[7]Ibid., p. 19.

More generally in their responses, teachers identified knowledge of the two different testaments, with emphasis being placed on the realization that the Old Testament is also the Jewish holy book and that its text comes from another tradition. Seventeen of the teachers also used the term 'story' in their definition. Others focused on the characters or people in the biblical text in the sense of being able to name them and give some account of their actions in the narratives.[8] It is important to add to this notion that a student would show biblical literacy not through being able to recite biblical verses or by giving a chronological account of the character or event as it happens in the biblical text, but should be able to retell the narrative orally, through a written piece or through use of pictures on a storyboard (dependant on age and normal levels of literacy in the student's principal language). It is noteworthy that many students believe that they are able to retell certain biblical stories, but on examination of their retelling the text is often confused and bears little if any resemblance to the biblical text. A good example of this is to assign the reading of the Genesis creation accounts to a group, preferably as a home assignment for their next class. The majority of the students will not complete the task, believing that they are already familiar with the biblical narrative. When asked to 'retell' the story, students will in the vast majority of cases blend the two accounts, holding on to the idea of the creation of the earth in seven days, the idea that God rested and at some stage created Adam and then Eve from his rib. Most are shocked at the idea that there are two accounts and cannot recall what made them think there was one coherent account. It must be supposed that they were first introduced to the narrative in a children's Bible or similar and had never readdressed it as a more mature individual – someone who would have viewed it as a story with structure.

Added to this definition would be the notion of recognizing a biblical reference in context and making connections with the word or phrase that is used. An oft-used example would be for a student to see the phrase 'turn the other cheek' and to realize that the phrase originated in the Bible and that it has a particular meaning in the biblical context. It should be possible to gauge if a person is biblically literate if he or she is able to link a ritual or event in their denomination to its biblical origins. For example, a Roman Catholic should be able to link the celebration of Mass with the events of the Last Supper as depicted in the gospels. Theological understanding should not be part of the definition, as this is a secondary activity when reading the Bible, even within a faith-based context. It is always, regardless of levels of faith, possible to hear or read a biblical text without hermeneutically engaging with it. If it were not, the text would have no relevance for smaller children or individuals who may not be able to grasp theological message. To understand the text on a theological level, and to appreciate

---

[8]Ibid.

this meaning, you must first understand what the text is saying on a literary level.

My interest in this topic stems from both my academic studies, which have taken place in Ireland, and my job as a secondary school teacher of Religious Education, teaching students in a school with a Catholic ethos governing its day-to-day running and enrolment policy. While my academic work has resulted in a desire for everyone to see how much the biblical texts impact our lives even outside of a religious sphere, my daily interaction with my students (mainly between the ages of 12 and 18) means that I am acutely aware of the pervading sense of biblical illiteracy that exists in our culture. For a country so proud of its rich narrative heritage and a cultural disposition to storytelling and oral traditions, it seems at variance with our cultural identity to know so little about the biblical text, even at the level of storytelling.

Recently, in a first-year class,[9] we were studying the gospels and different depictions of Jesus in each evangelist's account. We had encountered the idea that the Lukan gospel presents us with a picture of a caring and compassionate Jesus and I asked my students to think for a moment before giving me examples of times when Jesus was kind and caring towards others. One student volunteered the information about 'that funeral he was at with Mary where he did the stuff with the water and it was wine and they drank it'. I corrected the student as to the error regarding 'funeral' and enquired whether he had meant to say 'the wedding at Cana' instead. Before he could answer, another student had interjected with the question 'Who's Cana?'

While anecdotal evidence may give scholars (myself included) the impetus to attempt to examine why many Irish teenagers who subscribe to the Catholic Church in ways such as the sacraments know so little about biblical stories and narratives, it is only through careful examination of the path that led to this problem that any cause (or more likely several causes) may be identified. It is only by learning what brought about this illiteracy that a solution may be discussed or begun to be considered. To do this, it is necessary to take a brief look at the historical context of the Bible in Ireland.

Historical context

Very little major work has been conducted on the impact of the Bible in modern Ireland, but there exists excellent work on the historical use of the

---

[9] The 24 students in this class were all 12–13 years old. Not all were Irish citizens, with four having English as a second language, but all were Catholics and all students reported to me that they made their Confirmation in 2012, less than a year before the time of writing.

Bible and its impact on the religion, culture and politics of the country. Fearghus Ó Fearghail's recent work 'The Bible in Ireland' is perhaps the most comprehensive in terms of a chronological overview. Ó Fearghail highlights the fact that for 'nearly sixteen centuries the Bible has been an integral part of the religious and cultural situation of Ireland'.[10]

St Patrick is credited with bringing organized Christianity to Ireland in the early fifth century and his writings highlight how vital the biblical text would have been to his work. He used the Old Latin version and often quoted parts of the Bible directly. Frequently, he employed phrases from the Bible as a normal part of his writing.[11] Jerome's Vulgate was said to have been introduced to Ireland by St Finnian of Moville in the sixth century.[12] Ireland is probably most famous for its use of the Bible in the monasteries that were commonplace in the early days of Irish Christianity. John Ryan notes that 'it would be difficult to overestimate the place which the Bible held in the monastic system of education'.[13] Books of sacred scriptures were often lent between monasteries in order for copies to be made. Scriptoriums[14] would have produced books and manuscripts not only for their own monastery's use but to meet the needs of other monasteries. Normally, the most copied biblical texts would have been the psalms and the gospels. The *Cathach* (c. AD 600), the Psalter that is associated with Colum Cille (St Columba), is the earliest surviving biblical manuscript in Ireland and indeed the earliest example of Irish writing. The *Cathach* contains a Vulgate version of Psalms 30.10–105.13 and has an interpretative heading before each psalm. The text is normally attributed to St Columba, with legend having it that a copy was made of a psalter that had been lent to St Columba by St Finnian. A dispute subsequently arose as to the ownership of the copy. King Diarmait Mac Cerbhaill decreed the judgement 'To every cow belongs her calf; therefore to every book belongs its copy'. Unfortunately, this mediation failed, and the Psalter of St Columba passed into the hands of the O'Donnells after the battle of Cul Dremhne in AD 561.

Probably the best known work of the scriptoriums was the illuminated manuscripts. From the seventh to the ninth centuries, highly talented

---

[10] Fearghus Ó Fearghail, 'The Bible in Ireland', in Salvador Ryan and Breandán Leahy (eds), *Treasures of Irish Christianity: People and Places, Images and Texts*, Dublin: Veritas, 2012, p. 185.

[11] See Thomas O'Loughlin, *Celtic Theology: Humanity, World and God in Early Irish Writings*, London and New York: Continuum, 2000, pp. 25–47 for a thorough study of the use of the Bible in the writing of St Patrick.

[12] Martin Mc Namara, 'The Latin Gospels', in Barbara Aland and Charles Horton (eds), *The Earliest Gospels The Origins and Transmission of the Earliest Christian Gospels: The Contribution of the Chester Beatty Gospel Codex P⁴⁵*, London: T&T Clark International, 2004, p. 99.

[13] John Ryan, *Irish Monasticism*, Shannon: Irish University Press, 1972, pp. 378–9.

[14] The word 'scriptorium' literally means 'a place for writing' and is usually used to refer to a room within a medieval monastery where monastic scribes would have copied manuscripts.

illuminators painstakingly illustrated and decorated biblical manuscripts. The most well-known of these is the Books of Kells, a manuscript codex of the Latin text of the gospels that dates to the ninth century. It is by far the most lavishly decorated of the illuminated manuscripts, using the 'insular' artistic style common to the period.[15] The text is based on the Vulgate but is intermixed with the Old Latin translation. Rather than merely being viewed as beautiful illustrations, the book's illuminations can be seen as just that – as shedding light on the theology and spiritual aspects of the text, or an early form of exegesis. Important words and phrases are emphasized and the text is enlivened with decorated initials and interlinear drawings. Carol Farr highlights that much the Book of Kells' 'decoration functions to control, as well as to facilitate, understanding of text'.[16] For example, there are two full-page illustrations of the temptation and the arrest of Christ in the Book of Kells. In the temptation image (folio 202v)[17] in the Gospel of Luke, Jesus is depicted from the waist up on top of the Temple. To his right is a crowd of people, possibly the disciples, and to the left and below is a black figure of Satan. There is obviously dialogue between the two, as they gesture to each other. Jesus is holding a scroll in his left hand, possibly the Torah or the Pentateuch, which he seems to brandish at Satan. This raises the point that while lay people associated with a church or monastery may have viewed the images, and therefore gained understanding of them in their usual liturgical setting, the presentation of biblical texts such as this temptation scene would, as Farr suggests, lend themselves to a 'primary audience of élite ecclesiastics, possibly in the context of a monastic school or somehow connected with one'.[18]

The Book of Durrow contains an early medieval manuscript copy of the four gospels and is similar to the Book of Kells in its striking images depicted in insular art. It is usually dated to the late seventh century, which is more than a century prior to the Book of Kells, and makes it the earliest surviving fully decorated insular manuscript. It is traditionally associated with the monastery of Durrow, founded by St Colum Cille, giving rise to the belief that the saint created the book. What is interesting for this study, however, is its treatment in the 1600s by its custodian. It was a common notion in medieval hagiography (biographies of saints) that a book written

---

[15] Bernard Meehan, *The Book of Kells: An Illustrated Introduction to the Manuscript in Trinity College, Dublin*, New York: Thames & Hudson, 1994, p. 9.

[16] Carol Ann Farr, *The Book of Kells: Its Function and Audience*, London: British Library, 1997, p. 158.

[17] Cormac Burke, 'The Book of Kells: New Light on the Temptation Scene', in Colum Hourihane (ed.), *From Ireland Coming: Irish Art from the Early Christian to the Late Gothic Period and its European Context*, Princeton, NJ: Index of Christian Art, Department of Art and Archaeology, Princeton University in association with Princeton University Press, 2001, p. 49, with illustration on p. 50.

[18] Farr, *The Book of Kells*, p. 140.

by a saint was impervious to immersion in water.[19] In a translation of the Annals of Clonmacnoise in 1627, Connall MacEochagáin of Lismoyne recorded that the custodian of the Book of Durrow dipped the manuscript in water and gave the water to sick cattle as a cure.[20] This practice would seem to suggest that the Irish lent more credence to the idea of a relic and its purported healing properties than to the importance the biblical text may have had.

Jerome's Vulgate was the version of the Bible read in Ireland by the eleventh century and by the fifteenth century Irish had begun to be used in works such as *Leabhar Breac* (literally translated as 'speckled book'), which is a medieval Irish vellum manuscript containing Middle Irish and Hiberno-Latin writings. This is not a copy of any biblical text, but the work contains biblical quotations and references in the lives of saints, various ecclesiastical legends, hymns, catecheses and homilies. It is not recorded, but it seems likely that in the sixteenth and early seventeenth centuries, the Protestant translations of the Bible into English, which concluded with the King James Bible (1611), and the Catholic Douai-Rheims Bible (1582, 1609) would have circulated in Ireland.

The New Testament was first translated into Irish by the Church of Ireland in the sixteenth century by Uilliam Ó Domhnail and was published in 1602/3.[21] In his translation, Ó Domhnaill used Erasmus's Greek version, the *textus Receptus*, which was published in 1516. He also used the Latin Vulgate and the English Geneva Bible (1560). Demand for this carefully researched translation was not large (only 500 copies were published) and it was widely viewed as 'Protestant' or 'heretical', as it had been subsidized by an Old English, Dublin patrician family, the Usshers, and therefore not appealing to a Catholic audience.[22] While it may initially appear that the Roman Catholic Church was remiss in failing to produce an Irish-language Bible, it would seem that both the Roman Catholic hierarchy and scholars of that time did not see the need for such an undertaking, as anyone literate would have been literate in both Irish and Latin. Latin at this time and indeed for long into the future was the official language of the Roman Catholic Church. As liturgies were said in Latin until after the Second Vatican Council (1962–5), it would hardly have been useful for the lay people to have a copy of the biblical text in the vernacular.

[19] Bernard Meehan, *The Book of Durrow: A Medieval Masterpiece at Trinity College Dublin*, Boulder, CO: R. Rinehart, 1996, p. 14.
[20] Simon Eliot and Jonathan Rose (eds), *A Companion to the History of the Book*, Malden, MA: Blackwell, 2007, p. 484.
[21] Mícheál Mac Craith, 'Reformation Literature, Ireland', in John T. Koch and Antone Minard (eds), *The Celts: History, Life, and Culture*, Santa Barbara, CA: ABC-CLIO, 2012, p. 656.
[22] Ian Hazlett, *The Reformation in Britain and Ireland: An Introduction*, London: T&T Clark, 2003, p. 101.

The eighteenth century saw Cornelius Nary's revised translation of the Douai New Testament (1718, 1719) and Walter O'Kelly's history of the Bible in Irish (1726) as well as some printings of Catholic and Protestant versions of the Bible in both Dublin and Belfast. The number of printings increased in the early part of the nineteenth century. In the years 1810 to 1830, it is estimated that 67,000 Irish-language New Testaments and 25,000 Irish-language bibles were printed in Ireland for distribution among Irish speakers. While parts of the Bible were translated into Irish over the years, it was only in 1981 that a Catholic edition of the Bible in Irish finally appeared – the *Bíobla Naofa* (Holy Bible).[23]

It would seem therefore that the hierarchy of the Roman Catholic Church in Ireland never saw a real need to engage in any translation of the Bible (or even merely the New Testament or Gospels) for two principal reasons. Firstly, the official language of the church was Latin, and anyone who was fluent in this language (presumably only educated people, and more than likely the vast majority who wished to access it were in clerical formation or clergy) would have sufficient access to biblical texts in Latin for their needs. Secondly, the idea that 'Protestants read the Bible' would have been prevalent throughout the history of tensions between Catholics and Protestants, and therefore reading or indeed studying the Bible would have been seen as academically and spiritually less important. This is an idea that I still encounter today in my own work. When I began my undergraduate studies in the Pontifical University in Maynooth in 1997, my courses on Sacred Scripture were awarded fewer marks than those on Dogmatic and Moral Theology.

The modern situation

In the Roman Catholic Church in the Republic of Ireland, it is uncommon for Bible study groups to exist. In choosing what data to survey for this piece, I found it impossible to find Irish-specific church documents on the state of biblical literacy or even the importance of the Bible in liturgical or parish life. Rather than having a text that focused on the negatives and omissions, I chose to examine the Bible in education in Ireland, an area that I am familiar with as part of my occupation, and one that I knew would have substantially more data to survey.

The bible in education

In the Republic of Ireland, children normally attend primary school from 4–12 years of age. They then attend secondary school, where attendance is

---

[23] Pádraig Ó Fiannachta (trans.), *An Bíobla Naofa*, An Sagart: Maigh Nuad, 1981.

compulsory until their 16th birthday. After three years in secondary school they sit the Junior Certificate exam. The Senior Cycle caters for students in the 15 to 18-year age group. It includes an optional Transition Year, which follows immediately after the Junior Cycle. During the final two years of Senior Cycle students take one of three programmes, each leading to a State Examination: the traditional Leaving Certificate, the Leaving Certificate Vocational Programme (LCVP) or the Leaving Certificate Applied (LCA).

Primary education

The primary education sector in the Republic of Ireland includes state-funded primary schools, special schools and private primary schools. The state-funded schools include religious schools, non-denominational schools, multi-denominational schools and Gaelscoileanna (Irish-medium schools). For historical reasons, most primary schools are state-aided parish schools, although this pattern is changing. The state pays the bulk of the building and running costs of state-funded primary schools, but a local contribution is made towards their running costs. Teachers' salaries are paid by the Department of Education and Skills, and the schools are inspected by the department's inspectorate. The vast majority (96 per cent) of primary schools in Ireland are owned and under the patronage of religious denominations and approximately 90 per cent of these schools are owned and under the patronage of the Catholic Church.[24]

In 1999, Martin Kennedy reviewed the then programme for Primary Religious Education in the Republic of Ireland. He noted that the classroom was seen as a place where students engaged with religion in a way that was 'delightful' for them, but that 'the classroom is increasingly the only space where the students so engage with religion'.[25] Kennedy addressed the notion of the 'three islands of religious experience' for children: the school, the home and the parish. Children inhabit these three worlds and in terms of an experience of faith the most influential is that of the school. Increasingly, there is a division of the three 'islands'. Occasionally, the faith expressed in the school bears little or no relation to the faith that is witnessed (or indeed not) in the home or in the parish. In response to this, the current National Catechetical Programme was developed, resulting in the *Alive-O* series.[26] The title of the series was inspired by a phrase of St Irenaeus: '*Gloria Dei vivens homo*' (the glory of God is people fully alive).

---

[24] See www.education.ie [accessed 7 January 2013] for statistics. In 2010, 2,884 primary schools were listed as coming under the patronage of the Roman Catholic Church.

[25] Martin Kennedy, 'Islands apart: The religious experience of children', *The Furrow*, 50 (1999): 527.

[26] The series was first published in Dublin by Veritas and copyright is held by the Irish Episcopal Commission on Catechetics.

In terms of the Bible and knowledge of the biblical narratives, the notion of 'story' is important in the *Alive-O* programme. The majority of the stories in the programme are biblical in origin and are adapted to the comprehension and interest of the students. The story of the Lost Sheep from Luke 15.1–7 forms the core of the celebration of the Sacrament of Reconciliation, and is used in the classroom as a way of bringing the children to an understanding of the love of God. In *Alive-O 3* (for students in First Class, aged six years), the story is told firstly as it appears in the Bible, next from the point of view of the lost sheep and then from the point of view of the shepherd. In *Alive-O 4* (for students in Second Class, aged seven years) it is told from the point of view of the 99 left behind. The biblical text of the story is included in the teacher's handbook to each of the class books.

In each of the handbooks that are designated for teacher use there is a section in the introduction that discusses how to use the Bible with the particular age group the book is aimed at. For the purposes of brief discussion here, the handbook for *Alive-O 6* is used (for Fourth Class, student aged ten years). The title of the piece in this instance is 'Using the Bible with the Middle-Primary Schoolchild'.[27] The piece highlights the importance of the Bible as the Word of God, quoting from *Dei verbum* and noting that the Bible 'has something to say about every human situation'.[28] The text highlights that every lesson or theme that is to be addressed in the course will be accompanied in the teacher's handbook by 'an appropriate biblical text and a short reflection, which provide background information for the teacher'.[29] The justification for this is that the teacher can then approach the experiences of the child from a biblical and Christian standpoint. However, the text then immediately states that 'the biblical texts and reflections preceding each lesson are, of course, meant only for the teacher. They should not be taught to the children'. No rationale is given for this decision, though it is presumably linked with the text's initial statement that the biblical texts should be presented in an age- and developmental-appropriate manner. No reference is made to the use of a children's Bible or to any additional materials, such as online materials or animations of biblical texts.

The guidelines do encourage reverence for the Bible by suggesting a special place in the classroom where the Bible may be kept open, or a 'Bible Processional Ritual' that may be done in 'simple' or 'solemn' form. The methods for both forms are given much detail. The simple form is that 'a child takes the Bible from its place in the classroom and proceeds

[27] Peter O'Reilly, Clare Maloney, Elaine Campion and Jeanette Dunne, *Alive-O 6: Children of God: Teacher's Book for Fourth Class/Primary Six – a Re-Presentation of Grow in Love*, Dublin: Veritas, 2002, pp. 30–1.

[28] Ibid., p. 30.

[29] Ibid.

to a table where the Bible is placed reverently. The child bows and returns to his/her seat'.[30] The solemn form involves a procession with suggestions that children carry an unlit candle, flowers, incense stick or a cloth. The procession ends at a table where the items are placed, children bow and return to their seats. There are suggestions for hymns to be sung.[31]

This gives the impression that even among middle-primary children the idea is perpetuated that ritual and communal worship or celebration is the key to accessing the biblical texts and the message they contains rather than actually reading the Bible. This would fit into the idea that Irish Catholicism is very sacramental in its identity, perhaps harking back to the Penal Laws (1695–1829), when the British authorities attempted to forbid participation in the sacraments. Irish identity and its intricate link with Catholicism and participation in the sacraments would most likely stem from here.[32] I often ask my students (both teenagers and adults) where they might hear the Bible being read. Younger children sometimes suggest that their grandparents (or, in fewer cases, parents) might tell them about it or tell them some Bible stories, while the majority say 'at Mass'. When questioned further, they invariably confuse the Lectionary with the Bible.

Secondary schools

The post-primary education sector comprises secondary, vocational, community and comprehensive schools. Secondary schools are privately owned and managed. Vocational schools are state established and administered by Vocational Education Committees (VECs), while community and comprehensive schools are managed by Boards of Management of differing compositions. For schools with a Roman Catholic ethos, there are two choices for Religious Education. The document *Towards a Policy on RE in Post-Primary Schools* published by the Irish Catholic Bishops' Conference states that 'In non-examination classes Religious Education should be allocated a *minimum of two hours per week*'.[33] Therefore, if a school is a Catholic secondary school, students must either sit Religious Education as an examination subject, and/or have two classes of Religious Education a week for the duration of their time in the school, regardless of the age of the child. In looking at the inclusion of the Bible and instruction in the biblical texts, it is worth examining the two areas of teaching: examination and non-examination Religious Education.

---

[30] Ibid., p. 31.
[31] Ibid.
[32] Ted G. Jelen and Clyde Wilcox, *Religion and Politics in Comparative Perspective: The One, the Few, and the Many*, Cambridge: Cambridge University Press, 2002, p. 48.
[33] Irish Catholic Bishops' Conference, *Towards a Policy on RE in Post-Primary Schools*, Dublin: Veritas, 2003, p. 3.

Religious Education as an examined subject
The Junior Certificate

In 2012, 28,605 students sat the Religious Education examination paper in the Junior Certificate. This equates with just over 49 per cent of all students sitting the examinations taking the paper.[34] The Religious Education syllabus is quite broad and encompasses much information from Judaism, Christianity and Islam as well as introductory material on Hinduism and Buddhism. The syllabus is designed not to be faith based and not to examine any personal experience of faith a student may have. In this way, it is open to students of all faiths or those with none.

In terms of the biblical content of the syllabus, nowhere in the 47 pages of the document is the word 'Bible' used, nor is Qur'an, Tanakh, scripture or any other generic reference to a sacred or religious text. However, one of the key aims of the section devoted to 'The Foundations of Religion-Christianity' is 'to identify the Gospels as the main source of knowledge about Jesus'.[35] The educational rationale on the content of the course is not, however, to instruct any student on the doctrine of any particular faith, but rather to 'foster an understanding and critical appreciation of the values ... which have been distinctive in shaping Irish society and which have traditionally been accorded respect in society'.[36] There is the very welcome focus on seeking to promote 'an understanding and appreciation of why people believe, as well as tolerance and respect for the values and beliefs of all'.[37] One of the principal aims of Religious Education is stated as 'to identify how understandings of God, religious traditions, and in particular the Christian tradition, have contributed to the culture in which we live'.[38] In the five aims that are set out here, Christianity is the only religion that is mentioned by name and reference is made to the 'non-religious interpretation of life'.

When my Junior Certificate students are introduced to the Bible, usually within three or four months of starting the programme, I ask that they write down what they already know about the Bible anonymously on a sticky note and we put them on a board so that we can compare answers and check for common knowledge. This exercise also allows me to keep the notes. In 2013, the results were what I have come to expect. Out of a class of 24 students[39] three wrote that they knew nothing about the Bible.

---

[34] www.examinations.ie [accessed 5 January 2013].
[35] National Council for Curriculum and Assessment (Ireland), *Junior Certificate Religious Education (Ordinary and Higher Level)*, Dublin: Stationery Office, 2000, p. 14.
[36] Ibid., p. 3.
[37] Ibid., p. 4.
[38] Ibid., p. 5.
[39] Mixed boys (18) and girls (6); 22 were Catholic and made their Confirmation in 2012, less than 8 months before conducting this exercise. All would have attended a primary school with a Catholic ethos. Two students were Muslim but would have attended a primary school with a Catholic ethos.

Only two described it in clearly negative terms: one described it as 'very boring' and one 'too long'. One student described it as 'very long and has big words', which one has to presume would be negative for a 12 year old. Eleven students used the word 'story' or 'stories' somewhere on their note, mainly stories about Jesus, though one student wrote 'it is the story of Christianity'. Ten used the word 'holy' or 'sacred'. Sixteen used the word 'Jesus', while five used the word 'God'. One student wrote only 'Jesus got killed on a cross'. Several made reference to the idea that the Bible had two parts and four mentioned the Gospels. One student summarized: 'it's all about God and Jesus and you learn about their lives and other stuff', which as a biblical scholar is as succinct a definition as you will ever find. No student made any reference to having read the Bible or having encountered it in any form. No reference was made to any biblical 'character' other than God or Jesus and no mention was made of who composed the Bible. No student mentioned any specific event or narrative in the text. This finding would be typical for students I have encountered and anecdotal evidence among teachers would confirm this. As yet in the Republic of Ireland, there has been no further study on the religious knowledge of students of any age.

Obviously, it is impossible to thoroughly examine every Junior Certificate student to assess his or her knowledge of the Bible and biblical texts, but it could be safely assumed on examining the syllabus that this knowledge would be learned by students by the end of their three-year programme and final examination. The syllabus is paired with *Guidelines for Teachers*, published by the Department of Education and the National Council for Curriculum and Assessment, and offers support for teachers as well as an encouragement to use a wide range of teaching and learning methodologies and cross-curricular links with the programme. The guide also helps teachers and departments plan a Religious Education programme over three years.

The Guidelines offer much more in terms of the content of material on the Bible and its context that the syllabus does. The layout of the Guidelines is very practical and tends to treat each section with suggested lesson plans and ways in which students' understanding and learning may be assessed. In the section that was referenced above in the syllabus on gospels ('Evidence about Jesus'), there is a note for teachers on the versions or translations of the Bible to be used in class. It notes 'while any edition of scripture can be used in class, it is intended that questions in the exami-nation will draw on three: The Good News Bible, The Jerusalem Bible and the New Revised Standard Version'.[40] The reassurance is given that if any biblical text is to appear in an exam, the quote will be given in the three versions. In comparing how the synoptic gospels address the miracle of

---

[40] National Council for Curriculum and Assessment (Ireland), *Religious Education: Junior Certificate: Guidelines for Teachers*, Dublin: Stationery Office, 2001, p. 39.

Jesus calming the storm, the Guidelines suggest using three different voices to read the Gospel accounts (Mt. 8.18–27; Mk. 4.35–41; Lk. 8.22–5). The students are then asked to silently reread the accounts underlining words that are in common in one colour and words that are particular to a gospel with a different colour. When this information has been gathered and visually displayed by the teacher, the teacher is encouraged to facilitate the students in formulating generalizations or inferences about the context, the intended audience, the character of Jesus and the reasons for having such different stories.

In the section looking at Communities of Faith and the Founder of Judaism, the planned lesson revolves around group work and the Hebrew Bible. Each group is given either a Bible reference or a Bible story that has been depicted in words or pictures, which contains an account of one of 13 characters from the 'Hebrew Testament', as the text terms it on four occasions.[41] Each group then reads the life story and produces a storyboard with key events in the life of that person. Some of the characters include Abraham, Isaac, Moses, Solomon, Isaiah, Daniel and one female, Ruth.

It would seem to do little to increase biblical literacy for there only to be two concrete references to examining the biblical text in the syllabus. There is no reference to students being introduced to any other sacred text, such as the Qur'an or the Tanakh. Introductory material is covered on both these sacred texts, but considering that Christianity is deemed to be of particular interest, it would seem strange that more is not included on the Bible.

All textbooks introduce how to look up biblical references. Only one child in my three classes of first-year Religious Education this year – from a Christian denomination that values daily Bible reading – knew how to look up a biblical reference. His being able to look up the biblical references and his biblical knowledge made him a valuable resource to the other students, who looked to him for help, many boggling at the fact that he knew some of the biblical verses cited on their worksheet by heart.

The Leaving Certificate

At Senior Cycle, the Department of Education now provides two programmes for Religious Education:

a) a non-examination programme, which was introduced in 2005, and
b) the Leaving Certificate Religious Education syllabus (LCRE), which may be taken as an optional subject since September 2003.

In 2012 1,186 students sat the Leaving Certificate Religious Education paper. Compared to the number sitting English in the same year (50,517), only a

---

41 Ibid., pp. 47–8.

few decide to take Religious Education as an exam subject. Reasons for this are varied, including that it is not offered by all schools, most likely due to timetabling reasons. One of the optional sections of the coursework in this programme is dedicated to the Bible, under the title of 'The Bible: Literature & Sacred Text'. The inclusion of the Bible under this option means that it is possible to cover the syllabus without covering this topic, in which case the Bible would be minimal on the syllabus. Options may be covered for the exam or for pre-exam coursework that counts to the final grade. The aims of this syllabus in relation to the study of the Bible are quite wide and encompassing:

1   To explore how the Bible has functioned as a literary and sacred text since its formation.
2   To examine the impact of the Bible on contemporary society.
3   To examine how the Bible was formed as a text.
4   To introduce the variety of literary genres found in the Bible.
5   To explore the understanding of the Bible as Word of God and as expression of the relationship between God and humankind.[42]

In terms of non-examination Religious Education in the Senior Cycle, the Department of Education and the National Council for Curriculum and Assessment devised a Curriculum Framework Senior Cycle which recommends topics to be covered over whichever Senior Cycle programme the school offers. The framework has been designed with particular sensitivity to the variety of contexts in which it may be used – religious, social, school ethos, etc. In exposing students to a broad range of religious issues, religious traditions and ways of understanding the human search for meaning, the framework aims to contribute to the spiritual and moral development of students from all faiths and none. It wishes to help develop a healthy respect for the beliefs of others and openness to dialogue in search of mutual understanding. There is only one section on the Bible and sacred texts in this plan. Section H, 'Story', seeks to understand the 'power of story' to communicate truth on several levels, to explore the meaning of 'truth' in the Bible or another sacred text and finally to explore the transformative power of story past and present.[43] One of the exploration options for the section is to invite a Scripture scholar to talk to the class about modern approaches to reading sacred texts.[44]

The philosophy and rationale behind any inclusion of the biblical text in any programme of Religious Education is well meaning and to a certain

---

[42] National Council for Curriculum and Assessment (Ireland), *Leaving Certificate Religious Education Syllabus (Ordinary and Higher Levels)*, Dublin: Stationery Office, 2003, p. 75.
[43] National Council for Curriculum and Assessment (Ireland), *Framework Document for Senior Cycle Non-Examination Religious Education*, Dublin: Stationery Office, 2005, p. 168.
[44] Ibid., p. 168.

degree well thought out. However, there seems to be little effort made to build any knowledge or learning on what has actually taken place in a child's previous learning. There appears little or no coherency between primary education and its focus on story to secondary Religious Education, which for the most part presumes an ability to look up Bible verses or to know the basic structure of the Bible in terms of testaments. There is no sign in what is studied by the vast majority of students (Leaving Certificate-examined Religious Education aside) of any link being made with English (or even Irish) literature. The basis of English language in the Bible seems to be for the most part left aside, which in our definition of biblical literacy would appear a major failing.

Conclusion

Irish identity, whether the Irish like it or not, is inherently entangled with a Roman Catholic identity. Much public debate now centres on the relationship and influence of church over state and vice versa, especially concerning the current debate over abortion legislation.[45] Despite its beginnings as a country that had immense respect for and devotion to study of the biblical texts, the historical events that have shaped Irish cultural and religious identities have caused knowledge of the Bible and hence biblical literacy to suffer to the extent that Roman Catholics have little biblical knowledge beyond what they encounter in an educational setting.

It would be simplistic to hypothesize that if only there had not been British rule and the presence of Protestant denominations, then Ireland would have continued merrily along the path set out by the early monks who illuminated manuscripts. Perhaps the key to this is in the term often used for Ireland during the period AD 400–800 – the 'land of saints and scholars'. The phrase is normally used to depict the prevalence of saints and monasteries that existed at the time, but in my opinion it is indicative of the relationship that existed and still exists with the biblical text; namely that it is something that is only studied in an academic sense and rarely allowed to enter 'normal' life, where literacy is more easily gained.

Even in primary school, students are moved away from the biblical text, encouraged to see it as a 'holy' or 'sacred' book that has little meaning in their own lives. This continues throughout the education system, where little effort is made to show how the Bible permeates much of our culture and literature. Instead, the emphasis is placed on knowing the stories and narratives of the biblical text. However, this does little good when the student reaches the stage where he or she can engage with more theological

---

[45] Stephen Collins, 'Church's Abortion Broadside a Challenge to Democracy', *Irish Times*, 5 January 2013.

investigations of these narratives, as no link is made between the two. The tendency in terms of biblical literacy at least appears to allow literacy to develop towards the level of a child's understanding and recall, but does little to engender a more mature understanding and even critical engagement with the text. Without creating an association between the Bible and popular culture, even at the level of literature, without having to stray to the ever-changing cultures of music and social media, the impact and resonance of the biblical text is lost. While this obviously is a small matter in terms of the greater understanding of etymology and meaning in texts students may study, it seems anomalous that in programmes of Religious Education that do not hesitate in highlighting their Catholic identity greater emphasis is not placed on this essential area of biblical literacy.

Bibliography

Burke, Cormac, 'The Book of Kells: New Light on the Temptation Scene', in Colum Hourihane (ed.), *From Ireland Coming: Irish Art from the Early Christian to the Late Gothic Period and its European Context*, Princeton, NJ: Index of Christian Art, Department of Art and Archaeology, Princeton University in association with Princeton University Press, 2001, pp. 49–60.

Byrne, Máire, 'Rethinking Irish Catholic Identity', *Studying Faith, Practicing Peace*, Irish Peace Centres, 2010, pp. 25–8.

Central Statistics Office, Ireland, *Profile 7: Religion, Ethnicity and Irish Travellers*, Dublin, Ireland: Stationery Office, 2012.

Collins, Stephen, 'Church's Abortion Broadside a Challenge to Democracy', *Irish Times*, 5 January 2013.

Eliot, Simon and Jonathan Rose (eds), *A Companion to the History of the Book*, Malden, MA: Blackwell, 2007.

Farr, Carol Ann, *The Book of Kells: Its Function and Audience*, London: British Library, 1997.

Hazlett, Ian, *The Reformation in Britain and Ireland: An Introduction*, London: T&T Clark, 2003.

Irish Catholic Bishops' Conference, *Towards a Policy on RE in Post-Primary Schools*, Dublin: Veritas, 2003.

Jelen, Ted G. and Clyde Wilcox, *Religion and Politics in Comparative Perspective: The One, the Few, and the Many*, Cambridge: Cambridge University Press, 2002.

Kennedy, Martin, 'Islands apart: The religious experience of children', *The Furrow*, 50 (1999): 527–33.

Mac Craith, Michéal, 'Reformation Literature, Ireland', in John T. Koch and Antone Minard (eds), *The Celts: History, Life, and Culture*, Santa Barbara, CA: ABC-CLIO, 2012, pp. 656–7.

Mc Namara, Martin, 'The Latin Gospels', in Barbara Aland and Charles Horton (eds), *The Earliest Gospels The Origins and Transmission of the Earliest Christian Gospels: The Contribution of the Chester Beatty Gospel Codex P[45]*, London: T&T Clark International, 2004, pp. 88–206.

Meehan, Bernard, *The Book of Kells: An Illustrated Introduction to the Manuscript in Trinity College, Dublin*, New York: Thames and Hudson, 1994.

—*The Book of Durrow: A Medieval Masterpiece at Trinity College Dublin*, Boulder, CO: R. Rinehart, 1996.

National Council for Curriculum and Assessment (Ireland), *Junior Certificate Religious Education (Ordinary and Higher Level)*, Dublin: Stationery Office, 2000.

—*Religious Education: Junior Certificate – Guidelines for Teachers*, Dublin: Stationery Office, 2001.

—*Leaving Certificate Religious Education Syllabus (Ordinary and Higher Levels)*, Dublin: Stationery Office, 2003.

—*Framework Document for Senior Cycle Non-Examination Religious Education*, Dublin: Stationery Office, 2005.

Ó Fearghail, Fearghus, 'The Bible in Ireland', in Salvador Ryan and Breandán Leahy (eds), *Treasures of Irish Christianity: People and Places, Images and Texts*, Dublin: Veritas, 2012, pp. 185–7.

Ó Fiannachta, Pádraig (trans.), *An Bíobla Naofa*, An Sagart: Maigh Nuad, 1981.

O'Loughlin, Thomas, *Celtic Theology: Humanity, World and God in Early Irish Writings*, London and New York: Continuum, 2000.

O'Reilly, Peter, Clare Maloney, Elaine Campion and Jeanette Dunne, *Alive-O 6: Children of God: Teacher's Book for Fourth Class/Primary Six – a Re-Presentation of Grow in Love*, Dublin: Veritas, 2002.

Ryan, John, *Irish Monasticism*, Shannon: Irish University Press, 1972.

Setzer, Claudia and David A. Shefferman (eds), *The Bible and American Culture: A Sourcebook*, London: Routledge, 2011.

Wachlin, M., B. R. Johnson and the Biblical Literacy Project, 'Bible Literacy Report: What Do American Teens Need to Know and What Do They Know?', Front Royal, VA: Biblical Literacy Project, 2005; www.bibleliteracy.org/secure/documents/bibleliteracyreport2005.pdf

Websites

www.bibleliteracy.org/secure/documents/bibleliteracyreport2005.pdf [accessed 8 January 2013].

www.education.ie [accessed 7 January 2013].

www.examinations.ie [accessed 5 January 2013].

2

What the Bible Really Means: Biblical Literacy in English Political Discourse

James G. Crossley
(University of Sheffield)

Citing a report by Durham University's Centre for Biblical Literacy and Communication, Philip Davies noted that in Britain there is a notable lack of 'biblical literacy' in the sense of awareness of stories such as the Good Samaritan or figures from the Bible such as Abraham or Joseph.[1] Davies was provoking a debate about whether the cultural baggage of the Bible is a good or bad thing and Hector Avalos responded in praise of biblical *illiteracy*, adding that there has been a long history of it.[2] Of course, and as we will see, Davies and Avalos are not the only ones debating such ideas about biblical literacy and it is not the purpose of this chapter to wade into this debate as such. Instead, I want to change the question. The unifying assumption of these understandings comes close to being Protestant (as Avalos implies) in the sense that biblical literacy is understood as remembering specific details and wording of biblical narratives, in relation to decline. What I want to do is to move this discussion in a different direction and argue that if the assumptions of the debate are changed then the idea that there is a decline in biblical literacy might also be changed. More specifically, I want to argue that we should take seriously the widespread uses of and allusions to the Bible in contemporary culture, even if people cannot recite verses and stories in any precise detail. What I particularly

---

[1] P. Davies, 'Whose Bible? Anyone's?', *Bible and Interpretation*, July 2009.
[2] H. Avalos, 'In Praise of Biblical Illiteracy', *Bible and Interpretation*, April 2010.

want to focus on is the ways in which 'the Bible' is utilized in political discourse and what it is thought to 'really mean'. I will use the example of roughly contemporary British politicians to show that there are major traditions of understanding the Bible, which have an interrelated set of meanings that often precisely match dominant political positions.[3] The actual content of the Bible and biblical texts is close to being irrelevant; what matters is what the Bible *must* mean for political discourse. In many ways this is a decaffeinated Bible, a Bible deprived of its malignant product in order to be made compatible with democratic and largely Enlightenment and post-Enlightenment thought.[4] I will illustrate this with reference to three major assumptions of what the Bible 'really means' in contemporary political discourse: the Liberal Bible, the Cultural Bible and the Radical Bible.

The liberal bible

Looking at George W. Bush's use of the Bible, Yvonne Sherwood coined the phrase the 'Liberal Bible', which she described as an interpretative tradition developing since the sixteenth and seventeenth centuries.[5] The Liberal Bible is an understanding of the Bible as supportive of freedom of conscience, rights, law and consensus, and marks a shift from the Absolute Monarchist's Bible, where decisions made by the monarch were to be seen as proof of divine power. The Liberal Bible has also produced the (mistaken) assumption that the Bible is the foundation, and consonant with the principles, of Western democracies without acknowledging that such a view of the Bible has its roots in sixteenth- and seventeenth-century Europe. The Liberal Bible is able to endorse actions against its constructed opposite: the undemocratic, tyranny and terror, and unsurprisingly it can follow from this anachronistic perspective that the Bible and Jesus are more representative of democracy than the Qur'an and Muhammad. Because of its early modern origins, the Liberal Bible is continually vague. In the case of Bush's speeches, for instance, there were just enough biblical allusions to win key electoral support from Protestant Christians, with the specifics of faith left ambiguous. Indeed, Jacques Berlinerblau has argued that successful American politicians over the past 30 years have always used the Bible in a vague, non-polemical manner in order to signal to the electorate

---

[3] For a wide-ranging history of the Bible in English politics see N. Spencer, *Freedom and Order: History, Politics and the English Bible*, London: Hodder and Stoughton, 2011.

[4] I am alluding to S. Žižek, *The Puppet and the Dwarf: The Perverse Core of Christianity*, Cambridge, MA: MIT Press, 2003, p. 96: 'On today's market, we find a series of products deprived of their malignant property: coffee without caffeine, cream without fat, beer without alcohol …'.

[5] Y. Sherwood, 'Bush's bible as a liberal bible (strange though that might seem)', *Postscripts*, 2 (2006): 47–58.

that the politician is a decent God-fearing person while simultaneously trying to avoid controversial debates about the church/state distinction and a backlash from the liberal media.[6]

The Liberal Bible, along with the related rhetorical moves, is a common feature of all the major British and English politicians.[7] Although Margaret Thatcher placed great stress on interpreting the Bible in light of the developing neoliberalism, as her infamous exegesis of the Good Samaritan illustrates,[8] major features of the Liberal Bible were always and perhaps inevitably present. She claimed that Britain had gradually adopted a 'system of government and a way of living together which reflected the values implicit in that Book [the Bible]' and that 'the teachings of Christ applied to our national as well as personal life'. Thatcher acknowledged that there were 'considerable blotches' in British history but 'thanks to the patience and vision of people like Lord Shaftesbury and William Wilberforce', Parliament could be convinced that 'it was inconsistent for a nation whose life was based on Christ's teachings, to countenance slave labour, children and women working in the mines and criminals locked up in degrading conditions'.[9] Thatcher was, of course, aware that non-Christians were part of British history, particularly in more recent history, and even in her own party and among her own supporters. But this too could be reconciled with the idea of Britain as a country that 'most people would accept' as having a national 'way of life ... founded on Biblical principles'.[10] In her infamous speech to the General Assembly of the Church of Scotland, nicknamed the 'Sermon on the Mound', she argued that 'one of the great principles of our Judaic–Christian heritage is tolerance' but that people 'with other faiths and cultures' have 'always been welcomed' and 'assured of equality under the law, of proper respect and of open friendship ... There is no place for racial or religious intolerance in our creed'.[11]

This was exactly the kind of Bible Tony Blair believed he was also reading.[12] But Blair took positions only implicit in Thatcher's reading of the Bible: that non-Christian scriptures and non-Christian religions can been seen to share the same assumptions and that there might, after all, be some

---

[6] J. Berlinerblau, *Thumpin' It: The Use and Abuse of the Bible in Today's Presidential Politics*, Louisville, KY: Westminster John Knox, 2008.

[7] I have discussed this in detail in J. G. Crossley, *The Bible in English Politics and Culture Since 1968: Rethinking Reception History*, London: T&T Clark/Bloomsbury, forthcoming.

[8] '... no-one would remember the Good Samaritan if he'd only had good intentions; he had money as well'. Transcript available at M. Thatcher and B. Walden, 'TV Interview for London Weekend Television *Weekend World* (1980)'.

[9] M. Thatcher, 'Speech at St Lawrence Jewry', Margaret Thatcher Foundation (4 March 1981).

[10] Ibid.

[11] M. Thatcher, 'Speech to the General Assembly of the Church of Scotland', Margaret Thatcher Foundation (21 May 1988).

[12] For full discussion with bibliography see Crossley, *The Bible in English Politics and Culture*, Chapter 8.

problematic elements of the Bible. Indeed, Blair is aware that there is plenty in the Bible – and 'religion' more generally – which is not so easy to boil down to the essentials required for a modern liberal democracy and so he has focused on 'the values like love of God and love of your neighbour' as the core features of religion rather than 'doctrine and practice': 'one of the things I do through my [Tony Blair Faith] Foundation, through trying to bring different religious faiths together, to show how, actually, there is a huge common space around these values between the different religious faiths'.[13] This, inevitably perhaps, means that Blair is comfortable reading scriptures 'less literally' and 'more metaphorically'. But, in a hermeneutical move also made by Barack Obama in his famous Cairo speech in 2009,[14] there is a flexibility with the biblical texts whereby those controversial aspects for modern liberal democracies can also be problematized, attributed to radically different ancient social contexts, and compared with other alien practices that are not readily endorsed by contemporary Christians in liberal democracies. So, for instance, Blair can claim, in language curiously reminiscent of the so-called antithesis in Matthew (5.21–48) and his own relentless political rhetoric of 'modernizing' Labour from Old to New, that,

> when people quote the passages in Leviticus condemning homosexuality, I say to them – if you read the whole of the Old Testament and took everything that was there in a literal way, as being what God and religion is about, you'd have some pretty tough policies across the whole of the piece … and you've got the Old Testament kings with hordes of concubines, and so on. There's no way that you could take all of that and say, we in the 21st century should behave in that way.[15]

Yet there are still hermeneutical controls for Blair, even within the biblical (and Quranic) texts, though they are effectively general concepts compatible with liberal democratic values, and they involve the classic move towards the figure of Jesus, though Blair now logically has to extend this to include Muhammad. Again, Blair uses an antithetical argument and again these figures are, crucially for Blair's hermeneutic, tolerant and progressive so, no matter what the rest of the biblical and Quranic texts say, the core figures retain the essence of True Religion (and Politics):

> And actually, what people often forget about, for example, Jesus or, indeed, the Prophet Muhammad, is that their whole raison d'être was to change the way that people thought traditionally. Christianity was very

---

[13] J. Hari, 'A Civil Partnership: Interview with Tony Blair', *Attitude*, 8 April 2009, pp. 50–2 (52).
[14] B. Obama, 'Remarks by the President on a New Beginning', The White House: Office of the Press Secretary (2009), http://www.whitehouse.gov/the-press-office/remarks-president-cairo-university-6-04-09
[15] Hari, 'A Civil Partnership', p. 52.

much about saying, no, 'an eye for an eye, a tooth for a tooth' is not the right way to behave. And the Koran was, of course, an extraordinary, progressive – revolutionarily progressive – document for its time. That's why many of the old pagan practices that the Prophet was keen to wean people away from were dispensed with.[16]

David Cameron's inheriting of the Blair mantle likewise saw him adopt elements of the Liberal Bible in this even more social-liberalizing direction and with a particular focus on the ongoing 'de-toxification' of the Conservative Party. Cameron's premiership coincided with a significant celebration that would almost inevitably require him to comment on the Bible: the 400th anniversary of the King James Version in 2011. At the closing of the anniversary Cameron gave a speech where the major features of the Liberal Bible and the exegetical emphases of politicians such as Thatcher and Blair were present. Cameron suggested that Britain can still be understood as a *Christian* nation. What Cameron did not mean was equally important. He did not mean that Britain is, or should become, a theocracy, nor that the British people should all be going to church, singing hymns, praying to God, fasting, dealing with heretics appropriately, vigorously converting non-believers and so on. It would be a great surprise if Cameron did advocate such things given that he described his 'religious faith' as a 'typical member of the Church of England': it 'is a bit like the reception for Magic FM in the Chilterns: it sort of comes and goes'.[17] Instead, Cameron's vision of a Christian nation with the King James Bible at its heart is, as with Blair and Thatcher, a thoroughly liberalized notion of what a multicultural and multi-faith 'Christian country' ought to be, with anything unpalatable to this idea of the nation state removed:

> [From] human rights and equality to our constitutional monarchy and parliamentary democracy ... the first forms of welfare provision ... language and culture ... [T]he Judeo-Christian roots of the Bible also provide the foundations for protest and for the evolution of our freedom and democracy ... [They form] the irrepressible foundation for equality and human rights, a foundation that has seen the Bible at the forefront of the emergence of democracy, the abolition of slavery and the emancipation of women ... Responsibility, hard work, charity, compassion,

---

[16] Ibid.

[17] The full quotation is: 'I believe, you know. I am a sort of typical member of the Church of England. As Boris Johnson once said, his religious faith is a bit like the reception for Magic FM in the Chilterns: it sort of comes and goes. That sums up a lot of people in the Church of England. We are racked with doubts, but sort of fundamentally believe, but don't sort of wear it on our sleeves or make too much of it. I think that is sort of where I am'. See N. Watt and P. Wintour, 'Interview: How David Cameron is Trying to Reinvent the Tories', *Guardian*, 16 July 2008.

humility, self-sacrifice, love, pride in working for the common good and honouring the social obligations we have to one another, to our families and our communities – these are the values we treasure. Yes, they are Christian values. And we should not be afraid to acknowledge that. But they are also values that speak to us all – to people of every faith and none.[18]

Again, it would, presumably, be pointless asking what Cameron would have made of the details about Abishag the Shunammite keeping the ageing David warm in his bed, Joshua's conquest, posting parts of a chopped-up concubine, smashing babies' heads against rocks, labelling Gentiles 'dogs', condemning the rich to Hades, destroying idols, the weeping and gnashing of teeth, or, perhaps more pertinent still, using the King James Bible itself to convert heathens. Instead, the King James Bible and Christian values have to be understood in terms of liberal parliamentary democracy.

Today, this thoroughly liberalized (in both democratic and social terms) Bible is a dominant feature of political discourse and perhaps best illustrated in the parliamentary debate over same-sex marriage in February 2013.[19] Two now perhaps expected examples of biblical support came up: loving the neighbour and the singling out of Jesus. Toby Perkins (Labour, Chesterfield) claimed that 'as a Christian' he had 'no worries about voting for this Bill' because 'what greater example of the equalities agenda could there be than Jesus Christ himself? … Jesus Christ led the way on promoting equalities'. As we will see, there are also echoes of Radical Bible but the confrontational element of the Radical Bible is removed and the Bible is now more about defending victims of oppression which in turn provides the justification for equality: 'There are any number of stories in the Bible that make it absolutely clear that Jesus stuck up for groups that had been oppressed over the years'. The other use of Jesus came from David Lammy (Labour, Tottenham) and likewise we get the shift from Jesus the state criminal to Jesus defending victims of oppression: 'the Jesus I know was born a refugee, illegitimate, with a death warrant on his name, and in a barn among animals. He would stand up for minorities. That is why it is right for those of religious conviction to vote for this Bill'. Lammy also made sure that alternative understandings of the Bible which are not compatible with liberal democracies were assumed to be highly irrelevant: 'those on the extremes of our faith have poisoned what is an important debate with references to polygamy and bestiality'. Tellingly, this is close to the biblical justification for same-sex marriage given by the

---

[18] D. Cameron, 'Prime Minister's King James Bible Speech (16 December 2010)', Number 10 Downing Street.

[19] 'Marriage (Same Sex Couples) Bill', Hansard: Commons Debates (5 February 2013), Columns 125–230.

Conservative MP Peter Bottomley. The 'primary commandment is to love the Lord my God with all my heart, soul, mind and strength', he argued, and claimed that this 'should be used as a way of defining the second great commandment, which is to treat my neighbour as myself'. This was interpreted to mean that 'we are asking whether we can remove the barriers that stop same-sex couples enjoying the commitment – the "at one" meaning – of marriage. That is what the Bill comes down to. It does not redefine marriage; it just takes away barriers'. The Bible of Perkins, Lammy and Bottomley certainly has a contemporary nuance, but it is also part of the ongoing redefinition of the Liberal Bible and remains a Bible deprived of its malignant properties, the Bible shorn of any Otherness problematic for liberal democracy, tolerance and equality. This is what the Liberal Bible 'really means'.

The Cultural Bible

The one assumption that runs through all political persuasions is what we can call, following Jonathan Sheehan, the Cultural Bible.[20] Sheehan has shown in detail how the Enlightenment produced a Bible which was (sometimes contradictorily) a philological and pedagogical resource, a literary classic, a moral guidebook and a historical archive. These different strands were encapsulated by the Cultural Bible and biblical readers and interpreters interacted with developing ideas of secularization. That these developments were taking place at a time of developing nationalism and Orientalism, particularly in the nineteenth century, is of some significance. This Bible was part of 'our' Western culture and civilization and even an English classic. With the implicit nationalism of the Cultural Bible, it is little surprise that it gets repeatedly acknowledged in political discourse. Thatcher, for instance, believed that Britain is 'a nation whose ideals are founded on the Bible' and that this has been 'our very life blood'. This, she claimed, was a heritage which should be 'preserved and fostered'. She made the claim that without such an understanding 'it is quite impossible to understand our history and literature' and that there is a 'strong practical case' for 'ensuring that children at school are given adequate instruction in the part which the Judaic–Christian tradition has played in moulding our laws, manners and institutions'. How else, she asked, can we make sense of Shakespeare or Walter Scott, or seventeenth-century history in England and Scotland, without knowledge of the Bible?[21] She would also recall the story of Mary and Martha through one of her favourite poets, Kipling, as a

---

[20] J. Sheehan, *The Enlightenment Bible: Translation, Scholarship, Culture*, Princeton, NJ and Oxford: Princeton University Press, 2007, pp. 93–258.
[21] Thatcher, 'Speech to the General Assembly of the Church of Scotland'.

means of explaining the apparent practicality of her mother.[22] This Cultural Bible was, Thatcher argued, tied up with the political heritage of her own party. Thatcher explained that the Tory Party was not just a British party but *primarily* a church party whose concerns for church then state were then expanded to other fields such as economics.[23] In this context, Thatcher argued that the values that have driven this tradition were historically rooted in the Bible:

> For through the Old Testament our spiritual roots go back to the early days of civilisation and man's search for God. The New Testament takes us on through Greek philosophy, Roman law, the Church Fathers and the great flowering of a specifically Christian civilisation in the middle ages from which our own characteristic way of life emerged.[24]

This is not simply deference to tradition or an embrace of the importance of 'culture'. Thatcher believed that Tories have 'always believed' in the primacy of the church 'because it was concerned with those things which matter fundamentally to the destiny of mankind'.[25]

In the Age of Coalition, the King James Bible has also continued to survive through an emphasis on the Cultural Bible, which was brought to the fore in the 400th anniversary celebrations. The following are the main aims of the King James Bible Trust, as found in its Mission Statement:

> Reflect the global importance of the King James Bible and the role it has played in spreading the English language around the world.
> Promote events and celebrations throughout 2011 to ensure that as many people as possible can encounter the King James Bible by the year's end.

The Mission Statement concludes:

> The Trust, an education and arts Trust, will highlight and debate the significant contribution that the King James Bible continues to make. Fundamentally the Trust is here to leave a lasting legacy for future generations, by ensuring that this great work of literature and learning is still read and taught in years to come.[26]

---

[22] M. Stoppard and M. Thatcher, 'TV Interview for Yorkshire Television *Woman to Woman* (19 November 1985)', Margaret Thatcher Foundation. On the significance of using the Kipling version, see C. Moore, *Margaret Thatcher: The Authorized Biography, Volume One: Not for Turning*, London: Allen Lane, 2013, p. 9.
[23] Thatcher, 'Dimensions of Conservatism'; Thatcher, 'I Believe'.
[24] Stoppard and Thatcher, 'TV Interview for Yorkshire Television'.
[25] Thatcher, 'I Believe'.
[26] Available at www.kingjamesbibletrust.org/about-us/mission-statement

Developing her own views on the Liberal Bible, Yvonne Sherwood has noted the lack of concern in this Mission Statement for the historic role of the King James Bible in the combination of evangelism and empire.[27] And when the King James Bible Trust mention the King James Bible (and 'religion'), it is not about altars, blood or sacrifice but a very contemporary form of liberal multiculturalism in the form of Liberal or Cultural Holy Scripture: 'The Trust is hard at work developing projects which will include ... [d]iscussions about similar values in the texts of the world's major religions'.[28] The aesthetic and heritage angle was the position taken up by Richard Dawkins (a contributor to the promotional material of the Trust). Whereas the decaffeinating of the Bible – the King James Bible in this instance – is culturally implicit, Dawkins, following a standard New Atheist line, remained happy to be explicit in wanting to highlight any problematic moral elements in the Bible and 'religion'. But once this can be accepted, Dawkins argued:

> I must admit that even I am a little taken aback at the biblical ignorance commonly displayed by people educated in more recent decades than I was ... The King James Bible of 1611 – the Authorized Version – includes passages of outstanding literary merit in its own right ... But the main reason the English Bible needs to be part of our education is that it is a major sourcebook for literary culture ... Surely ignorance of the Bible is bound to impoverish one's appreciation of English literature ... We can give up belief in God while not losing touch with a treasured heritage.[29]

The present and the immediate, coupled with culturally short attention spans, and mapped on to a rapidly changing yet increasingly standardized world, may indeed be a distinctive feature of our postmodern and neoliberal age.[30] However, and probably because of this combination of unsettling, fragmentation and homogenization, it is also an age of individual and collective nostalgia, or, as Mark Fisher put it, 'an age given over to retrospection, incapable of generating any authentic novelty'.[31] Such uses of the King James Bible are clearly present in Cameron's speech, the Mission Statement of the King James Bible Trust and Dawkins' fight against what he perceives to be cultural ignorance.

---

[27] Y. Sherwood, 'This is Not a Bible/Ceci n'est pas une Bible', unpublished paper delivered to the Biblical Literacy and the Curriculum Conference, University of Sheffield, 25–28 May 2011.

[28] Available at http://www.kingjamesbibletrust.org/about-us

[29] R. Dawkins, *The God Delusion*, London: Bantam Press, 2006, pp. 340–1, 343, 344.

[30] D. Harvey, *The Condition of Postmodernity*, Oxford: Blackwell, 1989, pp. 201–323; F. Jameson, *Seeds of Time*, New York: Columbia University Press, 1994.

[31] M. Fisher, *Capitalist Realism: Is There No Alternative?*, Winchester and Washington, DC: Zero Books, 2009, p. 59; Harvey, *Condition of Postmodernity*, pp. 85–7.

Such fragmented memories, simultaneously nostalgic whilst forgetting other seemingly important, uncomfortable and even dangerous issues, have a ready-made cultural icon in the King James Bible with its antiquated language and gold lettering on a leather-bound cover, not to mention numerous cultured supporters of its historic and aesthetic qualities. In May 2012, Michael Gove, in his role as Education Secretary, and with the backing of private donors, took advantage of this cultural icon when he sent out copies of the King James Bible to English state schools with the following printed in gold on the spine: PRESENTED BY THE SECRETARY OF STATE FOR EDUCATION. Following the typical endorsements of the King James Bible in the 400th anniversary celebrations and beyond, Gove explained that he wanted this sent to schools because 'The King James Bible has had a profound impact on our culture ... Every school pupil should have the opportunity to learn about this book and the impact it has had on our history, language, literature and democracy'.[32] It is worth noting that the Gove Bible neatly complements one of the most controversial aspects of his time as Education Secretary, namely his early draft proposals for the history curriculum, which placed a strong emphasis on a patriotic narrative history of Britain and the importance of this history for national (effectively English) identity.[33]

The Gove Bible gained some weighty support. Once again, Dawkins got partly in the mood by declaring his double-edged support for the Gove Bible. 'A native speaker of English who has never read a word of the King James Bible is verging on the barbarian', proclaimed Dawkins, even if adding that his 'ulterior motive' was to expose the Bible for what it is: 'not a moral book and young people need to learn that important fact because they are very frequently told the opposite'.[34] The Gove Bible gained further endorsement in a 2012 Westminster discussion on Religion in Public Life featuring Tony Blair and Rowan Williams and chaired by the leading *Telegraph* journalist Charles Moore.[35] Once again, all the familiar positions from the Liberal Bible and Cultural Bible were present. Blair, for instance, denied that the Gove Bible was 'an act of proselytization ... we're not trying to convert anyone by doing it'. Rather, he claimed that

---

[32] 'Schools Get King James Bible to Mark 400th Anniversary', BBC News, 15 May 2012.

[33] See e.g. A. Philipson, 'Leading Historians Back Reforms to History Curriculum', *Telegraph*, 15 February 2013; R. J. Evans, 'The Wonderfulness of Us (the Tory Interpretation of History)', *London Review of Books* 33, 17 March 2011, pp. 9–12; R. J. Evans, 'Michael Gove's History Curriculum is a Pub Quiz Not an Education', *New Statesman*, 21 March 2013; R. Garner, '"Jingoistic and Illegal": What Teachers Think of Michael Gove's National Curriculum Reforms', *Independent*, 12 June 2013; W. Mansell, 'Michael Gove Redrafts New History Curriculum After Outcry', *Guardian*, 21 June 2013.

[34] R. Dawkins, 'Why I Want All Our Children to Read the King James Bible', *Observer*, 19 May 2012.

[35] The full debate (from which I have transcribed) is available at http://www.youtube.com/watch?v=1jE5z8UC_nk

it's 'part of our tradition and history as a country ... It's good that people understand it'.

And yet ... do plenty of schools not already have King James bibles? Does or will anyone actually read them at those schools where Gove's Bible is present? Was not Rowan Williams being implicitly cynical in arguing for the need for wider educational resources to understand such a complicated text? Would it be overly cynical to suggest that donating King James bibles to schools is an exercise in a PR, or a further exercise in promoting Govian history? In fact, comments of sceptical inner-city teachers who will not be using the Bible or those who see through the apparent PR purposes of the exercise are (predictably?) found in the same newspaper reports as Gove's plan, as well as sceptical liberal journalists and comedians, all providing outlets of cynicism in the same newspaper as the reports.[36] It would probably not be a great surprise if Cameron or Gove did not privately believe that the King James Bible would be taken up and read by even a handful of children in a given school. There was indeed a touch of scepticism when Dawkins wrote 'I am a little shocked at the implication that not every school library already possesses a copy. Can that be true? What do they have, then? Harry Potter? Vampires? ... But does anybody, even Gove, seriously think they will [read it]?'[37] Gove or Cameron would hardly write or speak openly like this at present, but if one day they were able to speak openly, who knows? Yet all the while the official narrative of a grand, democratic, cultured English civilization associated with the King James Bible continues comparatively unchallenged despite the popular cynicism over readership. Presumably this is the real ideological function of this story.

Broadly speaking, this perpetuation of the official story despite the cynicism can be tied in with the unconscious fiction of the Big Other, which we can in turn tie in with the more overtly cynical tradition of the Noble Lie, associated (rightly or wrongly) with figures from Plato through Machiavelli to Leo Strauss. Much of the Lacanian work on the Big Other has been carried out by Slavoj Žižek and others and applied to contexts of postmodern capitalism (as well as Soviet Russia). We can think of this Big Other symbolically functioning as a figure who 'believes' the official, expected or accepted public narratives, even if individuals really do not. Cynicism towards, disintegration and fragmentation of, and belief in, this Big Other have been a hallmark of postmodernity for Žižek.[38] Another

---

[36] J. Shepherd, 'Michael Gove's King James Bible Plan Rescued by Millionaire Tory Donors', *Guardian*, 15 May 2012; D. Mitchell, 'Michael Gove's Biblical Zeal is a Ruse', *Observer*, 20 May 2012.

[37] Dawkins, 'Why I Want'.

[38] E.g. S. Žižek, *The Ticklish Subject: The Absent Centre of Political Ontology*, London: Verso, 1999; S. Žižek, *For They Know Not What They Do: Enjoyment as a Political Factor* (2nd edn), London: Verso, 2008; Fisher, *Capitalist Realism*, pp. 44–50.

feature of a reliance on the Big Other who 'really believes' involves a
definition and function of 'culture', something particularly relevant to the
King James Bible-as-heritage arguments. Žižek has argued that 'culture'
has emerged as 'the central life-world category'. What this means is that
when we deal with the topic of religion (or the public presentation of the
Bible), people do not necessarily 'really believe' but rather 'just follow
(some) religious rituals and mores as part of respect for the 'lifestyle' of the
community to which we belong (nonbelieving Jews obeying kosher rules
'out of respect for tradition', etc.). As Žižek has suggested:

> 'I don't really believe in it, it's just part of my culture' effectively seems
> to be the predominant mode of the disavowed/displaced belief charac-
> teristic of our times. What is a cultural lifestyle, if not the fact that,
> although we don't believe in Santa Claus, there is a Christmas tree in
> every house, and even in public places, every December? ... 'culture'
> is the name for all those things we practice without really believing in
> them, without 'taking them seriously' ... Today, we ultimately perceive
> as a threat to culture those who live their culture immediately, those
> who lack a distance toward it. Recall the outrage when, two years ago,
> the Taliban forces in Afghanistan destroyed the ancient Buddhist statues
> at Bamiyan: although none of us enlightened Westerners believe in the
> divinity of the Buddha, we were outraged because the Taliban Muslims
> did not show the appropriate respect for the 'cultural heritage' of their
> own country and the entire world. Instead of believing through the other,
> like all people of culture, they really believed in their own religion, and
> thus had no great sensitivity toward the cultural value of the monuments
> of other religions – to them, the Buddha statues were just fake idols, not
> 'cultural treasures'.[39]

A distanced concern for 'our culture' and the cynical keeping up of
appearances helps explain in part the function of Gove's Bible in schools
and without, of course, recourse to anything too problematic like weighing
up the merits of casting out Girgashites, debating whether ageing rulers
should be warmed in bed by young women, or using the King James Bible
to convert and colonize. Again, recall Gove's explanation of the need
for the King James Bible in schools: 'Every school pupil should have the
opportunity to learn about this book and the impact it has had on our
history, language, literature and democracy'. Recall too Cameron's vocal
support for the cultural heritage of the King James Bible or Dawkins'
worries about the barbarianism of a life apart from the King James Bible.
    There is an assumption, then, that the King James Bible is, or should
be, an obvious part of British and English cultural heritage. But in the

---

[39] Žižek, *The Puppet and the Dwarf*, pp. 7–8.

case of both Dawkins and Gove there is clearly a fear that the ideological hinterland of the King James Bible could be under threat or even lost. In one sense, after going centuries unchallenged, the ongoing survival of the King James Bible is hardly a given and it could be seen as an unlikely survival story. The King James Bible is, after all, problematic in terms of its underlying Greek text-critical history, it is written in antiquated English, and it could potentially evoke scare stories of KJV-only 'fundamentalism'. Indeed, the standard explanation for the loss of its near monopoly in the English-speaking world is not particularly conducive to longer-term survival: by the turn of the twentieth century there was an increasing concern that the language of the King James Bible was too archaic for congregations and new Greek manuscript discoveries called into question *Textus Receptus*, thereby resulting in the King James Bible becoming one bible among many by the end of the twentieth century. Moreover, the idea of the King James Bible as *the* Bible – or indeed *the* Book – of the British Empire may have left its mark on the colonies, but the decline of the Empire might be another reason to think that its days of influence in Britain were always going to be numbered.

And yet the King James Bible has continued to survive, even if in radically different ways from its pre-twentieth-century dominance. There are a number of general ideological reasons for its survival in Britain and in an era of postmodernity, commercialization and neoliberalism.[40] The postmodern era has seen an explosion in different types of Bible with an accompanying fetish for (re-)packaging of already existing biblical translations for a targeted audience or market, neatly replicating the relentless postmodern interest in multiple identities and a relentless quest for more markets. The image has played a crucial role in the survival or perpetuation of what we might even call the Neoliberal Bible. As Katie Edwards has shown, the Bible in advertising only needs a split-second image to convey a range of 'common sense' meanings involving the intersection of (among other things) branding, gender and nationalism.[41] As an embedded cultural icon, the King James Bible was ready to survive the numerous different Bibles on the market and in one sense it can take its place among, or alongside, the *Queen James Bible*, *The Soldiers' Bible*, *The Teen Bible for Girls*, or any number of the Zondervan specialized Bibles whose 'true meaning' is instantly understood on sight. The distinctively branded King James Bible has managed to stand out and is instantly recognizable as a leather-bound text, with two columns, and a gold-coloured typesetting of 'Holy Bible' – possibly understood as *the* Bible – that might be bought for christenings. Whether we know precisely that it was a Bible published in

---

[40] On this and other reasons for the survival of the King James Bible see Crossley, *The Bible in English Politics and Culture Since 1968*, Chapter 1.

[41] K. Edwards, *Admen and Eve: The Bible and Advertising*, Sheffield: Sheffield Phoenix Press, 2012.

1611 is another issue – its branding and image retains a certain ancient and nostalgic mystique while, explicitly or implicitly, remaining the authoritative Bible of English or British nationalism and culture, and certainly so in the case of the Gove Bible.

The radical bible

Perhaps more surprisingly, the Cultural Bible has a long history in more radical politics in the sense that a specifically *English* or *British* radical tradition can be tied in with a politically radical understanding of the Bible, views which maintained the interest of Marxist historians such as Christopher Hill and E. P. Thompson in the Bible. In party politics, the most famous recent proponent of a radical English/British understanding of the Bible has been Tony Benn. This English or British (Benn mixed the two) tradition can be seen with particular reference not only to the Labour movement, but also the 17th-century Levellers and the English Civil War, a common point of reference in discussions of an English radical tradition. For Benn, the Levellers 'won wide public support among the people as a whole' and 'their ideas still retain a special place in the political traditions of the people of England'.[42] These 'political traditions', Benn argued, were very much socialist, though he acknowledged that the democratic ideals of the Levellers were also picked up by liberals, and have a lineage that stretches back further still:

> The Levellers can now be seen ... as speaking for a popular liberation movement that can be traced right back to the teachings of the Bible, and which has retained its vitality over the intervening centuries to speak to us here with undiminished force ... to understand what the Levellers said, and why, we must delve back far into our own history. For the Levellers drew many of their ideas, and much of their inspiration, from the Bible with its rich Jewish and Christian teaching.[43]

The Bible was the 'basic text' for Benn's Levellers and 'as now in many parts of the world' it was seen as a 'revolutionary book', partly because it was 'not to be trusted to the common people to read and interpret for themselves'.[44]

Benn went further still in placing the Bible prominently in the origins of British or English socialism. In his 1979 book *Arguments for Socialism*,

---

[42] T. Benn, *The Levellers and the English Democratic Tradition*, Nottingham: Russell Press, 1976, p. 7.
[43] Ibid., pp. 5, 7.
[44] Ibid., p. 9.

which sold over 75,000 copies,[45] Benn attempted to counter the suggestions that the origins of the Labour Party did not justify shifts to the Left by foregrounding the Bible, along with the Levellers, Marx and the Labour Party's Constitution, as some of the most important influences on the party.[46] The Bible and Jesus, traced through the Levellers, were a crucial part of 'democratic socialism', a form of socialism that 'is very much a home-grown British product which has been slowly fashioned over the centuries'. Benn added that its 'roots are deep in our history and have been nourished by the Bible, the teachings of Christ, the Peasants' Revolt, the Levellers, Tom Paine, the Chartists, Robert Owen, the Webbs and Bernard Shaw ...'.[47] The Bible also had another important aspect for Benn's socialism: to counter criticisms of atheism being integral to socialism. While socialism may be criticized for its atheistic element, Benn further added that this is 'not true as far as British Socialism is concerned' because 'the Bible has always been, and remains, a major element in our national political – as well as our religious – education', which Benn contextualized in terms of what we will see is his regular refrain of prophets-versus-kings.[48]

This Bible is part of what we might call the Radical Bible where it is roughly synonymous with socialism in its various radical forms, perhaps best known in terms of Liberation Theology. A number of themes about what the Bible 'really means' in the Radical Bible tradition include land and wealth redistribution, confrontation with power, communitarianism, egalitarianism, anti-clericalism and direct access to God, prophetic critique, and even 'apocalyptic' language, particularly with reference to a radical transformation of the social, economic and political order.[49] In English and British politics, it was, of course, radical Nonconformism that became one of the most important influences on the emerging Labour movement (and indeed the Communist Party[50]) at the turn of the twentieth century and with it came the influence of the Radical Bible in the Labour Party.[51] Again, in

---

[45] G. Dale, *God's Politicians: The Christian Contribution to 100 Years of Labour*, London: HarperCollins, 2000, p. 194.

[46] T. Benn, *Arguments for Socialism*, London: Jonathan Cape, 1979, p. 23.

[47] Ibid., p. 146.

[48] Benn, *Levellers*, p. 5; cf. Benn, *Arguments for Socialism*, pp. 23–4.

[49] The literature on radical interpretations of the Bible is vast, wide ranging and diverse. Two helpful summaries of key points in the history of politically radical biblical interpretation are R. Boer, *Rescuing the Bible*, Oxford: Blackwell, 2007, pp. 105–27; C. Rowland and J. Roberts, *The Bible for Sinners: Interpretation in the Present Time*, London: SPCK, 2008.

[50] R. Hilton, 'Christopher Hill: Some Reminiscences', in D. Pennington and K. Thomas (eds), *Puritans and Revolutionaries: Essays in Seventeenth-Century History Presented to Christopher Hill*, Oxford: Oxford University Press, 1978, pp. 6–10 (7); P. J. Corfield, '"We are All One in the Eyes of the Lord": Christopher Hill and the historical meanings of radical religion', *History Workshop Journal*, 58 (2004): 111–27.

[51] See e.g. Dale, *God's Politicians*; Spencer, *Freedom and Order*, Chapters 7–10.

more recent party politics, it was Benn who brought together virtually all the key themes from the Radical Bible.

Some of Benn's radicalism was influenced by his mother, Margaret 'Didi' Holmes, who was a feminist coming from a background of liberal Nonconformist (Congregationalist) dissent, a biblical scholar of some training (e.g. she read Hebrew and Greek) and contact of the American theologian Reinhold Niebuhr (whom Benn visited as a young man).[52] On meeting the Archbishop of Canterbury, Randall Davidson, Holmes said that she wanted her sons to grown up in a world where women would be given 'equal spiritual status',[53] a view that would chime with Benn's radical egalitarian democratic views and his understanding of the Bible with a radical Protestant spin. Citing texts such as Mark 12.29–31 in support,[54] Benn argued that the concept of the 'priesthood of all believers' was 'based on the belief that every person had a direct line to the Almighty and does not require a bishop to mediate concerning what to believe and what to do',[55] nor indeed the 'intervention of an exclusive priestly class claiming a monopoly right to speak on behalf of the Almighty, still less of a king claiming a divine right to rule'.[56] He labelled this religious dissent as 'a completely revolutionary doctrine because it undermined authority, disturbed the hierarchy and was seen as intolerable by the powers that be, in exactly the same way that, today, political dissenters are projected as trouble-makers and members of the "awkward squad", whose advice would lead to chaos'.[57]

The interconnected themes of individual conscience and confronting power and hierarchy are common ones in Benn's understanding of the Bible. Perhaps most famously, Benn recalled his father's fondness for the story of Daniel in the lions' den and the words from the Salvation Army hymn 'Dare to be a Daniel' ('Dare to be a Daniel, Dare to stand alone, Dare to have a purpose firm, Dare to make it known'). Benn claimed that that these sentiments 'greatly influenced my life' and 'taught me the importance of consistency and courage in the face of adversity – essential for anyone who is criticised for his convictions'. He even photographed a picture he saw in the YMCA in Nagasaki in 1983 of Daniel – head bowed, hands behind back and surrounded by lions – and hung the photograph in his office 'to remind me of those qualities that are most important in public life' [cites hymn].[58] Not everyone had Daniel's good fortune, however.

---

[52] T. Benn, *Conflicts of Interest: Diaries 1977–80*, London: Hutchinson, 1990, pp. 7–8; Dale, *God's Politicians*, p. 196. Benn parallels Niebuhr's views on democracy and sin with those of the Levellers, whom Benn also admired. See e.g. Benn, *Levellers*, p. 14.

[53] D. Powell, *Tony Benn: A Political Life*, New York and London: Continuum, 2001, p. 13; cf. T. Benn, *Dare to Be a Daniel: Then and Now*, London: Arrow Books, 2004, p. 5.

[54] E.g. Benn, *Arguments for Socialism*, pp. 24–5.

[55] Benn, *Dare to Be a Daniel*, p. 5.

[56] Benn, *Arguments for Socialism*, p. 25.

[57] Benn, *Dare to Be a Daniel*, p. 5.

[58] Ibid., pp. ix, 11.

Individuals, Benn argued, may always rebel against systems of power and think for themselves, but such people have been 'generally excommunicated or even killed'. Yet, Benn has added, 'teachers who explained the world without wanting to control it themselves' are of great importance in the development of ideas.[59]

Benn's mother continued to have an influence in reading biblical stories to Benn's children, as well as in Benn's remembering of her continued presence in his own radical politics, notably in standing up to power. He recalled:

> I was brought up on the Bible by my mother who told me about the age-old conflict between the kings who had power and the prophets who preached righteousness. She taught me to support the prophets against the kings, meaning that each of us had the responsibility for learning to differentiate between good and evil and make that our guide for action.

The prophets-versus-kings model may sound an abstracted kind of radicalism, but Benn immediately gave it contemporary application:

> She was right, we should all have the confidence to think things out for ourselves, and if we do it must be clear that Bush's plan to make war on Iraq is wrong, as is the conduct of Sharon in oppressing the Palestinians, or whipping up of hostility against asylum-seekers, or accepting the present grossly unfair division between rich and poor in a world dominated by globalization.[60]

These issues reflect well-known and precise causes most readily associated with the contemporary political Left, but this application of the Radical Bible also reflects deeply rooted ideas about the nature of political power and democratic ideals, which can often implicate the established church on the side of the 'kings'. A good example of this is found in Benn's diary entry for 25 April 1991. He recalled a 'crowded meeting' at Hartlebury Castle, the home of the Bishop of Worcester. After giving a speech, Benn engaged in questions of democracy, including the following incident:

> Then two Evangelicals got up and said, 'Do you accept that Jesus is our Lord?' I said, 'I don't like the word Lord. I don't believe in Lords'. This brought us on to the whole question of the Kingdom of God, and I did describe my Constitutional Reform Bill. What you realise is that an authoritarian Church, where power comes from the Creator mediated

---

[59] Ibid., pp. 4–5.
[60] T. Benn, *Free Radical: New Century Essays*, New York and London: Continuum, 2003, p. 226.

through the bishops to the clergy to the laity, can't really take on board democracy at all because everything is done from the top.[61]

But individual conscience did not, of course, lead to a Thatcherite reading of the Bible. Indeed, Benn contrasted Thatcher's Nonconformist roots and individualism as freedom from the state with his mother's Congregationalism and his 'grounding in both the Old and New Testaments of the Bible'.[62] More specifically, the idea of individual conscience transferred into more collective justice. In this respect Benn took the significant example of Marx, who he came to believe 'was the last of the Old Testament prophets, a wise old Jew ...'.[63] Applying ideas of eschatological judgement and justice familiar to both the Radical Bible tradition and the Labour movement, as well as elsewhere in Benn's thinking on the Bible,[64] he further argued that the idea of Heaven on Earth ('or justice in practice') is not only 'an integral part of the dissenting tradition' but also 'the trade-union movement, which recognised that you could only improve conditions by your on collective efforts'.[65] This integration of individual dissent and collectivism can be found throughout history. In a House of Commons debate on Socialism, Benn argued:

The Bible has led to many revolutionary ideas – for instance, that we were and are all equal in the sight of God – which is why, in 1401, the House of Commons passed the Heresy Act, which condemned any lay person reading the Bible to be burned at the stake for heresy. The Bible has always been a controversial document. At the time of the Peasants' Revolt and the English revolution, people started thinking of common ownership, based on the life of the apostles. (House of Commons debate on Socialism, 16 May 2000)[66]

What is also notable in this respect is that Benn rejected a famous view that we saw has been associated with Conservative understandings of the Bible and taken up by Thatcher but which has a long history of being questioned in radical theological thinking: Original Sin. Whereas Conservatives such as Thatcher saw Original Sin leading to misguided ideas of social utopianism and the perfectibility of humanity,[67] for Benn the very idea of Original Sin

---

[61]T. Benn, *Free at Last! Diaries 1991–2001*, London: Hutchinson, 2002, p. 17.

[62]Benn, *Dare to Be a Daniel*, p. 10.

[63]Ibid., p. 14.

[64]'Whether you believe that you are accountable on the Day of Judgement for the way you have spent your life, or have to account to your fellow men and women for what you have done during your life, accountability is a strong and democratic idea' (ibid., p. 17).

[65]Ibid., p. 7.

[66]Cited in ibid., pp. 268–78 (269).

[67]E.g. M. Thatcher, 'I Believe: A Speech on Politics and Politics (St Lawrence Jewry)', Margaret Thatcher Foundation, 31 March, 1978; Thatcher, 'Speech to the General Assembly

'is deeply offensive' because 'I cannot imagine that any God could possibly have created the human race and marked it at birth with evil that could only be expiated by confession, devotion and obedience'. Whereas Thatcher could associate the rejection of Original Sin with totalitarianism, Benn took the opposite view. This was a 'use of Christianity to keep people down was ... destructive of any hope that we might succeed together in building a better world'.[68]

The idea of later corruptions of an original purer message is common to all the major traditions of reading the Bible discussed here but Benn, of course, followed the standard rhetorical move of the Radical Bible. He saw Jesus (notably labelled 'the Carpenter of Nazareth') as 'one of the greatest teachers, along with Moses and Mohammed' and that Christianity, Judaism and Islam teach 'that we are brothers and sisters with a responsibility to each other'.[69] But these religions can distort the message of the great leader. While rejecting the 'implicit atheism' in Marx, Benn believed it was possible to accept the argument that religion is the opium of the people 'without in any way demeaning the importance of the teachings of Jesus'.[70] Benn's views of the Bible and faith may have changed over the years but, he claimed, they were not 'influenced by atheistic arguments, which were extreme and threw doubt on the value of the Bible and the historical truth of Jesus' life'. Rather the real challenge for Benn was 'the nature of the Church and the way in which it sought to use the teachings of the Bible to justify its power structures in order to build up its own authority'.[71] Benn, typically, has provided concrete examples of 'the one characteristic of most religions when they become established ... the entrenchment of authority at their heart', whether the Archbishop of Canterbury or the Pope, 'each in their time having great power over their respective churches and enforcing Christian doctrine, sometimes ruthlessly, as at the time of the Inquisition and on other occasions when heretics were burned at the stake'.[72] Benn also believed that this characteristic was part of the political arena, and perhaps not surprising given his views on Marx as Old Testament prophet, from Stalinism ('supposedly the teachings of Marx') to the 'Labour Party itself, which was inspired by men and women of principle, became corrupted by the same power structures, leading to the expulsion of different people on the grounds that they were not prepared to accept orders from the Party hierarchy'.[73]

---

of the Church of Scotland'. See also E. Filby, 'God and Mrs Thatcher: Religion and Politics in 1980s Britain', PhD thesis, University of Warwick, 2010, pp. 194–5.

[68] Benn, *Dare to Be a Daniel*, p. 13.

[69] Ibid., p. 15. The title 'Jesus Christ the Carpenter of Nazareth' and the 'revolutionary' nature of monotheism turn up elsewhere in Benn's reflections on the Bible. See e.g. Benn, *Levellers*, pp. 5–6.

[70] Benn, *Dare to Be a Daniel*, p. 14.

[71] Ibid., p. 13.

[72] Ibid., p. 4; cf. Benn, *Arguments for Socialism*, p. 39.

[73] Benn, *Dare to Be a Daniel*, p. 4.

Benn would narrowly lose the Labour Party Deputy Leadership election in 1981; this would mark the decline of the Bennite Left in the Labour Party and pushed such radicalism to the fringes of the party. By the end of the 1980s, the centrist ideas of Neil Kinnock were dominating the Labour Party, which was pushed further to the right by Tony Blair in the 1990s. As Blair was removing Clause 4 (a commitment to common/public ownership or nationalization) from the Labour Party Constitution, Benn was claiming that Clause 4 and public ownership owed at least as much to Acts of the Apostles as they did to Marx.[74] But any serious influence Benn had on the Labour Party had now gone and with it the Radical Bible was no longer the force it once was. Indeed, leading Labour users of the Bible slowly began embracing the some of the rhetoric of Thatcherism, which would become most fully developed in Blair's hermeneutics.[75] A significant moment came in 1993 in a Christian Socialist Movement (CSM) publication edited by Christopher Bryant (then press officer for the Christian Socialist Movement, later its chair) called *Reclaiming the Ground: Christianity and Socialism*, largely a collection of recent Tawney Lectures.[76] Along with the Bible, the book foregrounded the role of then Labour leader John Smith and included a foreword by Tony Blair. As might be expected, Smith's article contains anti-Thatcher polemics, but the ideas of individual freedom and their relationship with collectivism is the dominant theme. Along with Tony Blair, the editor Christopher Bryant and other contributors, such as Paul Boateng, would go on to be notable (to lesser or greater degree) New Labour figures. There was a still more radical voice of the Left in the volume, but notably it was from one outside party politics: John Vincent. This would foreshadow what would soon become the norm for the Radical Bible, which is now more at home on the fringes of party politics or outside Parliament altogether, though it regularly re-emerges in public debates, notably at times of controversy, whether the Occupy Movement at its use of Jesus and the money-changers, the dismantling of a Hawk Jet by East Timor Ploughshares group, or Peter Tatchell's use of Jesus as a figure of radical sexuality outside marriage.[77] As left-wing political radicalism has effectively left Parliament, so too has the Radical Bible.

---

[74] Dale, *God's Politicians*, p. 199.

[75] Crossley, *The Bible in English Politics Since 1968*, Chapter 8.

[76] C. Bryant (ed.), *Reclaiming the Ground: Christianity and Socialism*, London: Hodder & Stoughton, 1993.

[77] See e.g. P. Tatchell, 'Was Jesus Gay?', Peter Tatchell, 18 March 1996; S. Hill, 'Would Jesus Kick the Occupy London Protesters off St Paul's grounds?', *Guardian*, 20 October 2011; Catholic Social Teaching 'Seeds of Hope: East Timor Ploughshares'; H. O'Shaughnessy and M. Brace, 'Campaigners Face Jail for Raid on Military Jet', *Independent*, 21 July 1996; Hill, 'Would Jesus?; T. Eagleton, 'Occupy London are True Followers of Jesus, Even if they Despise Religion', *Guardian*, 3 November 2011; Crossley, *The Bible in English Politics Since 1968*, Chapter 9.

Conclusion

These are some – and only some – of the ways English and British politicians make assumptions about what the Bible 'really means'. In general terms, the political establishment continues to endorse the Liberal Bible and Cultural Bible with little in the way of detailed exegesis and plenty of assumptions about the compatibility of the Bible with liberal democracy and English or British nationalism. Given that studies of the Liberal Bible, Cultural Bible and Radical Bible are largely based on European and North American traditions, we should add that these assumptions are hardly restricted to English politics. Of course, these general ways of understanding the meaning of the Bible are, as suggested throughout, undergoing constant reinterpretation and it may be the case that we need to nuance the Liberal Bible further if, as seems likely, Thatcher's more overtly neoliberal reading of the Bible has longer-term influence.[78] It should also be added that the readings of the Bible outlined here (Liberal, Cultural, Radical) are not confined to party political or related discourses and there is evidence of such readings being part of wider cultural trends.[79] Thus, when we write or speak of the decline of biblical literacy, we need to be clear precisely what is meant by 'biblical literacy'. It may well be true that there is a more recent decline in awareness of passages such as the Good Samaritan or even seemingly major figures such as Abraham, but this does not mean that an understanding of what the Bible more generally means has disappeared from English or British culture – far from it. Quite why leading English politicians have felt the need to continue using the Bible when there are no obvious votes is a question beyond the scope of this essay but two things are clear: they do and they have inherited a series of major assumptions about 'what it really means'.

Bibliography

Avalos, H., 'In Praise of Biblical Illiteracy', *Bible and Interpretation* (April 2010); www.bibleinterp.com/articles/literate357930.shtml

Benn, T., *The Levellers and the English Democratic Tradition*, Nottingham: Russell Press, 1976.

—*Arguments for Socialism*, London: Jonathan Cape, 1979.

—*Conflicts of Interest: Diaries 1977-80*, London: Hutchinson, 1990.

—*Free at Last! Diaries 1991–2001*, London: Hutchinson, 2002.

—*Free Radical: New Century Essays*, New York and London: Continuum, 2003.

—*Dare to Be a Daniel: Then and Now*, London: Arrow Books, 2004.

---

[78] Crossley, *The Bible in English Politics since 1968*, Chapters 4, 7, 8 and 9.
[79] Ibid., Chapters 5–6.

Berlinerblau, J., *Thumpin' It: The Use and Abuse of the Bible in Today's Presidential Politics*, Louisville, KY: Westminster John Knox, 2008.

Boer, R., *Rescuing the Bible*, Oxford: Blackwell, 2007.

Bryant, C. (ed.), *Reclaiming the Ground: Christianity and Socialism*, London: Hodder & Stoughton, 1993.

Cameron, D., 'Prime Minister's King James Bible Speech (December 16, 2010)', Number 10 Downing Street, www.number10.gov.uk/news/king-james-bible/

Catholic Social Teaching, 'Seeds of Hope: East Timor Ploughshares'; www.catholicsocialteaching.org.uk/themes/peace/stories/seeds-hope-east-timor-ploughares/

Corfield, P. J., '"We are All One in the Eyes of the Lord": Christopher Hill and the historical meanings of radical religion', *History Workshop Journal*, 58 (2004): 110–27.

Crossley, J. G., *The Bible in English Politics and Culture Since 1968: Rethinking Reception History*, London: T&T Clark/Bloomsbury, 2014.

Dale, G., *God's Politicians: The Christian Contribution to 100 Years of Labour*, London: HarperCollins, 2000.

Davies, P., 'Whose bible? anyone's?', *Bible and Interpretation*, July 2009, www.bibleinterp.com/opeds/whose.shtml

Dawkins, R., *The God Delusion*, London: Bantam Press, 2006.

—'Why I Want All Our Children to Read the King James Bible', *Observer*, 19 May 2012.

Eagleton, T., 'Occupy London are True Followers of Jesus, Even if they Despise Religion', *Guardian*, 3 November 2011.

Edwards, K., *Admen and Eve: The Bible and Advertising*, Sheffield: Sheffield Phoenix Press, 2012.

Evans, R. J., 'The Wonderfulness of Us (the Tory Interpretation of History)', *London Review of Books* 33, 17 March 2011.

—'Michael Gove's History Curriculum is a Pub Quiz Not an Education', *New Statesman*, 21 March 2013.

Filby, E., 'God and Mrs Thatcher: Religion and Politics in 1980s Britain', PhD thesis, University of Warwick, 2010.

Fisher, M., *Capitalist Realism: Is There No Alternative?*, Winchester and Washington, DC: Zero Books, 2009.

Garner, R., '"Jingoistic and Illegal": What Teachers Think of Michael Gove's National Curriculum Reforms', *Independent*, 12 June 2013.

Hari, J., 'A Civil Partnership: Interview with Tony Blair', *Attitude*, 8 April 2009.

Harvey, D., *The Condition of Postmodernity*, Oxford: Blackwell, 1989.

Hill, S., 'Would Jesus Kick the Occupy London Protesters off St Paul's Grounds?', *Guardian*, 20 October 2011.

Hilton, R., 'Christopher Hill: Some Reminiscences', in D. Pennington and K. Thomas (eds), *Puritans and Revolutionaries: Essays in Seventeenth-Century History Presented to Christopher Hill*, Oxford: Oxford University Press, 1978.

Jameson, F., *Seeds of Time*, New York: Columbia University Press, 1994.

Mansell, W., 'Michael Gove Redrafts New History Curriculum After Outcry', *Guardian*, 21 June 2013.

Mitchell, D., 'Michael Gove's Biblical Zeal is a Ruse', *Observer*, 20 May 2012.

Moore, C., *Margaret Thatcher: The Authorized Biography, Volume One: Not for Turning*, London: Allen Lane, 2013.

Obama, B., 'Remarks by the President on a New Beginning', The White House: Office of the Press Secretary (2009), www.whitehouse.gov/the-press-office/remarks-president-cairo-university-6-04-09

O'Shaughnessy, H. and M. Brace, 'Campaigners Face Jail for Raid on Military Jet', *Independent*, 21 July 1996.

Philipson, A., 'Leading Historians Back Reforms to History Curriculum', *Telegraph*, 15 February 2013.

Powell, D., *Tony Benn: A Political Life*, New York and London: Continuum, 2001.

Rowland, C. and J. Roberts, *The Bible for Sinners: Interpretation in the Present Time*, London: SPCK, 2008.

Sheehan, J., *The Enlightenment Bible: Translation, Scholarship, Culture*, Princeton, NJ and Oxford: Princeton University Press, 2007.

Shepherd, J., 'Michael Gove's King James Bible Plan Rescued by Millionaire Tory Donors', *Guardian*, 15 May 2012.

Sherwood, Y., 'Bush's Bible as a Liberal Bible (Strange Though that Might Seem)', *Postscripts*, 2 (2006), pp. 47–58.

—'This is Not a Bible/Ceçi n'est pas une Bible', unpublished paper delivered to the Biblical Literacy and the Curriculum Conference, University of Sheffield, 25–28 May 2011.

Spencer, N., *Freedom and Order: History, Politics and the English Bible*, London: Hodder & Stoughton, 2011.

Stoppard, M. and M. Thatcher, 'TV Interview for Yorkshire Television *Woman to Woman* (19 November 1985), Margaret Thatcher Foundation, http://www.margaretthatcher.org/document/105830

Tatchell, P., 'Was Jesus Gay?', Peter Tatchell (18 March 1996), www.petertatchell.net/religion/jesus.htm

Thatcher, M., 'Speech at St Lawrence Jewry', Margaret Thatcher Foundation (4 March 1981), http://www.margaretthatcher.org/document/104587

—'Speech to the General Assembly of the Church of Scotland', Margaret Thatcher Foundation (21 May 1988), http://www.margaretthatcher.org/document/107246

Thatcher, M. and B. Walden, 'TV Interview for London Weekend Television *Weekend World* (1980)', Margaret Thatcher Foundation, http://www.margaretthatcher.org/speeches/displaydocument.asp?docid=104210

Watt, N. and P. Wintour, 'Interview: How David Cameron is Trying to Reinvent the Tories', *Guardian*, 16 July 2008.

Žižek, S., *The Ticklish Subject: The Absent Centre of Political Ontology*, London: Verso, 1999.

—*The Puppet and the Dwarf: The Perverse Core of Christianity*, Cambridge, MA: MIT Press, 2003.

—*For They Know Not What They Do: Enjoyment as a Political Factor* (2nd edn), London: Verso, 2008.

3

The Quest for Biblical Literacy: Curricula, Culture and Case Studies[1]

Iona Hine (University of Sheffield)

Introduction

Lost, missing or, as media reports tell us (less dramatically), in decline?[2] My title is a deliberate parody: the title of the English edition of Albert Schweitzer's now-famous book, *The Quest of the Historical Jesus* (1910), was appropriated by New Testament scholars seeking to construct a portrait of the 'historical Jesus', a quest that has produced a veritable 'marketplace of Jesuses'[3] but no hope of identifying anything more certain than early gospel traditions. The historical Jesus is beyond recovery. The case of biblical literacy, its quest, ought perhaps to be more straight-forward, because (while what is in it may be subject to debate, and its

---

[1]Based on a paper presented at the Biblical Studies Research Seminar, 5 November 2012. A companion article, 'Practicing Biblical Literacy: Case studies from the Sheffield Conference', is to be published in *Postscripts: The Journal of Sacred and Contemporary Worlds* (Special Issue: Biblical Literacy and The Curriculum, forthcoming).
[2]The following is intended as a representative sample: BBC, 'Knowledge of Bible "in Decline"', BBC, 12 July 2009; Presbyterian Church (USA), 'Newly Revised Study Encourages Congregation-wide Reading of Bible in Its Entirety as Bible Literacy in U.S. Sees Steep Decline', 24 August 2011; Smith, Greg, 'Declining Biblical Literacy', *Sowhatfaith.com*, 22 January 2012; Hardiman, Clayton, 'Bible Literacy Slipping, Experts Say', Religious News Service/Associated Press, 5 October 2009.
[3]J. Crossley, 'Jesus and the Chaos of History: Redirecting the Quest for the Historical Jesus', Paper delivered at the Department of Biblical Studies Research Seminar, University of Sheffield, 15 October 2012.

interpretation certainly is – or biblical scholars would have a less interesting occupation) we have 'the Bible' to hand in a way that we do not have the historical Jesus.

An iconic text

In 2006, the British government's Department for Media, Culture and Sport engaged the public in identifying icons of national identity. Using the internet, people were encouraged to nominate items they felt to be particularly English (perhaps an early sally in response to the pursuit of Scottish and Welsh independence). The aim was to 'paint a virtual portrait of England' by identifying things that represent Englishness; the project was supported by researchers working behind the scenes to provide historical information about the objects. When the initiative was launched by Culture Minister David Lammy, among the dozen items pre-selected to present the whole idea was the King James Version of the Bible. Positioned on the icons.org.uk website – now dismantled – it was set up as just that: an image, an icon of English identity.[4]

Though the government has changed, the rhetoric of an iconic Bible has not. When, in 2012, the Secretary of State for Education distributed 'an authentic copy' of the 1611 KJV to every primary and secondary school in England, this was endorsed on the Department for Education's website by various spokespeople. The Department commented:

> Representatives from a range of faith communities have lent their support to the King James Bible project. Cultural figures, academics and historians have also expressed their views on the importance of this national, historical, cultural and literary icon.[5]

But an icon is something to be looked at, and this devotion to the artefact is an odd mirror to the apparent desire that people should read it: if the complaint is that people are not biblically literate, that they are biblically illiterate, then iconification sends out the wrong message. Sleeping with the Bible under your pillow will not improve your biblical literacy; reading it might.

But that is to proceed on the assumption that what is said about the decline of biblical literacy is correct, that it should be taken at face value, that it is not worth more critical reflection.

---

[4]Culture Online, 'The King James Bible' Icons: A Portrait of England, 2006 (a project from the Department for Culture, Media and Sport).
[5]Department for Education, 'King James Bible Copies for Schools: King James Bible Project Comments', 21 May 2012.

Approach

Questions

If the notion of biblical literacy and its decline is to be explored, there are a number of questions that may be asked:

- Who should be biblically literate?
- Who says so? *Who cares?*
- And why?
- What would being 'biblically literate' look like? *What is the quest of biblical literacy?*
- And, if we accept – even partially – the assumptions that underlie the quest of/for biblical literacy, how might biblical literacy be improved, encouraged, or the decline reversed?

The limits of this study

The goal of my 'quest' here is not to form a definition of 'biblical literacy'; rather it is an opportunity to explore others' definitions. The content combines anecdotal material with commentary on others' studies, including case studies presented at the University of Sheffield's conference on Biblical Literacy & the Curriculum (held in May 2011 as part of a series of KJV anniversary events). In addition, I suggest some historical parallels that may better illuminate different perspectives on biblical literacy; in closing, I make a tentative proposal for a new approach to biblical literacy, through the engagement of other literacies.

Who should be biblically literate? (and who says so?)

The motif of the agricultural labourer is found in several layers of discussion about who should have access to the Bible, generally in the context of translation. The plough-boy, someone for whom both the need and opportunity for a lettered education made literacy a deeply improbable luxury, was depicted singing psalms in Jerome's idealized account of life in the holy land,[6] becoming an aspired reader for Erasmus's New

---

[6]Letter 46, 'On Visiting Jerusalem' (To Marcella, from Paula the elder, Eustochium and Jerome). 'Wherever you turn there is a farmer guiding his plough while singing Alleluia, or a man harvesting the crops, sweating from his labours but keeping himself cheerful with the

Testament[7] and a pawn in William Tyndale's (whose translations from Greek and Hebrew form the basis of what became the King James Version) dispute with Rome.[8] Nonetheless, the notion that it would be good if more people (could) read – or at least understand someone else reading – the Bible is not new.

Why did these people want others to read the Bible? A close reading of the prefaces to bibles from the 1500s suggests some lines of thought in common between the early modern Bible translator and some of the modern advocates of biblical literacy.[9]

'To lead a virtuous conversation'

Leading a virtuous conversation is the outcome Coverdale hoped for (from his readers) when his English Bible was published in 1535. This was not primarily about eloquence or avoiding inappropriate language (though some might feel a good bit of King James' English would help here) but something broader: 'conversation' in the 16th century was action, and what Coverdale seems to have been interested in was moral action, or perhaps

psalms, or a vineyard owner pruning his vines while singing one of David's compositions'. (¶12. Translation via Carolinne White [ed. and trans.], *Lives of Roman Christian Women*, Penguin, 2010, unpaginated ebook.)

[7]'I would wish that all women read the gospel and Epistles of Paul. If only they were translated into all human tongues, so that not only the Scots and the Irish but also the Turks and the Saracens could read and study them … If only the peasant sang something from them at the plough, the weaver recited something to the measure of the shuttle, the traveller dispelled the tedium of the journey with such stories!' From Paraclesis; that is, the preface to Erasmus' 1516 New Testament in Greek and Latin; cited in translation by Cornelis Augustijn, *Erasmus: His Life, Works, and Influence* (English translation from Dutch, Oscar Beck), London: University of Toronto Press, 1991.

[8]'I defie the Pope and all his lawes … if God spare my lyfe ere many yeares, I wyl cause a boye that dryveth the plough, shall knowe more of the scripture then thou doest' (emphasis added). The quotation appears in John Foxe's *Actes and Monuments of these latter and perillous dayes* (1563), STC (2nd edn) / 11222, EEBO, 514, image 297. For a discussion regarding its historicity, see J. James 'Establishing an English Bible in Henry VIII's England: Translation, Vernacular Theology, and William Tyndale', PhD, University of York, 2011, pp. 109–10, unpublished. Guido Latré has suggested that Tyndale's intention may have been more sincere than Erasmus' in this regard, at least in terms of his efforts to fulfil it. G. Latré, 'English Bibles in Antwerp (1526–38)', paper delivered at the Departmnet of Biblical Studies Research Seminar, University of Sheffield, 19 March 2012, unpublished.

[9]A compilation of Tyndale's earlier work and Coverdale's own translation from Latin and German sources, the Coverdale Bible was the first complete English Bible in print – *Biblia: The Bible that is, the holy Scripture of the Olde and New Teſtament, faithfully and truly tranlſlated out of Douche and Latyn in to Engliſhe* (trans. Miles Coverdale. Antwerp, Martin de Keyser) M.D.XXXV [1535].

better put, action devoted to God.[10] 'To lead a virtuous conversation', Coverdale wrote, 'is the greatest praise'.[11]

Traces of this attitude can still be found in the discourse of religious groups advocating biblical literacy. Thus, for example, this summary of biblical literacy taken from the Lutheran Bible Ministries (LBM) – published on their website in 2002:

> The foundation of biblical literacy is factual knowledge – knowing all the people, places, events and teachings in the Bible.
>
> A second and higher level is that of assent – accepting this knowledge as truth, and believing that the Bible is the word of God.
>
> The third and highest level is knowing the God of their Bible personally through a life changing commitment.[12]

The parallel here is that final phrase, 'a life changing commitment'.

That is, I think, what Coverdale hoped for in his readers. It would be unfair to term the finale to his prologue a manifesto, but he certainly laid out his hopes in terms of practical outworkings. These include:

> soliciting help for the poor (with the specified aim of getting beggars off the streets and finding labour for the unemployed) – the promotion of a social good;[13]
>
> advising any preachers professing limited knowledge of scripture that they were better to read the text aloud to their congregation than to rely on their own ideas and risk heresy – the promotion of a theological good;[14]
>
> asking parents (fathers) to teach their children ('bring them up in the nurture and information of the Lord') whether directly or by hiring a suitable tutor – promoting theology, employment and the realm.[15]

---

[10] The conflation of virtue and morality is more pronounced in current English, but may be traced back to the 1300s (cf. *OED*, 'virtuous, adj.' I.2).

[11] M. Coverdale, 'A Prologue: Miles Coverdale unto the Christian Reader'. Reprinted in modern spelling in G. Bray, *Translating the Bible: From William Tyndale to King James*, London: Latimer Trust, 2011, p. 72.

[12] Lutheran Bible Ministries. Quotation via B. Fisher. 'Promoting Biblical Literacy in the Elementary Classroom' (2005), Avondale College, http://research.avondale.edu.au/cgi/viewcontent.cgi?article=1020&context=edu_papers (emphasis added).

[13] '[L]ift up thine eyes, and see how great a multitude of poor people run through every town: have pity on thine own flesh, help them with a good heart, and do with thy counsel all that ever thou canst, that this unshameful begging may be put down, that these idle folks may be set to labor, and that such as are not able to get their living, may be provided for'. Coverdale, 'A Prologue', p. 72.

[14] '[R]ather than thou wouldest teach the people any other thing than God's word take the book in thine hand, and read the words even as they stand therein'. Ibid.

[15] Ibid., p. 78. The quotation (Eph. 6.4b in Tyndale's translation, reproduced in Coverdale's Bible) also appears with other biblical exhortations in Tyndale's *Obedience of a Christen Man*

These things would, Coverdale reckoned, not only end with people worshipping God,[16] but also be to the good of England's earthly kingdom. I suspect David Cameron would be nodding along in agreement to some of his sentiments: 'the bringing up well of children ... if it be diligently looked to, it is the upholding of all commonwealths: and the negligence of the same, the very decay of all realms'.[17]

Scriptural literacy, biblical literacy

There are two points emerging from this comparison: one is that although a good deal of what is said about biblical literacy does have religious origins, it will make more sense to distinguish this by a second term – scriptural literacy'. Within this lies the promotion of Bible reading to increase religiosity, whether this is framed with the same conservative 'truth' value as the LBM or something more liberal. The shift from 'biblical literacy' to 'scriptural literacy' could seem too fine a semantic move, but connotation is important, and I choose scriptural literacy not just because Coverdale employed the term 'Scripture', but because I do not think you would hear Richard Dawkins complaining that people don't know enough scripture.[18] (Scripture is the preserve of the religious.)

We will have cause to revisit some of what primarily religious stakeholders say about biblical literacy, not least because some of the (little) research that has been conducted into biblical literacy emerges from their work. For now, I want to pick up a second point – the notion that increasing biblical literacy (and for now let's appropriate the first point from the LBM as a working definition) will improve the moral behaviour of the population:

> The foundation of biblical literacy is factual knowledge – knowing all the people, places, events and teachings in the Bible.

We could probably recover the notion that better knowledge of the Bible leads to better behaviour from political rhetoric, too, but (in my own research) the most developed example found outside a directly religious context appears in the research of William Jeynes.

(1528), under the subheading 'The office of a father and how he should rule'; the reflection on practicalities is Coverdale's own.

[16] '[T]hat the holy scripture may have free passage, and be had in reputation, to the worship of the author thereof, which is even God himself', Coverdale, 'A Prologue', p. 78.

[17] Ibid.

[18] 18 See BBC News, 'Dawkins Backs School Bible Plan', 26 May 2012, sec. UK. http://www.bbc.co.uk/news/uk-18224114 [accessed 5 November 2012].

Jeynes, the behaviourists and moral gatekeepers

Jeynes, operating in an American context, does his best to advocate the inclusion of the Bible in the school curriculum by linking it with two important considerations: attainment and behaviour. Traditionally, the moral curriculum was guided by texts from the Bible such that when, in the early 1960s, new legislation prevented the religious use of the Bible in state-funded schools, it also affected the citation of biblical texts in contexts that were not directly religious and so (Jeynes and others argue) contributed to a decline in public morality. Jeynes' own research, published in 2009, found a strong correlation between biblical literacy and overall attainment, and a much weaker correlation between biblical literacy and behaviour – weak to the point of statistical insignificance. This technical insignificance does not prevent Jeynes from suggesting that Bible courses could have a positive effect on student behaviour as well as academic success. The following quotation is taken from his conclusions:

> If these [Bible] courses can substantially increase the Bible literacy of public school students *then* increased academic outcomes and *improved student behavior could possibly result*. Although this study *did not seek to determine, but only suggests, the direction of causality* specifically, many theories have been propounded about *the effects of religious expression* has [sic] on academic achievement and student behavior.[19]

Observe how Jeynes shifts between discourses, beginning with biblical literacy but ending with reference to others' research on religious expression. Some of that other research emerged from a British context; specifically, Lesley Francis conducted two large-scale studies of school children aged 13–15 and was able to demonstrate significant relationships between personal Bible reading and students' perspectives on drug-taking, and on the sense of meaning in life.[20] Though Jeynes does not acknowledge it, there is obviously a difference between personal Bible reading and studying the Bible in a classroom context (or in any guided manner); supporting that distinction, another research study has shown that personal Bible reading is a much higher indicator of biblical literacy among adults than participation in formal programmes.[21]

---

[19] W. H. Jeynes, 'The relationship between biblical literacy, academic achievement, and school behavior among Christian- and public-school students', *Journal of Research on Christian Education* 18, 1 (2009): 36–55. Consulted online in unpaginated form. www.tandfonline.com/doi/abs/10.1080/10656210902751826 [accessed 5 November 2012].

[20] L. J. Francis, 'The relationship between bible reading and attitude toward substance use among 13–15 year olds', *Religious Education* 97, 1 (Winter 2002): 44–60 and L. J. Francis 'The relationship between bible reading and purpose in life among 13–15-year-olds'; *Mental Health, Religion & Culture* 3, 1 (2000): 27–36.

[21] R. Filback and S. Krashen, 'The impact of reading the bible and studying the bible on biblical knowledge', *Knowledge Quest* 31, 2 (2002): 50–1. Filback and Krashen used the

Assessing biblical literacy

I have positioned the quest for, or rather the desire for, wider biblical literacy in the context of older campaigns for the dissemination of knowledge of the Bible or of scripture. The drive to give people access to the Bible in their own language motivated multiple translations in the 1500s, aided by the printing press. In part, those reponsible wanted to amend the behaviour of the church, so there was a moral concern in addition to (or involved with) the spiritual one; but that drive is not presented in terms of a decline in public biblical knowledge. For the specific argument that biblical literacy is in decline, let us shift to the late 1950s. This also provides us with an opportunity to see how biblical literacy has been assessed.

Thomas Roy Pendell, an Adventist pastor 'serving a college community'[22] in the USA conducted a written survey of his adult congregants, finding 63 per cent of them were 'biblically illiterate'.[23] He found that 75 per cent of them did not recognize Pentecost; nearly half did not know the significance of Gethsemane; and a third knew nothing of (the) Exodus. The test Pendell set had ten questions, and his congregants' median score was just three out of ten; that was in c. 1959. To what was this attributed? In January 1960, an editorial in the *Advent Review and Sabbath Herald* responded:

> What is the cause of the woeful state of Biblical ignorance that prevails in the popular churches today? For something more than half a century there has been a studied attempt on the part of a great many Protestant ministers to downgrade the reliability and importance of the Bible.[24]

This example predates the legislation that prevented devotional use of the Bible in American classrooms (and to which we saw Jeynes attribute a decline in moral behaviour). Notice also that the editorial regards the shift as having taken place more than 50 years earlier, around the turn of the previous century and, as it happens, the era when the KJV began to be displaced by newer, revised versions.

'Bible Character Recognition Test', administered through a questionnaire. They analysed responses from 102 adult subjects, all aged between 19 and 68 and affiliated with 'a multi-denominational Christian non-profit service organization' (p. 50).

[22] R. F. C., 'Editorial', *Advent Review and Sabbath Herald*, 1960, www.adventistarchives.org [accessed 5 November 2012]; author's full name not available.

[23] R. L. Saucy, 'Doing theology for the Church (the necessity of systematic theology)', *Journal of the Evangelical Theological Society* 16 (1973): 1–9 (1); T. R Pendell, 'Biblical literacy test', *The Christian Century* 76 (1959): 12–13.

[24] R. F. C, 'Editorial', For additional background information, cf. I. C. Hine 'Practicing Biblical Literacy: Case Studies from the Sheffield Conference', postscripts, forthcoming, 2012. Personally, I suspect that had the writer not been an Adventist, and therefore a minority Protestant, he or she might have targeted biblical scholars rather than the 'great many Protestant ministers'.

Surveys like Pendell's continue to be conducted and their results published with a firm assertion that biblical literacy is in decline. But such surveys have limited value: the samples are often small (Jeynes surveyed 180 pupils, Pendell 300 congregants); the interpreters are typically biased (*viz* Jeynes on moral behaviour);[25] and the studies are generally not repeated, so although we have snapshots that stretch over 60 years, they were not taken in the same way and often seem (at least superficially) to illustrate similar levels of 'illiteracy' rather than vastly different ones.

An exception is provided by Gallup polls, which provide comparative longitudinal data about personal Bible reading. Between 1990 and 2000, the number of US citizens reading the Bible at least once a week fell from 40 per cent to 37 per cent. Over a longer period, the number of 'occasional' readers fell from 73 per cent to 59 per cent. Although, as a cross-sectional study, the data presented cannot demonstrate whether this represents a change in individual lifestyles, or a generational shift, age was found to be a significant variable in Bible reading habits. The Gallup press release reported that '[f]ifty per cent of those over the age of 65 read the Bible at least weekly, compared to 27 percent of people between the ages of 18 and 29. Thirty-six percent of people in their 30s and 40s read the Bible that frequently'.[26] Given that Filback and Krashen found a strong correlation between such reading and biblical literacy among adults, this could be taken as implicit support for the claims of decline (see above). Extending the inter-generational picture, research from the CODEC project at Durham University, based on a sample of more than 900 people in England and Wales, found a significant difference between those under and over 45, having interviewed the subjects to see whether they knew anything about select Bible stories.[27] Results are, of course, highly dependent upon the methods used, the phrasing of questions, the atmosphere in which assessment is conducted, and other variables.[28]

---

[25] Jeynes also wholly fails to notice his Protestant bias in asking students to name the '66 books of the Bible'.

[26] Gallup, Alec and Wendy W. Simmons, 'Six in Ten Americans Read Bible at Least Occasionally: Percentage of Frequent Readers Has Decreased over Last Decade', Gallup, 20 October 2000, www.gallup.com/poll/2416/six-ten-americans-read-bible-least-occasionally. aspx [accessed 5 November 2012].

[27] '[F]indings show that the Church and politicians can no longer make assumptions about people's knowledge of the Bible, which in under-45s is in decline. Half of under-45s could not give accurate information about Samson and Delilah compared to a quarter of over-45s. Similarly 33 per cent of under-45s couldn't name anything about the Feeding of the 5,000 compared to 12 per cent of over-45s'. The interviewees represented faith and non-faith backgrounds. Durham University, 'Knowledge of the Bible is Declining, Researchers Say', 12 July 2009, www.dur.ac.uk/news/newsitem/?itemno=8234 [accessed 5 November 2012].

[28] Further evidence of lower biblical literacy among young adults is shown in 'The Bible in America Study', a telephone survey of 1,014 adults conducted by the Barna Group on behalf of the American Bible Society; in that case, however the distinction is between young adults (18–27) and those aged 28 or above, and demonstrates a decline in 'literacy' post-66 for two

The bible in education

Two of the studies presented at the Sheffield conference were concerned with the Bible's presence in British schools. The first involved a comparison of Religious Education in ten secondary schools (i.e. ages 11–16) and ten primary schools (ages 4–11) in Warwick. For the benefit of those not acquainted with the English system, Religious Education, or RE as it is commonly abbreviated, has an odd place in the curriculum. It is a statutory subject – all schools must provide religious education lessons for their students. However, its curriculum is governed not at a national level, but locally, with the syllabus agreed by an advisory council (there are around 200 in England and Wales). The national guidance is that 50 per cent of time should be spent on Christianity and 50 per cent on other faiths, that the lessons should give students opportunity to learn about religious practices and beliefs and to learn from them – to find some means to apply their learning to their own development. These lessons are not about being religious; that is, they are not in any way devotional or confessional, though the provision for faith schools is slightly different.

To continue, the comparison of primary and secondary schools found that teachers in primary school introduced and worked with whole passages from the Bible, often stories, and this was met by enthusiasm from the children. By secondary school, however, teachers operated with abbreviated Bible texts, typically in bullet-point form. In fact, Julia Ipgrave, lead researcher, observed: '*The Simpsons* cartoons had a more prominent place than the Bible in secondary RE lessons'.[29]

Also presenting at the Sheffield conference was Sarah Phillips, who teaches English at a secondary school in Cambridgeshire and who obtained research funding to explore ways to help her A level students make sense of biblical references in their core texts. During her project, Phillips worked with A level students at four different institutions, surveying their views about the relevance of the Bible and their knowledge of it prior to delivering a lesson designed to 'awaken' their thinking. Three findings are relevant here. Firstly, around 90 per cent of the 83-student cohort regarded RE

---

of the four survey questions: the reference of '3' in 'John three sixteen' and the main original language of the New Testament. Cf. American Bible Society/Barna Group. 'Football, Faith and John 3:16', 14 January 2012, www.barna.org/culture-articles/558-football-faith-and-john-316 [accessed 5 November 2012].

[29] J. Ipgrave, 'From Story Books to Bullet Points: Comparing the Status of Books in Primary and Secondary RE and the Implications for the Bible in School', at the Biblical Literacy and the Curriculum Conference, University of Sheffield, UK, 27 May 2011, unpublished. This was part of a research project carried out by the Warwick Religions and Education Research Unit and published by the Department for Children, Schools and Families; R. Jackson et al., 'Materials Used to Teach About World Religions in Schools in England', 2010. DCSF/ University of Warwick: Warwick. Available online at www.education.gov.uk/publications/ standard/publicationdetail/page1/DCSF-RR197

as a key source of their biblical knowledge, in spite of Ipgrave's observations. Secondly, scoring out of ten, students consistently placed the Bible's influence on literature higher than their own knowledge of the Bible, with an average of 2.5 points difference. Finally, while students initially showed little willingness to learn more, the suggestion (within a model lesson) that looking for biblical influence could improve their exam results led to a shift from 86 per cent approving a 'just tell us' approach to 83 per cent reporting they would make an increased effort to spot biblical influences in future.[30]

Returning, then, to the question of who should be biblically literate, and who wants it, the religious stakeholders are joined by another group.

Literary stakeholders

When Richard Dawkins declared that native English speakers who have never read (at least some of) the King James Bible were somewhat 'barbarian',[31] I assume that he meant this principally with regard to the fourth sense of the noun outlined by the *OED*: i.e. 'an uncultured person, or one who has no sympathy with literary culture' rather than 'one outside the pale of Christian civilization' (2.c) or a 'rude, wild, uncivilized person' (*OED* 3a), or perhaps even 'foreign' (*OED* 1).[32]

As you may infer from Philips' study and from Dawkins' remarks (though his endorsement for the donation of King James Bibles to England's secondary schools was presaged partly on the hope that anyone who actually read it would notice that its contents are less 'moral' than commonly supposed) there is a strong perception that knowledge of the Bible, epitomized by the King James Version, is a cultural asset and one

---

[30]These are not direct before/after comparators but give a sense of the shift in students' attitudes. Phillips' report is published in full on the Farmington Trust website: S. Phillips, 'The Bible and English: The Challenge of Teaching Biblically Rich Texts to Biblically Poor A-Level English Students' (2011, report TT272.) Farmington Trust, www.farmington.ac.uk [accessed 5 November 2012].

[31]'A native speaker of English who has never read a word of the King James Bible is verging on the barbarian.' R. Dawkins, 'Why I Want All Our Children to Read the King James Bible', *Observer*, 19 May 2012 www.guardian.co.uk/science/2012/may/19/richard-dawkins-king-james-bible [accessed 4 November 2012].

[32]'barbarian, n. and adj,' *OED* Online, September 2012. Oxford University Press, www.oed.com/Entry/15380 [accessed November 7, 2012]. The literary application is not recognized under the adjectival entry (barbarian, B), which lists only three meanings: (1) 'applied by nations, depreciatively, to foreigners'; (2) uncivilized, rude &c; and (3) 'Of or belonging to Barbary'. The context of Dawkins' earlier statement suggests he may also have intended something of sense 2.c: 'We are a Christian culture, we come from a Christian culture and not to know the King James Bible, is to be in some small way, barbarian'. (Dawkins/KJB Trust, 'Richard Dawkins Lends his Support to The King James Bible Trust', King James Bible Trust, 19 February 2010 www.kingjamesbibletrust.org/news/2010/02/19/richard-dawkins-lends-his-support-to-the-king-james-bible-trust [accessed 4 November 2012].

that will help those trying to make sense of English literature. Answering the questions for this clientele, the answer would run 'English students (and English-speakers more generally) should be biblically literate, according to cultural figures and those teaching English, so that they can understand biblical references in English-speaking culture and most especially in English literature'. This raises again the question of content: what would being 'biblically literate' look like in this paradigm? Is it more or less than 'knowing all the people, places, events and teachings in the Bible'?[33] To consider these questions, let us return to an earlier example; we will need to look also at the notion of cultural literacy.

The Bible Literacy Project

What lay behind Jeynes' study seems to have been the desire to promote the work of the Bible Literacy Project. Using the Bible in US classrooms has been, as implied earlier, a politically sensitive issue.

In 1962, a court ruling determined that any promotion of devotional activity by the state, including state-funded teachers, was incompatible with the First Amendment. Subsequent rulings from the Supreme Court made clear that teaching about the Bible was permissible provided that such teaching is 'presented objectively as part of a secular program of education'.[34] Nonetheless, the prohibition of devotional Bible reading created a hermeneutic of suspicion affecting any use of the Bible by teachers in the classroom.

That this is an ongoing problem was demonstrated by preparatory work for the Bible Literacy Project, a 'non-partisan, non-profit endeavor to encourage and facilitate the academic study of the Bible in public [i.e. state-funded] schools' in order to prevent students being '[left] in ignorance and cultural illiteracy'.[35] Teachers interviewed about their concerns using the Bible in class told the BLP that they were nervous and feared getting into trouble.[36] The BLP have tackled this by producing a textbook specifically designed for use in high schools entitled *The Bible and its Influence*. The textbook's publication in 2005 prompted a series of 'Bible Bills',

---

[33] Lutheran Bible Ministries.

[34] The quotation is taken from the case presented by the School District of Abington Twp v. Schempp, 374 U.S. 203, 225 (1963). See also Stone v. Graham, 449 U.S. 39, 42 (1980) (*per curiam*). Further references are available in *The Bible and Public Schools: A First Amendment Guide*, Front Royal, VA; Nashville, TN: Bible Literacy Project, and First Amendment Center, 1999.

[35] BLP, 'Frequently Asked Questions: About the Biblical Literacy Project'. Source www.bibleliteracy.org/site/Case/index.htm [accessed 4 November 2012].

[36] M. Wachlin, B. R. Johnson and the Biblical Literacy Project, 'Bible Literacy Report: What Do American Teens Need to Know and what Do They Know?', Front Royal, VA: Biblical Literacy Project (2005), p. 17.

each endorsing the delivery of appropriate elective courses. By February 2012, six US states had passed legislation encouraging Bible courses in government-funded schools, and a second edition of *The Bible and its Influence* was issued in 2011.[37]

Some of the legislation has been hostile to the textbook, with some feeling that the Bible should be its own textbook (generally in the guise of the King James Version). *The Bible and its Influence* has been attacked from another angle too, with an SBL reviewer criticizing it for failing to engage with historical–critical issues (e.g. dating, authorship).[38]

Broadening the biblical

Surveying teachers' views on critical Bible passages or references with which students need to be familiar, a BLP report suggests 25 items in Genesis and a further 25 in Matthew alone.[39] Yet, actually, the concept of 'biblical' for the literary scholar runs even wider. Nicky Hallett, Senior Lecturer in the School of English at the University of Sheffield, refers to the need for students to recognize the biblical 'reference' made by women spinning.[40] Another participant in a recent day symposium at the University of Sheffield, 'Beyond Belief: The Bible and Humanities Curriculum', remarked on the desirability of familiarity with the myriad hagiographies of the Golden Legend or at least its genre. The biblical in this instance goes beyond the confines of the Bible to include the post-biblical, too.

It is not that people in the early modern period, or the medieval world, were wholly illiterate in terms of theology or biblical knowledge; rather that they gleaned it from extra sources – whether mystery plays, the Legenda

---

[37] See Hine, 'Practicing Biblical Literacy'.

[38] S. L. McKenzie, 'Review of "The Bible and its Influence"', SBL Forum, November 2005, www.sbl-site.org/publications/article.aspx?articleId=465 [accessed 27 April 2012]. The angle of such critique raises questions about the role of the biblical academy as stakeholders in biblical literacy. For details of the politics surrounding the launch of *The Bible and its Influence* and its presentation within the Missouri, Alabama and Georgia legislatures, see Mark A. Chancey, 'Bible bills, bible curricula, and controversies of biblical proportions: legislative efforts to promote bible courses in public schools, *Religion & Education* 34 (2007): 28–47.

[39] See Wachlin et al., 'Bible Literacy Report', p. 20.

[40] Ibid., N. Hallett, discussion during 'Beyond Belief: The Bible and the Humanities Curriculum' symposium, the University of Sheffield, 7 March 2012. Hallett's primary association was with Eve, commonly depicted with a spindle in the medieval period; cf. the sermon attributed to the Lollard priest John Ball, 'When Adam dolve, and Eve span, / Who was then the gentleman?' (1381). The *OED* cites an earlier use of this rhyme (c. 1340) by the hermit Richard Rolle; cf. *OED* 'delve. v.' 7a. If there is a biblical antecedent, it may be the example of the valorous woman of Proverbs 31, whose use of the spindle is among her credits (cf. Prov. 31.19; 'spindle' appears in English bibles from the Wycliffite manuscripts, c. 1382, onward). I am grateful to Hilary Perry for this suggestion.

Aurea[41] or religious iconography. If we wish to interpret the past, we may need to equip ourselves not simply with a narrow 'biblical literacy' but with theological literacy, or some kind of historical–religious literacy.

Cultural literacy

The concept of 'cultural literacy' was formulated by E. D. Hirsch in the early 1980s. Examining the difficulties encountered by students from different backgrounds in American education, Hirsch observed that the obstacles were often not in the information on the page but the missing information – what the text-sender assumed that the recipient would already know (and thus would need to know to make sense of the information). 'The explicit meanings of a piece of writing', Hirsch argued, 'are the tip of an iceberg of meaning: the larger part lies below the surface of the text and is composed of the reader's own relevant knowledge'.[42]

Examining the links between cultural literacy and Bible translation, Ernst-August Gutt chose Luke 10.13–14 to demonstrate the depth of presupposed knowledge. The reader needs to know that Chorazin is Jewish, that Tyre and Sidon are the epitome of Gentile wickedness, that sackcloth and ashes are a sign of repentance, that 'mighty works' are a sign of divine interaction … and so on.[43] The receiver's relationship with the biblical text is thus more complex than the fact-knowing model proposed by the LBM. Consider another example, this time from the news archive of the Bible Literacy Project. A literature tutor at an American university reports being accosted by an anxious international student. The class have been studying T. S. Eliot's poem 'The Love Song of J. Alfred Prufrock'. Susan Froetschel describes the scenario:

> … the freshman was distraught, ready to drop the class.
>
> 'Everyone in class knew Lazarus and talked about him', he said in amazement, referring to the line in Eliot's haunting poem: 'To say: "I am Lazarus, come from the dead, Come back to tell you all, I shall tell you all.W
>
> 'How do they all know him?' he pressed me. 'Do you know who he is?'[44]

---

[41] Englished as the Golden Legend, the collection of saints' lives was among the first works printed in English, published by William Caxton in 1483.

[42] E. D. Hirsch, *Cultural Literacy: What Every American Needs to Know*; with an appendix, 'What Literate Americans Know' E. D. Hirsch, Jr., Joseph Kett and James Trefil., Boston: Houghton Mifflin, 1987, pp. 33–4.

[43] Via E-A. Gutt, 'Aspects of "cultural literacy" relevant to bible translation', *Journal of Translation* 2 (2006): 1–16 (4).

[44] Susan Froetschel, 'Back to School – with the Bible', *The Washington Post*, 11 September 2012.

As Froetschel explains, the encounter predates Wikipedia. One might argue that this anecdote contradicts the 'decline in biblical literacy', especially when I reveal that the international student was also Muslim. Yet the university in question was Yale; the anecdote refers to an exceptionally literate group of young people. Jeynes noted that attainment and biblical literacy were closely correlated. If biblical literacy is a subset of cultural literacy, it is fair to suppose that those with high attainment will typically show high levels of literacy across the board. (Were we inclined to be 'commercial' about it, the simplest argument for individual biblical literacy is that it may improve your grades, albeit in combination with other literacy competencies.)

At the time of the Sheffield conference, one strategy for extending biblical literacy was still a work in progress: Nicky Hallett has been the lead actor, advised to some extent by Hugh Pyper, and working with colleagues in the University of Sheffield's School of English, to design a new course module.

'What is a Jew?'
'How was paradise lost?'
'What genesis/exodus/epiphany?'
'A Judas? A thrice-crowing cock?'
'The voice of my beloved in the garden?'

These are the sort of questions lecturers in the School of English faced on a regular basis. Finding the right response proved difficult. Whether Eden or the Crucifixion, the subtle use of imagery in literature 'becomes', to quote Hallett, 'paradoxically over-important' when every reference has to be explained.[45] Prior to the introduction of the module, students would often show resistance to a perceived 'piety' if someone in their seminar group noticed religious imagery (and Hallett herself has been mistaken for a nun because some of her research focuses on medieval nuns' devotional writing).[46] Getting students to approach the Bible's role as a 'foundation of literary study' sympathetically and intelligently was thus a critical step.

The course is introduced by a 20-question quiz, providing a benchmark for both lecturers and students. The content of the module refers back to the quiz questions, giving students a clear sense of their developing knowledge and its relevance. Weekly lectures are delivered by different researchers, so each can exercise their own area of expertise (supplementing it with biblical material) and students gain an insight into the School's wider curriculum.

In each lecture, students are invited to consider the construction of a biblical text and its literary uses, in tandem. The module was intentionally

---

[45] N. Hallett, 'Case Study A: Beyond Belief – Teaching Religious Literature in a Secular Age' in Hine, *Practicing Biblical Literacy*, p. 45.
[46] N. Hallet, discussion during 'Beyond Belief' symposium, March 2012.

designed with a dual aim, not only to develop biblical literacy but also to develop learners' independent research skills (giving them skills for university in general). At the end of the course, students are assessed by a 45-minute paper. They receive three questions to prepare for in advance (three texts to research), but only one to write on. The paper requires them to provide an account of their research process, not just the content of their findings, ensuring that both aims are met (and that students have conducted their own research). The module ran for the first time in 2011–12, and it is too early to provide a detailed assessment of its effects, but student feedback was extremely positive – wanting more not less.

In earlier reflections on this subject, I observed that the promise of better grades often tempts the reluctant student,[47] but this is not actually the type of satisfaction the teacher is looking for. Every tutor likes to mark better papers, but the more satisfying outcome is students 'getting it' – being able to make sense of the detail, the background.

Engaging other literacies

The Sheffield English module is one possible solution for a particular issue with literacy, and though no longitudinal study of its outcomes is yet possible, it has been effective in terms of enthusiasm. Notice that the problem was partly resistance to learning – hostility to the piety of the seminar student who knew or recognized something 'biblical'. In the UK, there appears to be a cultural attitude that makes biblical literacy somehow unwelcome. At the same time, and somewhat contradictorily, we have figures like Richard Dawkins, David Cameron and Michael Gove calling for increased biblical literacy. There may be a problem there: it becomes something perceived as elitist, conservative, or perhaps even right-wing.[48]

Previously, I began to draw out parallels between the discourse of the early modern period, especially the Reformation era, and the present day. The potential for mass production of bibles was the result of a media revolution, the printing press, that made reading practically possible; and as a relatively new technology, the possibility of reading was valued. But we have taken mass production to a whole new level.

The mathematician Alfred Korzybski (1879–1950) attempted to calculate the multiplication of scientific knowledge beginning in the year 1 CE. His

---

[47] Hine, 'Practicing Biblical Literacy'.

[48] A large majority of readers of the *Guardian* newspaper, known for its left-wing leanings, voted 'no' when polled about the distribution of King James Bibles to English schools. Cf. 'Michael Gove to Send Copy of King James Bible to All English Schools', *Guardian*, 25 November 2011, sec. Politics, www.guardian.co.uk/politics/2011/nov/25/michael-gove-king-james-bible

calculations were popularized by Robert Anton Wilson (1932–2007), who named Korzybski's units 'jesuses'. According to Korzybski's calculations, it took until the year 1500 CE for the known facts of science to double (2 jesus), a further 250 years for them to double again (1750, 4j). By 1900, there were 8j; by 1950, 16j; and – by Wilson's extrapolations – in 1982, 512j. While these figures were intended only for scientific fact, the growth of the 'knowable' is obviously wider.

As the knowable grows, layers of literacy accrete, the peaks (and expectations) of literacy grow. If real, the decline in biblical knowledge may reflect multiplication of material not just in print but now also online – we cannot possibly ingest it all;[49] increasing access to internet resources such as Wikipedia may engender the perception that little ingestion is really necessary. More than this, the expectation that all should aim for the highest levels of 'written' literacy should not go wholly unquestioned; our peculiar ways of being literate may fail to attend to, to value other literacy practices, other literacies.

There is a standard question in the Early Church History exams at Cambridge University: to what extent was St Augustine's conversion typical of Christians in his period? The answer is 'not very'. In his Confessions, Augustine describes hearing a childlike voice calling to him: 'Tolle lege, Take up and read!' He was a book-led man, moving progressively from Cicero through Manichaeism and neo-Platonism before arriving at Christianity. In contrast, Socrates had pooh-poohed 'written speech', the latest media revolution, partly because books were impersonal and could not adjust to the audience's needs. Augustine's literacy was writing-based, and he embraced a religion focused on the written word, on scripture. But oral literacy is itself a prize – as we intuit from the awe we feel for people who speak without notes, or from Moses' response to his call and the engagement of Aaron as a spokesperson.[50] There are other real literacies too, and other places the Bible is found today.[51]

Some of the best research on literacy and pedagogy begins from the recognition that we learn in real situations. People read the news they expect to discuss: in the words of Lauren Resnick, 'what one chooses to

---

[49] The perception of 'decline' in biblical knowledge may be symptomatic of a greater awareness of or interest in those who do not know, those now judged 'illiterate' by the literate elite; it might also reflect the widening of participation in higher education – those from less-literate families typically have less exposure and so lower cultural literacy, but have been encouraged to engage with higher levels of education (thus increasing the numbers of non-biblically literate students within higher education). On the latter point, cf. D. A. Jameson, 'Literacy in decline: untangling the evidence', in Business Communication Quarterly 70 (March 2007): 16–33.

[50] Exodus 4.10–16.

[51] One example is Cheryl Exum's call for the addition of 'visual criticism' to the biblical scholar's toolkit, a tool that relies upon visual literacy. J. C. Exum, 'A Role for the Arts in Biblical Studies', paper delivered at the Department of Biblical Studies Research Seminar, University of Sheffield, 29 October 2012.

read in a newspaper probably depends to an important degree on what kinds of conversations one anticipates'.[52] Reading occurs where we have external motivation, because there is some practical application. A child learns to read recipes or bedtime stories with the parents' assistance or 'scaffolding' because they enjoy cake and stories.

If *The Simpsons* is in the RE classroom, it could be there for good reasons: a critical, analytical approach to the cartoon is found in the online forums. Discussion of a season 10 episode, 'Simpsons Bible Stories', covers everything from God's hand having the wrong number of fingers (apparently, five is the done thing for the divine in Springfield; this is Simpsons-literacy at work), to the fig leaves arriving before Homer and Marge have eaten any fruit in Eden.[53] In this instance, people are voluntarily engaging their own biblical literacy as part of a shared discourse. Wherever the Bible appears in popular culture, or culture more broadly, somebody is using it knowingly or it would not be there to spot, and if it was not going to be spotted it would be less meaningful. (While an artist may incorporate references that he or she realizes may not be spotted, it is not quite the same with advertising or comedy.)

Resnick argues that literacy is best learned through apprenticeships – participating in something meaningful. There are two examples, shared at the Sheffield conference and published as case studies on the proceedings, that I think take this forward. The first is that of a lecturer in economics who uses the Joseph cycle (Gen. 39–45) and Nehemiah 5 to engage his students in critical reflection on debt cycles – who benefits, and so forth. From the account given, it is clear that this is is a personal quest conducted on the part of the lecturer, but involving the students in that quest.[54]

The second example is that of Carl Tighe, Professor of Creative Writing at the University of Derby in the UK. Creative writing is a new subject in universities, and sometimes demeaned for that. In response, Tighe invites students to consider the effort and discipline of scribes in the ancient world. They examine the relationship between Jeremiah and Baruch, his scribe, an illustration of the early movement between oral and written word (Jer. 36). They also consider the example of Nahash's inexplicable siege in 1 Samuel 11.1–2, reflecting on how critical the transmission of the written word can be; in this case, the omission of Hebrew words by an ancient copyist presented an inexplicable scenario and a mystery resolved only by a complete text found among the Dead Sea Scrolls. The use of such stimuli is intended not only to provoke students' imaginations, but also to present creative writing as 'the oldest, the original subject' without which

---

[52] L. B. Resnick, 'Literacy in school and out', *Daedalus* 119, 2 (1990): 169–85 (177).

[53] 'Simpsons Bible Stories', *The Simpsons*, Archive, n.d., www.snpp.com/episodes/AABF14 [accessed 5 November 2012].

[54] See J. L. Lopez-Calle (Case-study B) in Hine, 'Practicing Biblical Literacy'.

others would not operate. Tighe's account provides the sense of a quest for meaning shared with his students.[55]

Towards a conclusion

To summarize, in this 'quest' I have focused on two major proponents of, or stakeholders in, biblical literacy: the religious, who hope for an impact on morality and conversation, and whose desire is more precisely that of 'scriptural literacy', and the literary academic, for whom the ability to recognize the biblical is its own satisfaction, but whose notion of 'biblical' extends beyond the limits of the printed Bible. Unfortunately, the latter is accompanied at times by a form of cultural philistinism – though this is to slander the Philistines! – because it places high value on written literacy to the neglect of other forms, sometimes with a political edge. There are others with a stake in the quest for biblical literacy, not least the biblical academy, but such stakes remain to be explored elsewhere.

Compared with the eras of Jerome, Coverdale or the 1611 King James Version, it is far easier to read the Bible today: it is available in multiple forms, and in fonts that are more accessible than the heavy type of the sixteenth and seventeenth centuries. Yet it is fairly surely less read or heard by the average individual. This is in spite of the statistic that '3 Bibles [are] sold or given away every second'.[56] Perhaps it is time to call for apprenticeships (whatever they would look like)!

Bibliography

Augustijn, Cornelis, *Erasmus: His Life, Works, and Influence* (English translation from Dutch, Oscar Beck), London: University of Toronto Press, 1991.

Bray, G., *Translating the Bible: From William Tyndale to King James*, London: Latimer Trust, 2011.

Chancey, Mark A., 'Bible bills, bible curricula, and controversies of biblical proportions: legislative efforts to promote bible courses in public schools, *Religion & Education*, 34 (2007): 28–47.

Crossley, J., 'Jesus and the Chaos of History: Redirecting the Quest for the Historical Jesus', paper delivered at the Department of Biblical Studies Research Seminar, University of Sheffield, 15 October 2012.

Dawkins, R., 'Why I Want All Our Children to Read the King James Bible', *Observer*, 19 May 2012.

---

[55] See C. Tighe (Case-study C) in ibid.

[56] D. Cameron. 'Prime Minister's King James Bible Speech: Commemorating the Version's 400th Anniversary'. Number 10, 16 December 2011, www.number10.gov.uk/news/king-james-bible/ [accessed 5 November 2012].

Exum, J. C., 'A Role for the Arts in Biblical Studies', paper delivered at the Department of Biblical Studies Research Seminar, University of Sheffield, 29 October 2012.

Filback, R. and S. Krashen, 'The impact of reading the bible and studying the bible on biblical knowledge', *Knowledge Quest* 31, 2 (2002): 50–1.

Francis, L. J., 'The relationship between bible reading and attitude toward substance use among 13–15 year olds', *Religious Education* 97, 1 (Winter 2002): 44–60.

—'The relationship between bible reading and purpose in life among 13–15-year-olds', *Mental Health, Religion & Culture* 3, 1 (2000): 27–365.

Froetschel, Susan, 'Back to School – with the Bible', *The Washington Post*, 11 September 2012.

Gallup, Alec and Wendy W. Simmons, 'Six in Ten Americans Read Bible at Least Occasionally: Percentage of Frequent Readers Has Decreased over Last Decade', Gallup, 20 October 2000.

Gutt, A., 'Aspects of "cultural literacy" relevant to bible translation', *Journal of Translation*, 2 (2006): 1–6.

Hine, I. 'Practicing biblical literacy: Case studies from the Sheffield Conference', *Postscripts: The Journal of Sacred and Contemporary Worlds* (special issue, Biblical Literacy and the Curriculum; forthcoming, 2013).

Hirsch, E. D., *Cultural Literacy: What Every American Needs to Know*, Boston: Houghton Mifflin, 1987.

Ipgrave, J., 'From Story Books to Bullet Points: Comparing the Status of Books in Primary and Secondary RE and the Implications for the Bible in School', Biblical Literacy and The Curriculum Conference, University of Sheffield, UK, 27 May 2011. Unpublished.

Jackson, R. et al, Materials Used to Teach About World Religions in Schools in England, 2010. DCSF/University of Warwick: Warwick. Available online at www.education.gov.uk/publications/standard/publicationdetail/page1/DCSF-RR197

Jameson, D. A., 'Literacy in decline: Untangling the evidence', *Business Communication Quarterly* 70 (2007): 16–33.

Jeynes, W. H., 'The relationship between biblical literacy, academic achievement, and school behavior among Christian- and public-school students', *Journal of Research on Christian Education* 18, 1 (2009): 36–55.

Latré, G., 'English Bibles in Antwerp (1526–38)', paper delivered at the Department of Biblical Studies Research Seminar, University of Sheffield, 19 March 2012, unpublished.

Pendell, T. R, 'Biblical Literacy Test', *The Christian Century*, 76 (1959): 12–13.

Phillips, S., 'The Bible and English: The Challenge of Teaching Biblically Rich Texts to Biblically Poor A-level English Students' (Report TT272.) Farmington Trust, 2011, www.farmington.ac.uk

Resnick, L. B., 'Literacy in School and Out', *Daedalus* 119, 2 (1990): 169–85.

R. F. C., 'Editorial,' *Advent Review and Sabbath Herald*, 1960, www.adventistarchives.org

Saucy, R. L., 'Doing theology for the Church (the necessity of systematic theology)', *Journal of the Evangelical Theological Society*, 16 (1973): 1–9.

'Simpsons Bible Stories', *The Simpsons* Archive, n.d., www.snpp.com/episodes/AABF14

Vasagar, J., 'Michael Gove to Send Copy of King James Bible to All English Schools', *Guardian*, 25 November 2011.

Wachlin, M., B. R. Johnson and the Biblical Literacy Project, 'Bible Literacy Report: What Do American Teens Need to Know and what Do They Know?', Front Royal, VA: Biblical Literacy Project, 2005.

White, Carolinne (ed. and trans.), *Lives of Roman Christian Women*, Penguin, 2010, unpaginated e-book.

PART TWO

Visual Literacies

4

Loss of the Bible and the Bible in *Lost*: Biblical Literacy and Mainstream Television

Matthew A. Collins
(University of Chester)

Introduction

Recent well-publicized efforts to encourage biblical literacy have emerged as a direct response to its perceived 'decline'. There appears, for instance, to be a marked difference between levels of biblical literacy in the nineteenth century and the present. The prominence of the Bible within the Victorian education system and the 'mass exposure to Scripture' beyond it gave rise to a widespread remarkable familiarity with the biblical text and its themes, characters and motifs.[1] This stands in apparent stark contrast to the 'biblically illiterate world' of today,[2] where the ostensible 'absence' of the Bible has 'contributed to a steady disintegration of ... basic awareness of biblical stories and characters'.[3]

Acknowledging the indebtedness of much of Western culture to the Bible, Timothy T. Larsen suggests that familiarity with the text 'decodes

---

[1] T. T. Larsen, 'Literacy and biblical knowledge: The victorian age and our own', *Journal of the Evangelical Theological Society*, 52/3 (2009): 519–25.
[2] J. S. Lang, *The Bible on the Big Screen: A Guide from Silent Films to Today's Movies*, Grand Rapids, MI: Baker Books, 2007; S. Prothero, 'We Live in a Land of Biblical Idiots'/'Reading, Writing and Revelation', *Los Angeles Times*, 14 March 2007.
[3] K. K. Manzo, K. K., 'The bible makes a comeback', *Education Week*, 26/37 (2007): 25; G. M. Burge, 'The greatest story never read: Recovering biblical literacy in the Church'. *Christianity Today*, 43/9 (1999):

our own cultural inheritance' and 'serves as the gateway ... to advanced literacy and high literary culture for a western society'.[4] Conversely, biblical illiteracy constitutes something of a stumbling block, rendering inaccessible the countless scriptural allusions that (even unseen) continue to saturate our culture and society. The assumed (or feared) gradual 'loss' of the Bible to modern society at large has given rise to a renewed determination in some quarters to ensure an ongoing engagement and familiarity with what ex-poet laureate Sir Andrew Motion calls 'an essential piece of cultural luggage'.[5] Amid claims that religious literacy generally, and biblical literacy in particular, are not only desirable but specifically beneficial educational objectives, having both academic and behavioural impacts,[6] concerted efforts have been made in recent years to redress and encourage biblical literacy within the education systems of both the UK and the US. In May 2012, the UK Secretary of State for Education, Michael Gove, sent a copy of the King James Bible to every state school in the country, with the express purpose of underscoring 'the impact it has had on today's English-speaking society',[7] an undertaking backed even by renowned atheist Richard Dawkins,[8] while in the US attempts have been made to introduce regular Bible courses to public schools, a move aimed specifically at the promotion of biblical literacy.[9]

The established position appears, therefore, to be one which posits the 'loss' of the Bible as a self-evident problem to be rectified in our modern, biblically illiterate society. However, while the average person's overall familiarity with the minutiae of the Bible has undoubtedly reduced over the past 150 years (an inevitable result of the less prominent role played by the text in daily life),[10] is it necessarily the case that we live now in a

---

[4]Larsen, 'Literacy and biblical knowledge', p. 528.
[5]J. Bingham, 'Poet Laureate Andrew Motion Calls for All Children to be Taught the Bible', *Telegraph*, 17 February 2009.
[6]D. Carr, 'Religious education, religious literacy and common schooling: A philosophy and history of skewed reflection', *Journal of Philosophy of Education*, 41/4 (2007); W. H. Jeynes, 'The relationship between biblical literacy, academic achievement, and school behavior among Christian- and public-school students'. *Journal of Research on Christian Education*, 18 (2009); W. H. Jeynes, 'The relationship between bible literacy and behavioral and academic outcomes in urban areas: a meta-analysis', *Education and Urban Society*, 42/5 (2010).
[7]Vasagar, J., 'Michael Gove to Send Copy of King James Bible to all English Schools', *Guardian*, 25 November 2011; J. Crossley, 'Biblical Literacy and the *English King James Liberal Bible*: A twenty-first century tale of capitalism, nationalism and nostalgia', *Postscripts* (forthcoming).
[8]R. Dawkins, 'Why I Want All our Children to Read the King James Bible', *Observer*, 19 May 2012.
[9]Gallagher, E. V., 'Teaching for religious literacy', *Teaching Theology and Religion*, 12/3 (2009): 208–21; Jeynes, 'The Relationship Between Biblical Literacy'; Manzo, 'The Bible Makes a Comeback'; S. Mehta, 'Bible Finds a Place in Schools', *Los Angeles Times*, August 2007, p. 5; Prothero, 'We Live in a Land of Biblical Idiots'.
[10]Larsen, 'Literacy and biblical knowledge'.

'biblically illiterate world'? Katie Edwards has demonstrated the continuing impact of biblical allusion and symbolism within the context of marketing and advertising,[11] the presence and implied usefulness of which assumes a degree of (at least subconscious) recognition on the part of the consumer. Contributors to the present volume have likewise explored a range of alternative avenues (or 'ways of knowing') by which biblical literacy might be recognized in cultural uses and appropriations of the Bible. Thus, when it comes to biblical or religious literacy, as Elaine Graham notes:

> [I]t may be that media and popular culture are as influential as more formal sectors such as education. Such a suggestion is reinforced by trends in contemporary scholarship in religion, media, and culture which argue that popular culture and media perform an increasingly influential role in articulating and constructing people's perceptions and orientations to the sacred.[12]

Taking this as our cue, we address the question of biblical literacy from the perspective of mainstream television, further problematizing a straightforward assumption of its decline. Focusing on the popular US television series *Lost* (2004–10, ABC), we highlight the surprising prominence of biblical allusion (both implicit and explicit) throughout. This in turn raises questions about biblical literacy on the part of the writers and audience, as well as the extent to which the programme itself might function as an unwitting tool for the promotion of biblical literacy.

The world of *Lost*

Lost was the brainchild of Jeffrey Lieber, J. J. Abrams and Damon Lindelof. Under the direction of its head writers, Damon Lindelof and Carlton Cuse, the story spanned six seasons and 121 episodes (totalling some 91 hours), airing between 22 September 2004 and 23 May 2010. In addition, there were 13 short 'mobisodes' ('Missing Pieces', released November 2007 to January 2008, between Seasons 3 and 4) and a 12-minute epilogue ('The New Man in Charge', released August 2010, three months after the end of Season 6).

When it originally aired in the US, the programme averaged 15.69 million viewers per episode in Season 1 and retained an overall average of

---

[11] K. B. Edwards, *Admen and Eve: The Bible in Contemporary Advertising*, Sheffield: Sheffield Phoenix Press, 2012.

[12] E. Graham, 'Religious Literacy and Public Service Broadcasting: Introducing a Research Agenda', in G. Lynch and J. Mitchell with A. Strhan (eds), *Religion, Media and Culture: A Reader*, London: Routledge, 2012, p. 230.

nearly 14 million viewers per episode over the course of the six seasons. In addition, it was one of the most watched shows online, as well as one of the most frequently downloaded or recorded.[13] The results of a survey carried out in 2006 suggested it was the second most popular television show internationally,[14] and in 2012 it was declared the highest-ranking show of the previous 10 years.[15] In 2010, the White House even decided against holding the State of the Union Address on 2 February in order to avoid a clash with the premiere of the show's final season. In return, Lindelof and Cuse offered President Barack Obama the opportunity to ask them any question he wanted, an offer he reportedly took them up on.[16]

The show centred on the survivors of a plane crash (Oceanic Flight 815 from Sydney to Los Angeles) who find themselves stranded on a mysterious Pacific island. No attempt to summarize *Lost* can really come close to doing justice to its complexity or depth, but some key points may help to provide a general overview of the plot. In Season 1, the survivors soon realize that this is no ordinary island – they encounter polar bears in the jungle, hear the roars of an unseen 'monster' and see apparitions of dead people. One character, John Locke, finds that, while paralyzed and confined to a wheel-chair before the crash, he is now able to walk again. Flashbacks to their lives before the crash reveal peculiar coincidences that seem to connect the various survivors in some way, hinting at some larger purpose behind events. Deep in the jungle, they discover a sealed metal hatch set into the ground and begin to realize that they are not alone on the island.

In Season 2, the group discovers that the hatch leads to an underground research station built in the 1970s by a group called the Dharma Initiative, where an 'incident' in the past has meant that a button must now be pushed every 108 minutes. They continue to encounter the 'monster', revealed to be an ominous cloud of black smoke, and a number of the survivors are captured or killed by the mysterious 'Others' living on the island. In Season 3, they learn that the Dharma Initiative were wiped out years ago by the Others who, although nominally led by a man named Benjamin Linus, ultimately answer to an as-yet-unseen figure known as Jacob. Meanwhile, the survivors find a way to contact a nearby freighter. In Season 4, it becomes clear that the freighter crew are not there to rescue them and the survivors have to join forces with

---

[13] Ratings retrieved from http://en.wikipedia.org/wiki/List_of_Lost_episodes, http://lostpedia. wikia.com/wiki/Ratings and http://en.wikipedia.org/wiki/Lost_(TV_series) [accessed 27 March 2013].

[14] BBC, 'CSI Show "Most Popular in World"', *BBC News*, 31 July 2006.

[15] S. Schillaci, 'Johnny Depp, "The Dark Knight," "Lost" Named to IMDb's Top 10 of the Last Decade', *The Hollywood Reporter*, 25 January 2012, from www.hollywoodreporter. com/news/brad-pitt-johnny-depp-dark-knight-lost-imdb-top-10-284912 [accessed 27 March 2013]. On *Lost* as 'mainstream television', see A. Letak, 'Accidental Intellectuals: *Lost* Fandom and Philosophy', in P. Moore (ed.), *LOST Thought University Edition: Leading Thinkers Discuss LOST*. Scotts Valley, CA: CreateSpace, 2012, esp. pp. 93–5.

[16] See B. East, 'Fans May Forever be Lost for Answers', *The National*, 18 January 2010.

Benjamin and the Others in order to repel them. Six of the survivors manage to make it off the island before seeing it disappear in a flash of light.

In Season 5, those left on the island find themselves in the 1970s alongside the Dharma Initiative, their actions in the past causing the very 'incident' that necessitated the function of the hatch in Season 2. In the present, the few who made it off the island are eventually persuaded to return, while a mysterious 'Man in Black' orchestrates the death of Jacob. In Season 6, it is revealed that Jacob and the nameless 'Man in Black' were once twin brothers, an ancient conflict between the two resulting in the latter's 'death'. Jacob became the island's ageless guardian, responsible for protecting the 'light' at the heart of the island (the source of its healing properties, and inferred to have a wider significance for the world at large), while his brother returned as the vengeful 'smoke monster', able to assume the shape of dead people and determined to both extinguish the light and destroy the island. The survivors realize that they were each brought to the island for a purpose, as 'candidates' to replace Jacob. Ultimately, the 'Man in Black' is destroyed, one of the group becomes the island's new guardian and the remaining few still alive manage finally to escape.

Against this backdrop of an ancient 'cosmic conflict' between good and evil, light and dark, a number of other prominent themes emerge throughout the series, including science vs. faith, fate vs. coincidence and determinism vs. free will. The creation of a *Lost* mythology is seen perhaps most readily in 'the Numbers' (4, 8, 15, 16, 23, 42), which play a key role in Season 2 and are hidden in plain sight throughout all six seasons (found, for instance, on the hatch, a winning lottery ticket, a sports team at the airport, the mileage of a car, etc., as well as in the immediate context of Flight 815 itself, which left Sydney from Gate 23). Devices such as these cleverly imbue everything which is seen or heard with potential significance, thereby encouraging (over-)analysis of the minutest details of the series. The programme is furthermore saturated with symbolism and allusion, being filled to the brim with intertextual references to literature, philosophy and culture. Sarah Clarke Stuart notes with regard to the show's intricate and pointed use of literary texts:

> [W]hether through a recirculation and appropriation of story lines and dialogue, or on-screen appearances of the stories ... *Lost* re-contextualises these traditional narratives, bestowing new cultural significance on them.[17]

Similarly, many characters share names with prominent philosophers (e.g. Locke, Hume, Bentham, Rousseau, Bakunin) or scientists (e.g. Faraday,

---

[17] S. C. Stuart, *Literary Lost: Viewing Television Through the Lens of Literature*, New York: Continuum, 2011, p. 5.

Hawking).[18] This alerts us to the potential significance of some of the biblical names used (Jacob, Benjamin, Aaron, Isaac, etc.), not to mention the religiously loaded name of one of the main protagonists, Jack Shephard (or indeed his father, Christian Shephard). Closer examination reveals that the Bible sits firmly alongside the other literary works utilized and referred to within the series, with frequent explicit and implicit allusions to the biblical text throughout having an undeniable bearing upon the complex issue of contemporary biblical literacy.

Explicit allusion to the bible in *Lost*

Several episodes of *Lost* have names that reference the Bible. Most prominent are 'Exodus' (S1E23–24/25), in which a group of survivors trek across the island towards a pillar of smoke (recalling the pillar of cloud that guided the Israelites in Exod. 13.21–2), and 'The 23rd Psalm' (S2E10), in which Psalm 23 is at one point recited over a funeral pyre.[19] Other more indirect allusions might include 'Numbers' (S1E18; though ostensibly about 'the Numbers' themselves, the biblical connotations have been picked up on),[20] 'Fire + Water' (S2E12; an episode featuring baptism, the title seemingly referencing Mt. 3.11 and Lk. 3.16), and '316' (S5E06; ostensibly referring to a flight number, though promotional materials make clear that Jn 3.16 is here in focus).[21]

There are also numerous explicit references to biblical figures and events, often utilized as a point of comparison or illustration. In the Season 1 episode 'House of the Rising Sun' (S1E06), the survivors discover two skeletons lying side by side in a cave. Upon realizing that one of them is female, they are quickly nicknamed 'Adam and Eve', their true identities remaining a mystery until near the end of Season 6 (S6E15).[22] On separate occasions, both Jack Shephard and John Locke are compared to Moses (Jack by Naomi Dorrit in the finale of Season 3 [S3E22/23], and Locke by Benjamin Linus in the finale of Season 5 [S5E16/17]). In each case this is in the context of them leading a large group across the island, prompting parallels with the biblical exodus.

---

[18] See further, S. F. Parker, 'Appendix: Who are Locke, Hume, and Rousseau? The Losties' Guide to Philosophers', in S. Kaye (ed.), *The Ultimate Lost and Philosophy: Think Together, Die Alone*, Hoboken, NJ: Wiley, 2011.

[19] The shorthand 'S#E##' is used here throughout to refer to season and episode number.

[20] For instance, Stuart, *Literary Lost*, pp. 17–18, 54 and http://lostpedia.wikia.com/wiki/Numbers_(episode)

[21] See http://lostpedia.wikia.com/wiki/316 and http://lostpedia.wikia.com/wiki/Ajira_Airways

[22] When in 2010 offered the opportunity to ask Lindelof and Cuse any question he liked, President Barack Obama reportedly asked about the identities of 'Adam and Eve' (see n. 16 above).

Similarly, in the Season 2 episode 'Adrift' (S2E02), a character's situation is explicitly compared to the story of David and Goliath.

In a flashback towards the beginning of 'Catch-22' (S3E17), Desmond Hume and Brother Campbell discuss the story of Abraham and Isaac (Gen. 22). Noting that the wine produced by the monastery where he is staying is labelled 'Moriah Vineyards', Desmond questions the peculiar choice of name, further suggesting that 'God need not have asked Abraham to sacrifice his son in the first place'. In response, Brother Campbell counters: 'Well then it wouldn't have been much of a test, would it brother? Perhaps you underestimate the value of sacrifice'. This frank discussion of Genesis 22 forms a backdrop to the episode as a whole, where the theme of sacrifice is especially prominent.[23] On the island, Desmond experiences a series of prophetic visions in which it is suggested that he must sacrifice the life of his friend, Charlie Pace, in order to bring about the group's rescue.[24] Despite having led an unwitting Charlie to the ordained location under false pretences (just as Isaac is led by Abraham), Desmond ultimately finds that he cannot go through with it, sparing his life and sacrificing instead his own opportunity to be reunited with his beloved Penny. This is just one of a number of instances where biblical themes are adopted but ultimately inverted or in some way reconfigured in the course of appropriation, reflecting an apparent degree of creativity in the use of the biblical text.

In 'What Kate Did' (S2E09), Mr Eko relates to Locke the story of Josiah and the discovery of the 'book of the law' in the temple (2 Kgs 22 and 2 Chr. 34). Although he wrongly equates the book with the entirety of the Old Testament ('What the secretary had found was an ancient book, the Book of Law. You may know it as the Old Testament'), Eko draws a direct parallel between this biblical discovery and his group's own discovery (in S2E07) of a copy of the Bible in another hatch on the island:

Eko: On the other side of the island we found a place much like this, and in this place we found a book.
[Eko unwraps the Bible and passes it to Locke.]
Eko: I believe what's inside there will be of great value to you.

In this contemporary parallel, however, it is not the book itself which is significant, but its literal contents. Upon opening it, Locke discovers that the pages have been hollowed out in order to conceal a piece of film – the missing part of the 'Orientation' reel for the hatch. In the biblical account,

---

[23] In terms of wider biblical allusion, it is also surely no coincidence that the two new female characters introduced in this episode are called Naomi and Ruth, both names occurring together in the book of Ruth.
[24] Elsewhere the death of the character Boone Carlyle (S1E20) is frequently referred to as 'a sacrifice that the Island demanded' (e.g. S1E24/25; S2E21; S3E03).

the discovery of the book reveals that there are laws that are not being followed ('for great is the wrath of the LORD that is kindled against us, because our ancestors did not obey the words of this book, to do according to all that is written concerning us' [2 Kgs 22.13]). Similarly, the missing piece of film specifically forbids attempting to use the computer in the hatch for communication purposes; unknown to Locke and Eko, one of the other survivors, Michael, is at that very moment attempting to do just that – an act which will have dire consequences for the group.

In a flashback to Charlie's childhood at the beginning of 'Fire + Water' (S2E12), a copy of Andrea del Verrocchio's *Baptism of Christ* (1475) hangs innocuously on the wall in the background. Later in the episode, while on the island, Charlie has a dream/vision in which this scene is recreated, with his mother and Claire in the role of the angels, a dove descending from above, and Hurley in biblical-looking robes, seemingly appearing as John the Baptist. Charlie subsequently tries to persuade Claire to have her newborn baby, Aaron, baptized. Towards the end of the episode, Claire approaches Eko (a Nigerian drug smuggler turned priest), who tells her the New Testament story of Jesus' baptism by John the Baptist and the appearance of the dove (Mt. 3.13–17; Mk 1.9–11; Lk. 3.21–2), before baptizing Claire and Aaron together. Forming the culmination of the subplot, this renders explicit the various implicit allusions to the story of Jesus' baptism that have appeared throughout the episode.

In the Season 5 episode '316' (S5E06), we find yet a further example of one character recounting to another a story from the Bible. Sitting in a church in Los Angeles and preparing for their imminent attempt to return to the island, Jack Shephard (the eponymous 'man of science' from the Season 2 premiere, 'Man of Science, Man of Faith' [S2E01]) has been asked by Eloise Hawking to take 'a leap of faith'. Benjamin Linus draws his attention to the copy of Caravaggio's *The Incredulity of Saint Thomas* (1601/02) hanging on the wall:

> Ben: Thomas the Apostle. When Jesus wanted to return to Judea, knowing that he would probably be murdered there, Thomas said to the others, 'Let us also go, that we might die with him'. But Thomas was not remembered for this bravery. His claim to fame came later, when he refused to acknowledge the resurrection. He just couldn't wrap his mind around it. The story goes that he needed to touch Jesus' wounds to be convinced.
> Jack: So was he?
> Ben: Of course he was. We're all convinced sooner or later, Jack.

The use of this particular biblical illustration (drawing on Jn 11.16 and 20.24–9) plays on Jack's own doubt and inability to believe, while, more subtly, the return to the island is reflected in the return of the disciples to Judea. The full extent of its appropriateness is only revealed later on, however, with the apparent resurrection of John Locke (S5E07) and in its foreshadowing of Jack's 'ultimate transformation to a man of faith' in Season 6.[25]

As well as these explicit discussions of biblical episodes, there are a number of other occasions where biblical passages are referenced or cited. In a flashback in 'The Moth' (S1E07), both 'the meek shall inherit the earth' (cf. Mt. 5.5; Ps. 37.11) and 'I bring good tidings of great joy' (cf. Lk. 2.10) are spoken by Charlie's brother, Liam, as he reveals that they've been offered a recording contract. On the island, Psalm 23 is recited by Eko on at least two separate occasions: over a funeral pyre in the appropriately named episode 'The 23rd Psalm' (S2E10), and then again, immediately before his own death at the hands of the smoke monster, in 'The Cost of Living' (S3E05). Further significance is lent to this particular biblical passage by the fact that 23 is one of 'the Numbers', and on account of the opening words, 'The LORD is my shepherd', in the light of the prominent role played by Jack Shephard (as well as his father, Christian Shephard) in the series. Indeed, it is later revealed that the candidate number assigned to Jack by Jacob is 23 (S6E04 and S6E05), another probable allusion to the shepherd motif of this passage.

By far the most concentrated and conspicuous occurrence of biblical references in the programme comes, however, from Eko's staff. In 'The Other 48 Days' (S2E07), 'The 23rd Psalm' (S2E10) and 'Live Together, Die Alone' (S2E23/24), Eko is seen carving chapter and verse numbers into it ('Things I need to remember'), prompting Charlie to describe it as his 'Jesus stick' (S2E10). The references carved into it include Genesis 13.14, Psalm 23; Psalm 144, Habakkuk 1.3, Luke, John 3.5, Acts 4.12, Romans 6.12, Galatians 3.16, Colossians, Titus 3 and Revelation 5.3. The potential significance of these specific passages has been a fertile topic of speculation for fans of the show, its prominence in online discussion forums attesting to the programme's apparent capacity for engendering interest in the biblical text.[26]

Finally, in terms of explicit allusions to the Bible in *Lost*, we should not forget the numerous occasions upon which Bibles themselves appear (i.e. as physical objects). On the island: Boone discovers a bible with the body of one of the Nigerian drug smugglers (S1E19); Desmond has one with him in the hatch (S2E01); a Bible is found in the Arrow station (S2E07) and later given by Eko to Locke (S2E09). Off the island: Jack has a Bible in his office (S3E01); Eko finds his brother's Bible on the floor of the church confessional, containing a childhood photo of Eko and Yemi tucked between Isaiah 4 and 5 (S3E05); Cassidy poses as a bible salesperson (S3E15);

[25] Stuart, *Literary Lost*, p. 56.

[26] J. Ankerberg and D. Burroughs, *What Can be Found in Lost*, Eugene, OR: Harvest House, 2008, pp. 67–70; C. Seay, *The Gospel According to Lost*, Nashville, TN: Thomas Nelson, 2009, pp. 107–12.

Desmond is shown reading a Bible in the monastery (S3E17); Richard reads a Bible while in prison, later opened to Luke 4.24–9 by the priest who visits him (S6E09). The Bible is thus depicted not only as a book that is referenced and alluded to, but as one which is read.

Implicit allusion to the bible in *Lost*

In addition to these explicit allusions to the Bible, *Lost* appears to contain a large number of implicit allusions to biblical themes, characters and motifs. These are, for obvious reasons, rather more difficult to detect and we can be somewhat less certain as to whether or not they are truly intended. Nevertheless, the frequency with which they appear to occur, coupled with the extent to which the Bible is *explicitly* alluded to, suggests that at least some are likely to be deliberate allusions to the biblical text. Moreover, whether intended or not, that these perceived allusions can and have been interpreted in this way (an observation not irrelevant to our focal question concerning levels of biblical literacy) lends them, in any case, an undeniable significance in terms of a 'reader–response' approach to the series, which moves beyond the world of authorial intent and towards a shared mythology co-created by writer and audience.[27]

We have already noted the potential significance of the use of biblical names within the show, comparable to the way in which the names of prominent philosophers (e.g. Locke, Hume, Bentham, Rousseau, Bakunin) and scientists (e.g. Faraday, Hawking) are used (Parker 2011). Although many names occurring in *Lost* can also be found in the Bible (e.g. Daniel, Michael, Sarah, Rachel, Elizabeth, John, James, Thomas), their commonplace nature means that it is not always justifiable to infer a *deliberate* allusion to the biblical text (not that this has stopped these possible connections being the topic of speculation, as can readily be seen from a cursory glance at websites such as *Lostpedia*).[28] However, where rather less common

---

[27] This two-way enterprise can be further seen, for instance, in the phenomenon of fan fiction (expanding upon the 'canonical' work), as well as in the involvement of fan communities (or 'fandoms') in the creation of cooperative projects such as online discussion forums, wikis (e.g. *Lostpedia: The Lost Encyclopedia*, http://lostpedia.wikia.com), and even a virtual rendering of the island in Second Life (C. Bancroft, 'Web Ensnares "Lost" Souls"', *Tampa Bay Times*, 10 January 2006; J. Mittell, 'Sites of Participation: Wiki Fandom and the Case of Lostpedia', *Transformative Works and Cultures*, 3 (2009); M. Wagner, 'Lost Fans find Internet Thrills via Wikis, Games, Second Life', *InformationWeek*, 26 April 2008. See further, L. S. Clark, 'Religion, philosophy, and convergence culture online: ABC's *Lost* as a study of the processes of mediatization', *Northern Lights*, 6 (2008): 143–63; L. S. Clark, 'You Lost Me: Mystery, Fandom, and Religion in ABC's *Lost*', in D. Winston (ed.), *Small Screen, Big Picture: Television and Lived Religion*. Waco, TX: Baylor University Press, 2009, pp. 319–41; Letak, 'Accidental Intellectuals'.

[28] See n. 27 above. Also, Ankerberg and Burroughs, *What Can be Found in Lost*, pp. 71–2; L.

names are used, or in a context which appears to in some way mirror the biblical text, we might surmise that these are indeed intended to allude to the Bible. Names that fall into this category might include Jacob, Benjamin, Aaron and Isaac. In fact, in the case of Aaron, the implicit allusion (Claire names him in S1E24/25) is later made explicit, when Eko observes that it was the name given to the brother of Moses and proceeds to tell Claire a little about the role played by the biblical Aaron (S2E10).

In the course of the episode 'Catch-22' (S3E17), two new female characters, Naomi and Ruth, are introduced. Although seen in very different contexts (Naomi on the island in 2004, Ruth off the island in 1995) and with neither character displaying any obvious affinity with their biblical namesakes, the occurrence of these two figures together in this episode seems unlikely to be coincidental, constituting instead an implicit allusion to the book of Ruth. Further names that might be interpreted as alluding to the Bible include Matthew Abaddon (cf. Rev. 9.11) and Hugo/Hurley Reyes ('Reyes' being Spanish for 'Kings', as in 1–2 Kings).

In particular, much has been made of the name given to one of the main protagonists, Jack Shephard, especially in the context of both Psalm 23 ('The LORD is my shepherd') and John 10.1–18 ('I am the good shepherd'). As already seen, the former passage is recited twice in *Lost* (S2E10 and S3E05), with 'The 23rd Psalm' also appearing both as an episode title (S2E10) and as a scriptural reference carved into Eko's stick. The relevance of this passage is seemingly further underlined in Season 6, with the revelation that 23 is the candidate number assigned to Jack (S6E04 and S6E05). John 10.1–18, on the other hand, speaks of the shepherd leading the sheep, further noting that 'The good shepherd lays down his life for the sheep' (10.11). Jack quickly becomes the *de facto* leader of the survivors and is, on occasion, even depicted literally leading them like sheep across the island (e.g. the 'exodus' march of S3E22/23).[29] Long before the final season, the assumed association with John 10.11 led many fans to speculate that Jack would ultimately be seen to lay down his life for the group, something which did indeed come to pass in the final episode (S6E17/18).[30]

Use of the names Jacob and Benjamin also seems significant. 'The Others' are frequently depicted as constituting something of a 'tribe' (also described as 'the Natives' or 'the Hostiles'). In Season 3, we discover that this tribe is nominally led by Benjamin (S3E02), though he apparently answers to an even higher authority known as Jacob (S3E06; S3E07; S3E16; S3E20). The biblical overtones of this Jacob–Benjamin dynamic are further hinted at in

---

Porter and D. Lavery, *Lost's Buried Treasures* (3rd edn), Naperville, IL: Sourcebooks, 2010, p. 5; Stuart, *Literary Lost*, p. 18.

[29] Interestingly, one of the pieces of music on the soundtrack for this episode is actually titled 'The Good Shepherd', http://lostpedia.wikia.com/wiki/The_Good_Shepherd

[30] See, for instance, the various forum discussions at *The Fuselage* (www.thefuselage.com), dating from the show's launch in 2004 right through to its conclusion in 2010.

the episode 'Not in Portland' (S3E07), where the line 'God loves you as He loved Jacob' flashes up briefly in the brainwashing video in Room 23 (cf. Mal. 1.2; Rom. 9.13).

However, it is the relationship between Jacob and his brother, the unnamed 'Man in Black', which appears to provide the most fertile ground for speculation regarding the implicit influence of the Bible, seemingly drawing upon a number of different elements. Their backstory was finally seen in 'Across the Sea' (S6E15), where it is revealed that the brothers were twins, born some 2,000 years ago. Brought up by the then-guardian of the island, it is Jacob who eventually inherits the job, despite being a role initially intended for his brother. This usurpation of his brother's 'inheritance', coupled with the subsequent antagonism between them (the brother wishes to kill Jacob [S5E16/17]), has strong parallels with the biblical tale of twins Jacob and Esau (Gen. 25.19–34; 27.1–45). Even the comparative descriptions of these two biblical figures ('Esau was a skilful hunter, a man of the field, while Jacob was a quiet man, living in tents' [Gen. 25.27]) matches rather exactly the depiction of their *Lost* counterparts while growing up, their oppositeness further reflected visually in the fact that Jacob is always shown wearing white, while his brother wears black. The island's Jacob is moreover referenced in Season 3 by the phrase 'God loves you as He loved Jacob' (S3E07), which seems to deliberately echo the first part of Malachi 1.2-3 and Romans 9.13 ('I have loved Jacob but I have hated Esau'), thereby both implicitly associating him with the biblical Jacob and further implying the existence of a counterpart 'Esau'.[31]

The apparent fratricide that occurs shortly after Jacob is appointed guardian of the island hints at some additional parallel with the biblical story of Cain and Abel (Gen. 4.1–16). This is even more striking when it transpires that the brothers' (adoptive) mother is in fact the 'Eve' whose skeleton was discovered by the survivors in Season 1 (S1E06; cf. S6E15). One might also argue that there is an implicit allusion to the story of Job. We discover that the brothers disagree about human nature; over the course of the centuries, the 'Man in Black' remains convinced that people are inherently wicked ('They come, they fight, they destroy, they corrupt. It always ends the same' [S5E16/17]), while Jacob brings people to the island in order to try to prove him wrong (S6E09):

Jacob: That man who sent you to kill me believes that everyone is corruptible because it's in their very nature to sin. I bring people here to prove him wrong. And when they get here, their past doesn't matter.

---

[31] Chris Seay suggests that the word 'hateth' carved into Eko's staff may be a further reference to Mal. 1.2-3 (C. Seay, *The Gospel According to Lost*, Nashville, TN: Thomas Nelson, 2009, p. 111.)

Richard: Before you brought my ship, there were others?

Jacob: Yes, many.

Richard: What happened to them?

Jacob: They're all dead.

Richard: But if you brought them here, why didn't you help them?

Jacob: Because I wanted them to help themselves, to know the
     difference between right and wrong without me having to tell them.
     It's all meaningless if I have to force them to do anything. Why
     should I have to step in?

Richard: If you don't, he will.

It turns out that behind much of what happens on the island lies a 'cosmic
dispute' between the immortal figures of Jacob and his brother, who
(clothed in white and black respectively) appear to reflect in some way
the YHWH and 'Satan' characters of the book of Job. While everyone
brought to the island is 'tested' in this manner, Sarah Clarke Stuart[32] notes
an especially strong parallel between Job and Richard Alpert, including a
remarkable correspondence between the 140 subsequent years Richard lives
on the island (1867–2007 [S6E09; S6E17/18]) and the 140 years Job lives
after his trial (Job 42.16).

Thus, the relationship between Jacob and his brother would appear to
allude implicitly to three separate biblical pairings: Jacob and Esau (Gen.
25.19–34; 27.1–45), Cain and Abel (Gen. 4.1–16) and YHWH and 'Satan'
(Job 1–2). These dynamics are, however, each in some way inverted or
reimagined. On the island, Jacob is the older twin (cf. Gen. 25.24–6),
his (adoptive) mother prefers his brother (cf. Gen. 25.28), and neither
brother actually wants to inherit the role as guardian of the island (S6E15).
Similarly, it is the white-clad Jacob who commits fratricide, 'killing' his
brother (cf. Gen. 4.8; S6E15), and who, in the context of the later Job-like
dispute, is described by his brother as 'the devil' (S6E09). It may be that
we should identify a similar inversion in the frequent depiction of the 'Man
in Black' as a pillar of smoke, an image which in the Bible is reserved for
God (e.g. Exod. 13.21–2; 33.9–10).[33] In the same way that the biblical
'pillar of cloud' aids the escape of the Israelites from the Egyptians (Exod.
14.19–25), so too does the 'pillar of smoke' aid the escape of the survivors
from the mercenaries (S4E09) and later Charles Widmore's team (S6E14).
These apparent inversions or re-imaginings undermine neither the value
nor veracity of these biblical allusions. Instead, they seemingly betray the
creative ways in which the biblical text is being utilized and subtly manipulated in order to problematize a straightforward dichotomy of light and

---

[32] Stuart, *Literary Lost*, pp. 56–7.

[33] While often appearing as an amorphous cloud, he is explicitly described as a '*pillar* of black
smoke' on at least two occasions (S6E03 and S6E04).

dark, good and evil, thereby reflecting a tension which could be said to underlie the thrust of the series as a whole.[34]

Further examples of implicit allusions to the Bible might include the various 'miracles' which take place. There are a number of healing miracles attributed to the island itself, such as Locke regaining the ability to walk (S1E04) and Rose being cured of cancer (S2E19), while others are attributed to either Jack (S2E01) or Jacob (S3E16; S6E06). While all are in some way reminiscent of the New Testament healing miracles of Jesus, Locke's in particular (occurring towards the very beginning of Season 1, and thus the most prominent and unexpected) recalls the story of the healing of the paralytic (Mt. 9.2–8; Mk 2.3–12; Lk. 5.18–26; cf. Jn 5.2–9). Echoing the prominent biblical theme of 'barrenness' and miraculous conception (e.g. Gen. 20.17–21.3; 25.21; 29.31; 30.22–3; Judg. 13.2–5; 1 Sam. 1.2–6; 2.20–1; Lk. 1.7, 24), Sun and Jin Kwon, who had previously been told they were infertile, find out in Season 2 that Sun is pregnant (S2E16), while in the Season 3 episode 'Not in Portland' (S3E07) Rachel Carlson is also miraculously cured of her infertility (the choice of name perhaps a deliberate allusion to the biblical Rachel, who is similarly 'barren' [Gen. 29.31] but who later conceives [30.22–3]).

The topic of resurrection is alluded to on several occasions and appears as a major theme in the episode '?' (S2E21). In a flashback in 'The Incident' (S5E16/17), Locke appears to die in the event that caused his paralysis, but is restored to life when Jacob touches him, while in 'LA X' (S6E01/02), Sayid Jarrah is dead for two hours before mysteriously being brought back to life. The first instance in particular recalls Jesus' resurrection miracles, involving the agency of another (e.g. Lk. 7.11–15, 8.49–56), while it is notable that, prior to his return from the dead, Sayid's body is carried from the water with arms outstretched, in a conspicuous 'crucifixion' pose – an allusion to Jesus' own resurrection? Jacob is himself temporarily resurrected in order to speak to the remaining candidates ('disciples'?) one last time before finally moving on (S6E16). Locke's apparent (second) resurrection (S5E07), on the other hand, is eventually revealed to be a ruse by Jacob's brother, who has assumed Locke's form (S5E16/17). Perhaps even more significantly, we might note the various appearances of a 'risen' Christian Shephard as well as the discovery of his empty coffin (S1E05; cf. Mt. 28; Mk 16; Lk. 24; Jn 20).

A number of the visions experienced on the island have detectable biblical undertones. Starting in 'Further Instructions' (S3E03), Desmond finds himself experiencing visions of the future (cf. S3E08; S3E17; S6E11) and, having awoken naked in the jungle, clothes himself in the only thing

---

[34] Note, for instance, the weighing scale, with white and black stones, in Jacob's cave (S6E04), as well as Dogen's comments that, 'For every man there is a scale. On one side of the scale there is good. On the other side, evil' (S6E06). Ultimately, no character in *Lost* is presented as being wholly good or wholly evil – instead all are flawed.

to hand, an overly large tie-dyed t-shirt. Might we here infer some allusion to the biblical Joseph and his 'multi-coloured' coat (Gen. 37.2–11)? In this context, it is perhaps of some significance that Desmond is later cast into a well (S6E12/13; cf. Gen. 37.22–4).[35] Immediately before Charlie's vision recreating Verrocchio's *Baptism of Christ* (S2E12; discussed above), he has a vision of Aaron's cradle in the water, mirroring imagery of Moses in the bulrushes (cf. Exod. 2.3–5), while when John Locke decides he needs to commune with the island and starts having a series of visionary experiences (S3E03; cf. S1E19), it is similarly tempting to draw links with John of Patmos (cf. Rev. 1.9–11).

In addition to these, we might draw attention to the claim that Locke was 'immaculately conceived' (S1E19; cf. Mt. 1.18–25; Lk. 1.26–35), Eko's 40 days of silence (S2E07; cf. Mt. 4.2; Mk 1.13; Lk. 4.1–2), Hurley's hallucination of 'Dave' tempting him to eat and to throw himself off a cliff (S2E18; cf. Mt. 4.1–11; Lk. 4.1–13), the marking/branding of Juliet for having killed someone (S3E09; cf. Gen. 4.15), the frequently recurring 'exodus' imagery (e.g. S1E23–24/25; S3E22/23; S5E15–16/17; cf. Exod. 13–19), and even, at a push, Jacob's ladder (S6E04; cf. Gen. 28.10–17). There are also several possible 'second-hand' biblical allusions, such as 'an eye for an eye' and 'stranger in a strange land' (S3E09; cf. Lev. 24.20; Exod. 2.22), which have their roots in the Bible but which have found their way into popular parlance.[36]

Finally, we should acknowledge the use of the Bible in promotional and marketing materials for *Lost*. In particular, a series of promotional images from January 2010 heralding the imminent arrival of the final season have become known as 'The *Lost* Supper'. These recreate Leonardo da Vinci's *The Last Supper* (1495–98), albeit in a jungle setting, with a piece of plane wreckage in place of a table, and key characters from *Lost* seated around it. The 'Man in Black' (assuming the appearance of Locke) appears in the centre in the place of Jesus – another 'inversion' troubling our distinctions between good and evil. It is perhaps interesting to note that Jack appears to his left, in the place of Thomas (cf. S5E06 and the discussion above), while Sayid, who eventually betrays the 'Man in Black' (S6E13; S6E14), appears to be in the place of Judas.[37] Furthermore, the viral marketing website created for Ajira Airways (the fictional airline with which some of the survivors return to the island in Season 5 [S5E06]) contains hidden references to John 3.16 throughout, betraying the flight number (and episode title), '316', as an implicit biblical allusion to this passage.[38]

---

[35] Note also that he reveals and explains these visions to a select group of companions, all of whom he calls 'brother' (e.g. S3E08; S3E17; cf. Gen. 37.5–11).

[36] Stuart (*Literary Lost*, p. 36) suggests that the latter example may come via Robert Heinlein's novel *Stranger in a Strange Land* (1961).

[37] See further http://lostpedia.wikia.com/wiki/The_Lost_Supper

[38] The website for the fictional airline can be found here: www.ajiraairways.com See further

Biblical literacy and *Lost*

The examples highlighted here make clear the extent to which *Lost* is suffused with biblical allusion, both explicit and implicit.[39] The broad range of passages or motifs alluded to (from Genesis right through to Revelation), as well as the intricate and subtle ways in which the text is manipulated and appropriated, certainly attest to some estimable degree of biblical literacy on the part of the writers.[40]

> The sacred narratives of Christian-Judeo origin permeate the mythology of *Lost* to such an extent that some of the story's meaning would be unrealized without the connections to these texts.[41]

Perhaps more pertinent to our overarching question, however, is what this pervasive use of the Bible might say about the extent to which biblical literacy is similarly assumed on the part of the audience. Are viewers expected to recognize implicit biblical allusion when they see it? Adele Reinhartz, in discussing the use of the Bible in film, suggests that the existence of biblical allusion onscreen does not in and of itself equate to or necessitate a biblically literate audience.

> One of the most difficult questions relates to whether audience knowledge of the Bible is essential, desirable, or even helpful when viewing these films. In most cases, one would guess that filmmakers do not assume that viewers will necessarily identify the biblical references.[42]

While recognition of these allusions might provide 'added value', thereby enabling a 'deeper understanding'[43] or 'richer reading'[44] of the show, it is not unequivocally required.[45] Nevertheless, the numerous *explicit* allusions

---

http://lostpedia.wikia.com/wiki/Ajira_Airways

[39] John Ankerberg and Dillon Burroughs note that 'every scene of *Lost* is rich in multiple layers of meaning' (Ankerberg and Burroughs, *What Can Be Found in Lost*, p. 100). For discussion of non-biblical allusion (e.g. to film, music, literature, etc.), see initially Porter and Lavery (*Lost's Buried Treasures*, esp. pp. 1–173) and Stuart, *Literary Lost*.

[40] Cf. B. C. Patterson, 'The New Narnia: Myth and Redemption on the Island of Second Chances', in S. Kaye (ed.), *The Ultimate Lost and Philosophy: Think Together, Die Alone*, Hoboken, NJ: Wiley, 2011, p. 279; Porter and Lavery, *Lost's Buried Treasures*, p. 5.

[41] Stuart, *Literary Lost*, p. 17.

[42] A. Reinhartz, *Scripture on the Silver Screen*. Louisville, KY: Westminster John Knox, 2003, p. 186.

[43] Stuart, *Literary Lost*, p. 3.

[44] Parker, 'Appendix: Who are Locke, Hume, and Rousseau?, p. 339.

[45] Indeed, Reinhartz goes further and suggests that, 'In some cases, however, one suspects that the filmmakers themselves do not have thorough or complete knowledge of the passages or images they themselves draw on … In such cases both viewers and filmmakers would benefit from a higher level of biblical literacy' (Reinhartz, *Scripture on the Silver Screen*, pp. 186–7).

to the Bible alert viewers to the presence and prominence of the text in both the narrative and the minds of the writers, thereby simultaneously alerting them to the potential for additional (less obvious) *implicit* allusions throughout. In this way, the explicit references hint at the existence of the implicit ones. This is further reinforced on those occasions where implicit references are subsequently rendered explicit (e.g. the baptism imagery in 'Fire + Water' [S2E12] or the naming of Aaron [S1E24/25 and S2E10]). The writers are thus careful to ensure that viewers cannot be entirely oblivious to the presence of biblical allusion in the programme. Indeed, we have already seen that perceived implicit biblical allusions have been widely identified by fans and commentators of the show whether or not they were all deliberately intended as such by the writers! This prompts us to acknowledge an even more important function of *Lost* – as itself a tool for promoting biblical literacy.

Much has been written about the participatory role of fan communities (or 'fandoms') in relation to *Lost*.[46] The very nature of the programme encourages a close attention to detail on the part of its viewers and (over-) analysis of everything seen and heard. The extent of discussion and speculation this has generated (reflected in the sheer number of dedicated websites and forums to be found online) has meant that '*Lost*'s fans have a connection to the show that is unrivalled in television history'.[47] Just one

---

Is then the decision to cast the white-clad Jacob as the older twin (cf. Gen. 25.24–6), the least favoured by his mother (cf. Gen. 25.28), and as the one responsible for fratricide (cf. Gen. 4.8) truly an example of deliberate inversion and textual manipulation (see the discussion above), or merely the result of unrigorous application of the underlying biblical text? An accidental confusion of the well-known Cain and Abel roles, at least, certainly seems unlikely, while the frequency of these inversions likewise suggests some deliberate attempt to problematize a straightforward light/dark dichotomy. Nevertheless, in this context, we might note that when Eko and Charlie recite Psalm 23 in 'The 23rd Psalm' (S2E10), they both say 'the shadow of the valley of death' (cf. Ps. 23.4). In the DVD commentary for this episode, the writers, Lindelof and Cuse, acknowledged this as an accidental error (though felt retrospectively that it was appropriate, since Eko was a drug smuggler who had assumed the identity of a priest and thus might display some unfamiliarity with the text).

[46] For example, L. S. Clark, 'You Lost Me: Mystery, Fandom, and Religion in ABC's *Lost*', in D. Winston (ed.), *Small Screen, Big Picture: Television and Lived Religion*, Waco, TX: Baylor University Press, 2009; Letak, 'Accidental Intellectuals'; M. Ramos and J. Lozano, 'Promoting Lost: New Strategies and Tools of Commercial Communication', in M. A. Pérez (ed.), *Previously On: Interdisciplinary Studies on TV Series in the Third Golden Age of Television*, Seville: Biblioteca de la Facultad de Comunicación de la Universidad de Sevilla, 2011. See also n. 24 above.

[47] B. East, 'Fans May Forever be Lost for Answers', *The National*, 18 January 2010. For commentary on some of the key websites, see: Ankerberg and Burroughs, *What Can Be Found in Lost*, pp. 130–6; C. Bancroft, 'Web Ensnares "Lost" Souls', *Tampa Bay Times*, 10 January 2006; Letak, 'Accidental Intellectuals', pp. 97–8; Mittell, *Sites of Participation*; Porter and Lavery, *Lost's Buried Treasures*, pp. 274–5; M. Wagner, 'Lost Fans find Internet Thrills via Wikis, Games, Second Life', *InformationWeek*, April 26, 2008. A fuller list can be found here: http://lostpedia.wikia.com/wiki/Websites

of those websites, DarkUFO (http://darkufo.blogspot.co.uk/), received 173 million page visits, and was reportedly still receiving over 75,000 page visits per month more than a year and a half after the final episode was screened.[48] Recognizing the tendency of the writers to hide clues and 'Easter eggs' throughout each episode, visitors to these sites would discuss theories, analyse screenshots and audio files, and consider the potential significance of every detail seen.[49] A number of viewers have since reflected on the phenomenon and how it affected their engagement with the programme:

> We not only watched the show, we participated in it. We tried to get ahead of the characters by following the clues and solving the puzzles before they could ... I miss the mad Google searches after every episode seeing if I caught a hidden anagram or reference to a piece of literature.[50]

> [I've] analysed freeze frames of key scenes, contributed to Lostpedia. com, zoomed in on Jack's crossword puzzle and Eko's Jesus Stick for a closer read ...[51]

> [It] was a history and literature lesson disguised as a television series ... I can't think of another series that has been as influential regarding the promotion of literature, mythology, and history.[52]

These comments (the last in particular), coupled with the prominence of biblical allusion throughout, clearly highlight the show's potential for encouraging and nurturing biblical literacy amongst its audience. As Abby Letak notes:

> Lost has indeed dragged cult into the mainstream and along with it, cult audience activity. Behavior previously reserved for fans of shows like Star Trek and Buffy is now seen in viewers of a mainstream hit ...

---

[48] A. Page, 'Chased by Polar Bears: How an English Bloke Got to Run the Largest Lost Fan Site', in P. Moore (ed.), LOST Thought University Edition: Leading Thinkers Discuss LOST, Scotts Valley, CA: CreateSpace, 2012, p. 81.

[49] Note writer/producer Javier Grillo-Marxuach's pertinent observation that 'Lost fans are like Talmudic scholars. They have created a body of scholarship about every episode' (cited in Ankerberg and Burroughs, What Can Be Found in Lost, p. 5.

[50] Stafford, 'Haikus for the Journey', pp. 40, 42.

[51] Ankerberg and Burroughs, What Can be Found in Lost, p. 9.

[52] E. Olson and J. Garfein, 'Culture Disguised as Television: Lost in Conversation', in P. Moore (ed.), LOST Thought University Edition, p. 47. With regard to the promotion of literature, a survey carried out in May 2010 found that, out of 752 respondents, 582 had read one or more of the literary works referenced in Lost as a direct response to its appearance on the show (Stuart, Literary Lost, pp. 9–12). Communities of viewers even established a number of Lost book clubs specifically in order to read and discuss the works of literature featured or alluded to in the series (Stuart, Literary Lost, pp. 7–14).

Mainstream viewers are solving puzzles and hunting clues in ways they never have before.[53]

The result is that mainstream audiences are, as part of this larger process, actively following up the biblical allusions in *Lost*, carefully analysing the explicit references and speculating about the existence and meaning of implicit ones. Thus viewers are, for instance, tacitly encouraged to look up the chapter and verse numbers carved into Eko's 'Jesus stick', prompting extensive online discussions about their potential significance.[54] Similarly, Jacob's unnamed brother (the 'Man in Black') quickly acquired the nickname 'Esau' amongst the online community, with fans picking up on (or perceiving) an allusion to the biblical twins (cf. Gen. 25.19–34; 27.1–45).[55] Moreover (and somewhat remarkably), numerous posts commenting on the relationship between Jacob and his brother did so under the subject heading 'My brother's keeper' (in at least one instance, with no subsequent explicit discussion of Cain and Abel), betraying familiarity and association with Gen. 4.1–16 (cf. v. 9).[56]

The nature of the show, together with the participatory role of its fan communities, means that 'unsuspecting viewers become *accidental intellectuals*'.[57] As Sarah Clarke Stuart puts it, '*Lost*'s instruction and its entertainment are inextricable'.[58] Not only does the programme's extensive use of the Bible appear to reflect an admirable degree of biblical literacy on the part of the writers, it also actively encourages it on the part of the audience. Regardless of whether or not a biblically literate audience is anticipated,[59] the evidence of the online fan discussions would appear to suggest that it is, in end effect, nevertheless produced. The enthusiasm of viewers to engage with the show translates (via the wealth of explicit and implicit allusion) to enthusiasm to engage with the biblical text. In this

---

[53] Letak, 'Accidental Intellectuals', p. 94.

[54] See initially: http://lostpedia.wikia.com/wiki/Eko%27s_stick and the various forum discussions at www.4815162342.com and www.thefuselage.com (all of which explicitly attest to contributors picking up and engaging with the biblical text). Also, Ankerberg and Burroughs, *What Can Be Found in Lost*, pp. 67–70, and Seay, *The Gospel According to Lost*, pp. 107–12.

[55] See Dougherty, R., 'Jacob and Esau Bible Story Puzzled Over by Puzzled Lost Fans', *Yahoo! Voices*, 14 May 2009, and Porter and Lavery, *Lost's Buried Treasures*, p. 197, as well as the forums indicated above (n. 47).

[56] See for instance: (i) http://tomontv.typepad.com/tom_on_tv/2010/05/lost-may-11.html; (ii) www.losttv-forum.com/forum/showthread.php?t=68563; (iii) http://static-am.blogspot. co.uk/2010/05/lost-is-on-am-i-my-brothers-keeper.html

[57] Letak, 'Accidental Intellectuals', p. 87.

[58] Stuart, *Literary Lost*, p. 148. So too B. Addey, '"Don't Mistake Coincidence for Fate": Lost Theories and Coincidence', in S. Kaye (ed.), *The Ultimate Lost and Philosophy: Think Together, Die Alone*. Hoboken, NJ: Wiley, 2011, p. 106 and Porter and Lavery, *Lost's Buried Treasures*, p. 172. Cf. E. Graham, 'Religious Literacy and Public Service Broadcasting: Introducing a Research Agenda', in G. Lynch and J. Mitchell with A. Strhan (eds), *Religion, Media and Culture: A Reader*, London: Routledge, 2012, p. 230.

[59] cf. Reinhartz, *Scripture on the Silver Screen*, p. 186.

way, *Lost* fandom has seemingly created an environment, within the realm of mainstream television and popular culture, where biblical literacy can flourish.

Conclusions

While comparisons of biblical literacy in the nineteenth and twenty-first centuries may suggest an ostensible decline,[60] it is clear that rumours of the Bible's 'loss' to modern society are greatly exaggerated. It may no longer play such an explicitly prominent role in daily life, yet nevertheless continues to saturate our culture and heritage. Biblical literacy may likewise function somewhat differently in our postmodern digital age, yet it remains. Our examination of explicit and implicit biblical allusion in *Lost* confirms 'the degree to which biblical narratives have shaped the ways in which Western culture tells its stories'.[61] Moreover, the extent of the Bible's use in this mainstream television programme[62] reveals something of both the actual and anticipated levels of biblical literacy in contemporary society (on the part of the writers and audience respectively). Most startlingly, however, whether or not *Lost* assumes continued familiarity with the biblical text, it would intriguingly appear to play a (perhaps unintentional) part in actively encouraging and promoting it.

Thus, while recent government and educational efforts to bolster biblical literacy in the UK and US are certainly laudable, we may justifiably problematize a straightforward assumption of its decline, as well as the labelling of our society as 'biblically illiterate'.[63] The issue is clearly far more complex. Although our examination of *Lost* constitutes but an individual example, it demonstrates at least some of the ways in which biblical literacy might continue to function in the twenty-first century, highlighting thereby the potential educational impact of contemporary popular culture.[64] We may, therefore, recognize a plurality of 'ways of knowing' about the Bible, acknowledging that at least one of the places biblical literacy can most certainly be *found* is in *Lost*.

---

[60] Larsen, 'Literacy and biblical knowledge'.

[61] Reinhartz, *Scripture on the Silver Screen*, p. 186.

[62] Letak, 'Accidental Intellectuals', pp. 93–5.

[63] E.g. Burge, 'The Greatest Story Never Read'; Lang, *The Bible on the Big Screen*; Manzo, 'The Bible Makes a Comeback', p. 25; Prothero, 'We Live in a Land of Biblical Idiots'.

[64] Graham, 'Religious Literacy', p. 230; Letak, 'Accidental Intellectuals', p. 87; Stuart, *Literary Lost*, p. 148. See also n. 54 above.

Bibliography

Addey, B., '"Don't Mistake Coincidence for Fate": *Lost* Theories and Coincidence', in S. Kaye (ed.), *The Ultimate Lost and Philosophy: Think Together, Die Alone*. Hoboken, NJ: Wiley, 2011, pp. 91–106.

Ankerberg, J. and Burroughs, D., *What Can be Found in Lost*, Eugene, OR: Harvest House, 2008.

Bancroft, C., 'Web Ensnares 'Lost' Souls', *Tampa Bay Times*, 10 January 2006. Retrieved March 27, 2013, www.sptimes.com/2006/01/10/Floridian/Web_ensnares__Lost__s.shtml

BBC, 'CSI Show "Most Popular in World"', *BBC News*, 31 July 2006, http://news.bbc.co.uk/1/hi/entertainment/5231334.stm [accessed 27 March 2013].

Bingham, J., 'Poet Laureate Andrew Motion Calls for All Children to be Taught the Bible', *The Telegraph*, 17 February 2009 www.telegraph.co.uk/education/educationnews/4678369/Poet-Laureate-Andrew-Motion-calls-for-all-children-to-be-taught-the-Bible.html [accessed 27 March 2013].

Burge, G. M., 'The greatest story never read: Recovering biblical literacy in the Church', *Christianity Today*, 43/9 (1999): 45–9.

Carr, D., 'Religious education, religious literacy and common schooling: A philosophy and history of skewed reflection', *Journal of Philosophy of Education*, 41/4 (2007): 659–73.

Clark, L. S., 'Religion, philosophy, and convergence culture online: ABC's *Lost* as a study of the processes of mediatization', *Northern Lights*, 6 (2008): 143–63.

—'You Lost Me: Mystery, Fandom, and Religion in ABC's *Lost*', in D. Winston (ed.), *Small Screen, Big Picture: Television and Lived Religion*, Waco, TX: Baylor University Press, 2009, pp. 319–41.

Crossley, J., 'Biblical literacy and the English King James liberal bible: A twenty-first century tale of capitalism, nationalism and nostalgia', *Postscripts* (forthcoming, 2013).

Dawkins, R., 'Why I Want All Our Children to Read the King James Bible', *Guardian*, 19 May 2012. www.guardian.co.uk/science/2012/may/19/richard-dawkins-king-james-bible [accessed 27 March 2013].

Dougherty, R., 'Jacob and Esau Bible Story Puzzled Over by Puzzled Lost Fans', *Yahoo! Voices*, 14 May 2009, http://voices.yahoo.com/jacob-esau-bible-story-puzzled-over-puzzled-3320550.html [accessed 27 March 2013].

East, B., 'Fans May Forever be Lost for Answers', *The National*, 18 January 2010, www.thenational.ae/arts-culture/fans-may-forever-be-lost-for-answers [accessed 27 March 2013].

Edwards, K. B., *Admen and Eve: The Bible in Contemporary Advertising*, Sheffield: Sheffield Phoenix Press, 2012.

Gallagher, E. V., 'Teaching for religious literacy', *Teaching Theology and Religion*, 12/3 (2009): 208–21.

Graham, E., 'Religious Literacy and Public Service Broadcasting: Introducing a Research Agenda', in G. Lynch and J. Mitchell with A. Strhan (eds), *Religion, Media and Culture: A Reader*, London: Routledge, 2012, pp. 228–35.

Jeynes, W. H., 'The relationship between biblical literacy, academic achievement, and school behavior among Christian- and public-school students', *Journal of Research on Christian Education*, 18/1 (2009): 36–55.

—'The relationship between bible literacy and behavioral and academic outcomes in urban areas: A meta-analysis', *Education and Urban Society*, 42/5 (2010): 522–44.

Lang, J. S., *The Bible on the Big Screen: A Guide from Silent Films to Today's Movies*, Grand Rapids, MI: Baker Books, 2007.

Larsen, T. T., 'Literacy and biblical knowledge: The victorian age and our own', *Journal of the Evangelical Theological Society*, 52/3 (2009): 519–35.

Letak, A., 'Accidental Intellectuals: *Lost* Fandom and Philosophy', in P. Moore (ed.), *LOST Thought University Edition: Leading Thinkers Discuss LOST*, Scotts Valley, CA: CreateSpace, 2012, pp. 83–122.

Manzo, K. K., 'The bible makes a comeback', *Education Week*, 26/37 (2007): 25–7.

Mehta, S., 'Bible Finds a Place in Schools', *Los Angeles Times*, 5 August 2007, from http://articles.latimes.com/2007/aug/05/local/me-bible5 [accessed 27 March 2013].

Mittell, J., 'Sites of Participation: Wiki Fandom and the Case of Lostpedia', *Transformative Works and Cultures*, 3 (2009), from http://journal. transformativeworks.org/index.php/twc/article/view/118/117 [accessed 27 March 2013].

Olson, E. and Garfein, J., 'Culture Disguised as Television: *Lost* in Conversation', in P. Moore (ed.), *LOST Thought University Edition: Leading Thinkers Discuss LOST*, Scotts Valley, CA: CreateSpace, 2012, pp. 47–57.

Page, A., 'Chased by Polar Bears: How an English Bloke Got to Run the Largest *Lost* Fan Site', in P. Moore (ed.), *LOST Thought University Edition: Leading Thinkers Discuss LOST*, Scotts Valley, CA: CreateSpace, 2012, pp. 73–82.

Parker, S. F., 'Appendix: Who are Locke, Hume, and Rousseau? The Losties' Guide to Philosophers', in S. Kaye (ed.), *The Ultimate Lost and Philosophy: Think Together, Die Alone*, Hoboken, NJ: Wiley, 2011, pp. 321–39.

Patterson, B. C., 'The New Narnia: Myth and Redemption on the Island of Second Chances', in S. Kaye (ed.), *The Ultimate Lost and Philosophy: Think Together, Die Alone*, Hoboken, NJ: Wiley, 2011, pp. 253–79.

Porter, L. and Lavery, D., *Lost's Buried Treasures* (3rd edn), Naperville, IL: Sourcebooks, 2010.

Prothero, S., 'We Live in a Land of Biblical Idiots'/'Reading, Writing and Revelation', *Los Angeles Times*, 14 March 2003, from http://articles.latimes. com/2007/mar/14/opinion/oe-prothero14 [accessed 27 March 2013].

Ramos, M. and Lozano, J., 'Promoting Lost: New Strategies and Tools of Commercial Communication', in M. A. Pérez (ed.), *Previously On: Interdisciplinary Studies on TV Series in the Third Golden Age of Television*. Seville: Biblioteca de la Facultad de Comunicación de la Universidad de Sevilla, 2011, pp. 421–32.

Reinhartz, A., *Scripture on the Silver Screen*. Louisville, KY: Westminster John Knox, 2003.

Schillaci, S., 'Johnny Depp, "The Dark Knight," "Lost" Named to IMDb's Top 10 of the Last Decade', *The Hollywood Reporter*, 25 January 2012, www.hollywoodreporter.com/news/brad-pitt-johnny-depp-dark-knight-lost-imdb-top-10-284912 [accessed 27 March 2013].

Seay, C., *The Gospel According to Lost*. Nashville, TN: Thomas Nelson, 2009.

Stafford, N., 'Haikus for the Journey: The Life-Changing Reality of *Lost*', in P. Moore (ed.), *LOST Thought University Edition: Leading Thinkers Discuss LOST*, Scotts Valley, CA: CreateSpace, 2012, pp. 39–45.

Stuart, S. C., *Literary Lost: Viewing Television Through the Lens of Literature*, New York: Continuum, 2011.

Vasagar, J., 'Michael Gove to Send Copy of King James Bible to All English Schools', *The Guardian*, 25 November 2011, www.guardian.co.uk/politics/2011/nov/25/michael-gove-king-james-bible [accessed 27 March 2013].

Wagner, M., 'Lost Fans find Internet Thrills via Wikis, Games, Second Life', *InformationWeek*, 26 April 2008, www.informationweek.co.uk/personal-tech/science-tech/lost-fans-find-internet-thrills-via-wiki/207401542 [accessed 27 March 2013].

5

Streetwise About the Bible: Unexpected Allusions (to the Text) in Unusual Places

Amanda Dillon (Mater Dei Institute)

Angels and prophets cower in street corners. They lament over the person sleeping rough. They point to the poor. They plead with deep eyes for an acknowledgement. They carry the sick and dying. These are among the most moving images emerging as contemporary Street Art, on cracked walls and peeling plaster in cities all over the world. Who are these silent, new-yet-ancient messengers? Where do they come from and what message do they bring? Why and how are these biblical characters; angels, prophets and the anawim used, to such great effect, to critique the prevailing culture and engage the imagination of passers by? What does it reveal about biblical literacy among this particular group of artists and their perceived audience?

We are living in a tumultuous time of unprecedented paradigm shifts in every fundamental aspect of life on earth: ecological, political, financial, technological, moral, social and religious. This phenomenon finds something of a historical parallel in previous cataclysmic epochs. Phyllis Tickle offers an interesting theory in her book *The Great Emergence*, suggesting there is a discernible cyclical pattern of reform or renewal that has taken place in the Jewish and Christian religions reaching far back into the first millennium before the common era. She suggests that this pattern of momentous change seems to occur roughly every 500 years and is characterized by major challenges to the authority and structure of the prevailing religious hegemony, and these reflect changing socio-political developments in the surrounding culture. Positing the Reformation as the previous occurrence of such a shift, she demonstrates that the result is usually a split or fragmentation of some sort that, positively, results in reformed structures with a greater diversity of theologies and spiritualities, interpretations of scripture, and greater democratization within and revitalization and spread of these reformed churches (including the post-Reformation Roman Catholic Church), throughout the world. To the extent that a primary driving impulse behind the Reformation was the invention of printing in Europe – allowing for the mass distribution of the Bible, a parallel is obvious in the impact of the current digital and technological revolution. This, likewise, has profound and far-reaching implications for biblical literacy. If we follow her theory, this contemporary digital evolution places the biblical text ever more instantly and accessibly, and with more background resources, before more people – and therefore could potentially see biblical literacy expanded to the power of 'n' again – rather than diminished.

Another characteristic of the last half century has been civil unrest and protest against secular governing systems and ideologies. Civil rights, women's rights, peasants' rights and animal rights have all charged the political atmosphere and these movements are now experiencing renewed vigour, in this next generation, aided by the ease of global social networking. The last few years alone have seen campaigning groups such as Avaaz, the Occupy Movement, One Billion Rising, to mention but a few, emerge simul-taneously online and on the street, in large numbers, impacting political decisions at both a local and a global level. What is common to all of these movements is the insistent call for a recognition of the fundamental equality of all people and a much fairer redistribution of all resources. Unfettered capitalism has come under review and been found wanting when weighed against the ethical demands of the Common Good. The fiscal ideology of endless year-on-year growth, that benefits the few, is clearly unsustainable on a finite planet with fast-diminishing natural resources and a burgeoning population and where the global urban/rural ratio has officially tipped towards urban for the first time in human history. Projections to 2030 conservatively suggest five billion out of a global population of eight billion will be made up of megacity-dwellers. This paradigmatic change that we are all living in is infinitely vaster, faster and epochal than a gradual philosophical or cultural drift, from modernism to postmodernism, slowly percolating through the collective consciousness of Westerners.

Street Art is located at the juncture between this evolving digital cyber-realm and its necessary opposite – the material; the gritty, grounded, concrete frames of our urban existence. It mixes up the instantly downloaded, Photoshopped and stencilled image with cheap spray-can acrylics on a free substrate in public, urban space. This chapter explores biblical literacy as expressed in the Street Art of artists such as Faith47, Ernest Pignon-Ernest and C215 from Paris to Soweto. I suggest that the appropriation of the biblical motifs of message, prophecy and social justice are not incidental but prophetic in and of themselves; critiquing the status quo, demonstrating in action the emergence that is taking place and serving as harbingers of these emerging directions in global religious sensibilities.

What is Street Art?

Norman Mailer sensed in the early days of the 'scourge' of subway graffiti in New York that there was a rich anthropological backstory to this supposedly 'antisocial' activity. Mailer's intuitive recognition that anger at their social exclusion and disempowerment was central to these young mens' need to mark and thereby claim a space in the city prompted his seminal essay 'The Faith of Graffiti', reflecting on New York subway graffiti in the 1970s:

> From what combat came these curious letters of graffiti, with their Chinese and Arabic calligraphies; out of what connection to the past are these lights and torches of flame so much like the Hebrew alphabet where the form of the letter itself was worshipped as a manifest of the Lord ...[1]

Beyond the sometimes ugly tagging of buildings and bridges, a far more socially aware and constructive movement is underway to re-appropriate public space by and for the communities that live there – to claim back the city. Contrary to the commonly held belief that graffiti is always and everywhere antisocial and cynical, or grossly misunderstood as Mailer claimed, much emerging Street Art has social critique, social justice, community building and interpersonal relationships at its core. There is much about Street Art that allows it to function in this way as a generator of new metaphors by its very outsider nature. Street Art is an intervention, often dangerous to execute, usually performed at night under cover of darkness and the risk of being caught in an illegal act. Even when it is commissioned, in the case of some community murals, it may be defaced and ultimately either erased or covered over. It is not permanent, it is transient, speaking of present issues in an immediate way, unselfconsciously and unafraid of its impermanence. Street artists talk of 'giving up their art to the city, to the world'. These momentary poetic interludes are intended to transform the experience of life in the city and as such serve as an antidote to cynicism. These works of art are also 'a political act which aims to reinstate the lived experience as the true map of the city'.[2]

There are two 'turns' that are receiving attention from scholars presently, most especially those working in the broad area of theology and its related disciplines. The first is the 'spatial turn' and the second is the 'aesthetic turn'. In many ways Street Art is a simultaneous manifestation of both. Cultural Studies professor Nicolas Whybrow writes:

> The city has become effectively the 'new body'. In other words, as an object of study – it promises to supersede in significance a previous

---

[1] Norman Mailer, *The Faith of Graffiti*, New York: Harper Collins, 1974/2009, p. 31.
[2] Nicolas Whybrow, *Art and the City*, London: I. B. Tauris, 2011, p. 123.

preoccupation within critical discourse with the signifying human body as both implicated and expressive locus. Instead cities with their rising populations and complex transitory configurations have become the prime embodiments and therefore indices of a fast changing modernity.[3]

'Sometimes graffiti is an irritant, an unwanted autograph or tattoo anonymously etched onto the body of official urban culture'.[4] But it is also a temporary yet durable 'writing' of the city. Graffiti asserts some form of fundamental right to the freedom of expression in public places. It is important to distinguish between 'tagging' and those subversive acts of creativity intent on displaying artistic skill and dialoguing with the viewer. Much Street Art is intended as an interruption of the homogenizing and hypnotizing effects of capitalism's standardization – what Naomi Klein described as 'the pervasive colonisation of our mental space as well as our public spaces'.[5] These incursions on the cityscape are an invitation to notice the extraordinary within the ordinary.[6]

'Any gesture that has not been granted permission and yet commands public address needs to be understood primarily as a kind of discourse', writes street-art commentator Carlo McCormick.[7] These are some of the motivations described by contemporary British artists. Cyclops says: 'When I paint in the street, it's because I want to engage with the city I live in. Any time I'm painting on the street, it's as a participatory action, it is a response to the notion that I should be a vacant consumer, the property laws that are in place to benefit those who own said property, and the idea that I should abide in silence'.[8] ROA says: 'I like to paint in big cities because it's a totally different way to experience a city. You spend a couple of hours on a certain spot and get involved in that specific corner of a hood, you get to know the locals, the all day life of that particular micro space'.[9] And Pixel Pancho explains, 'I paint on the street because the streets ask me to do it. All the places I have painted have a story behind them and each place and its surface have told me what I should paint there'.[10]

---

[3] Ibid., p. 7.
[4] Ibid., p. 114.
[5] Naomi Klein, *No Logo*, London: Flamingo, 2001, p. 66.
[6] Whybrow, *Art and the City*, p. 113.
[7] Carlo McCormick 'Where Angels Fear to Tread', in Ethel Seno (ed.), *Trespass: A History of Uncommissioned Urban Art*, Cologne: Taschen, 2010, p. 16.
[8] W. G. Romany, *Burn After Reading*, Durham: Carpet Bombing Culture, 2012 (unpaginated).
[9] Ibid.
[10] Ibid.

Exploring Biblical Themes in the Work of
Three Street Artists

FIGURE 1   *The Freedom Charter by Faith47, at Grey Street, Woodstock, Cape Town, 2010. Left-hand Gate.*

FIGURE 2   *The Freedom Charter by Faith47, Cape Town, 2010. Right-hand Gate.*

Faith47

Faith47, who hails from Cape Town, South Africa, is a one of few female street artists to have achieved international recognition. Her work is characterized in part by human characters, especially female characters, such as 'Our Lady Poverty',[11] who bear golden halos and appear to be pierced in the heart by a light source coming from above. She also makes striking calligraphic work, emblazoning selected sentences (articles) from the Freedom Charter across the walls of downtown Cape Town and Johannesburg.

The work I want to examine here involves a pair of lamenting angels painted over a set of rusting metal gates, possibly the entrance and exit gates (about 30–50 metres apart) to an industrial site adjoining a railway line.[12] On the left-hand gate one angel of the pair (Figure 1) is slumped over a headstone, in a posture of mourning or lament. The words: 'The Freedom Charter' appear as though carved into this headstone or sarcophagus. Reference in this way to the perceived death of the Freedom Charter makes this a highly charged political piece. The Freedom Charter was first introduced in 1955 at a congress of liberation movements in South Africa, just prior to the banning of the African National Congress. Its obvious antecedent was the Universal Declaration of Human Rights launched just six short years earlier by the newly formed United Nations in the wake of the Second World War. The Freedom Charter articulated the deepest desires of oppressed South Africans and animated 'The Struggle' for equality for four decades. Sadly, for the mostly poor and black South Africans today, little has changed materially in their lives in the almost two decades since this liberation was achieved. Rather, reports of widespread and large-scale corruption dog the government as it frantically clamours to override, change and undermine what was once lauded as one of the most progressive national constitutions in the world.[13] For South Africans, the Freedom Charter is in some ways not unlike something between the Ten Commandments (Exod. 38.24) and the Beatitudes (Mt. 5.3–5.11) – with a political twist. It is an aspirational ethical code for a society that earnestly desires reform and longs for these fundamental rights to be realized.

---

[11] www.faith47.com/inhale/-character/ [accessed 2 March 2013], scroll through to 'rhapsody, rochester, 2012' to see a type of religious female character that reappears frequently in Faith47's work. Another: '"the hunter" cologne – 2011', is also an example.

[12] This pair of angels can be viewed on Google Maps by entering 'Grey Street, Woodstock, Cape Town' into the browser and then going to the street-level view and moving, in a westerly direction, towards the corner of the street [accessed 2 March 2013].

[13] The 4 March 2013 edition of *TIME* magazine has a lead article on violence in South Africa, 'the ruling African National Congress (ANC) is tarred by corruption and criminality. Scandals involving government ministers seem like a weekly occurrence. About a tenth of South Africa's annual GDP – as much as $50 billion – is estimated to be lost to graft and crime': www.time.com/time/magazine/article/0,9171,2137420,00.html#ixzz2MaQwYCnU [accessed 4 March 2013].

On the right-hand gate an angel with large wings holds her head in her hand and clutches her side – as though weeping uncontrollably. This angel is also in a gesture of profound grief, mourning or lament. She is similar to the concrete or marble statues that one finds standing over headstones in old graveyards. Thick black outlines mark out the form, the grey of the gates is allowed to act as the mid-tone, with darker shadow areas added and white highlights on the shoulder and top tip of the wings – a light source that comes from above. Previous graffiti has been worked over. This artwork, in a derelict corner adjacent to the railway line, is in a historically disadvantaged area of Cape Town. The potency of the lamenting angel on this right-hand gate is brought into sharp relief in the photograph of a woman shown sleeping rough and uncovered at the foot of this angel. The stark reality of this grinding poverty, the failure of this government to realize freedom from poverty for this woman, among millions more, is brought home. This photograph (even if one allows for the possibility that it may be posed and not an authentic happen-chance), is still altogether believable as this is a common sight in South African cities. The two figures, the human and the angel, mirror each other in posture. The photograph carries great pathos and serves to further illuminate the message of the Street Art.

These angels are not the heralds of 'Good News'. They do not annunciate the incarnation of God into this circumstance. These angels are beside themselves with sadness for the hope that has been squandered and for those who continue to suffer as a result. This covenant, between the warrior-leaders of the liberation struggle and the citizen-soldiers who toyi-toyied them into power has been broken – not by the citizens but by those who were democratically elected to make real this Freedom Charter.[14] In an allegorical reading of the biblical text, especially among indigenous churches, the biblical Exodus motif was widely appropriated to illustrate the liberation of 'non-white' South Africans from racial oppression. Mandela was a Moses-figure leading the people out of Apartheid – and the Freedom Charter – the 'golden rule' laying out the new social order. These angels are like the cherubim that Moses was commanded to make; to stand facing each other, at either side of the seat of mercy of the ark of the covenant, overshadowing it with their outstretched wings (Exod. 25.18–25, 37.9). The mercy seat is the place of encounter with God, the place to which Moses goes, in the tent of meeting to speak to the Lord (Num. 7:89). But this seat of mercy has been desecrated by corruption; the cherubim have all but dropped their wings and collapse with grief over this broken covenant.

---

[14] 'Toyi-toyi' is the name given to the foot-stomping, weapon-brandishing, song and dance style of protest march that became commonplace during mass demonstrations against Apartheid in South Africa.

FIGURE 3   *'Rest, Leisure and Recreation' by Faith47, Newtown, Johannesburg,*
2010.

Other pieces relating to the charter abound throughout the city, again exposing the sad irony. Alongside Khayelitsha, one of the most well-known informal settlements in the world, is visible Faith47's calligraphic illumination: 'The People Shall Share In The Country's Wealth'. Another Freedom Charter piece painted in Johannesburg, beneath the overpass of a freeway, proclaims: 'Rest, Leisure and Recreation Shall Be the Right of All'. But this is not a leisure venue: again the people who live under this bridge are sleeping rough. In the background are other beds and belongings suggesting a small community eking out an existence in this exposed environment. Most probably these people do not have employment, hence their precarious living arrangements. Rest, leisure and recreation belong to those who can afford it and do not have the constant worry of where their next meal is coming from. Commenting on this typographic piece, Faith47 reflected, '... painted under a bridge in Newtown – a cathedral of a home to about 60 of Joburg's lost people, bedroom to the lowest economic spectrum of our society. Now I have painted many areas that have left me startled but this place is just too much. ... My heart was so heavy from the energy there'.[15]

Many of Faith47's own descriptions of her work and creative process are striking in her use of metaphorical language that derives from the

---

[15] Faith47, *Faith47, On the Run, No.12*, Berlin: From Here to Fame Publishing, 2011, p. 73.

'semiotic cathedral'[16] of religion. In her book she writes, 'i am not religious but i pray through my work to unknown devils and gods. i look for my soul in colors and empty my being through parables of rusted, lost metal doors ...'.[17] In another interview she describes having painted for hours 'in empty buildings that felt like spiritual experiences, exploring holy chambers of neglected architecture ... finding something so beautiful in what society disregards, and bringing to life that which people usually throw away or ignore'.[18] Her own moniker: 'Faith47' and her own words: 'cathedral', 'pray', 'unknown devils and gods', 'soul', 'parables', 'holy chambers', evince a vital spirituality deeply engaged with people and place; a religious sensibility and, I suggest, a biblical literacy. Is it fair to assume then that she aims to invoke this in her audience?

C215

C215 is the signature pseudonym of Christian Guémy, a prolific French street artist based in Paris, who travels and paints internationally.[19] His vibrant and fluid graphic style is easily recognizable and his work can now be found in cities all over the world with many pieces in Barcelona, Amsterdam, London, Dublin, Rome and Oslo. His current technique is stencil based and characterized by graphic, close-up portraits of people. C215's favoured subjects are street kids, beggars, homeless people, refugees and the elderly. The rationale behind this, as he frequently points out in interviews, is precisely to draw attention to those that society has chosen to forget.

This frontal portrait of a young African boy has a powerful, ethereal quality, set against the gritty texture of the wall. The right-hand side of the boy's face is lit as though from a source on the right, the other side is in shadow. The focal point is his eyes – most especially the highly defined right eye. The lit side of his face is clearly defined whereas the other side fades into darker background colours abstractly obscuring the details of his face. There is no suggestion of any other contextual details, clothes, etc., just this utterly alluring portrait. It is clear this work has been done in a spontaneous and gestural style; spraying arcs of colour quickly and confidently. Sharp, crisp, beautifully defined shapes have been sprayed over the background colour, through a four or five part stencil, working from the lightest to

---

[16] Gerd Theissen, *The Bible and Contemporary Culture*, trans. David E. Green, Minneapolis: Fortress Press, 2007, p. 36

[17] Faith47, *Faith47, On the Run*, No.12, p. 11.

[18] http://davidkrutprojects.com/exhibitions/2012-11-2_faith-47_proj-js [accessed 6 February 2013].

[19] A wonderful Flickr photostream of C215's work is available to view at www.c215.com/ [accessed 6 February 2013].

FIGURE 4   *Untitled by C215, in France, 2010.*

darkest colour. Fluid and arching lines define the contours of his face in a
sensuous graphic style. Scratchy bits of raw texture in the background have
been left exposed, while smooth, clear and almost luminescent colours like
lime green are juxtaposed with turquoise. These electric, modern colours,
quite artificial in one sense – the colours of surf culture; purple, lime green
and turquoise – all add to the striking luminosity of this arresting image.
The clever use of colour, dark and light, lets the face jump right off the

wall while also simultaneously receding. It is quite simply remarkable in this regard. There is an iconographic quality to this piece of work. I suggest it is the street-art version of a Louis-le-Brocquyesque portrait in its abstract cubes of colour converging to create a penetrating portrait. It is both receding and emerging, quite magically, all at once – as he holds us in his gaze.

Who is this young boy? He seems to project forward towards us from the past; like a ghost, a vague shard of memory, a reminder, an omen. And what is he doing here? When we think of the French colonial engagement with Africa we have to think of slavery and its present-day consequences; thousands of second, third, fourth generation, diaspora Africans and many more refugees trying to create new lives in France. Civil unrest in Paris, especially in recent years, has shown that all is not well among these immigrant communities – especially the angry, young men. The 'cultural carnage' of colonization in many former Francophone African countries has been corruption, coups and civil war. This together with international debt burdens, HIV and AIDS, famine, drought, poverty, and the myriad other contingent problems that plague contemporary African countries have left a legacy of millions of displaced orphans and street children.

This boy is at once innocent and yet wise. If we choose to consider him through a biblical lens, his perceptive gaze and pronounced ear might suggest a visionary, a future leader; perhaps Ishmael (Gen. 17.20) or a young Joseph (Gen. 30.24), or the young Samuel (1 Sam. 3.4) hearing the call of the Lord? Or the future King David (1 Sam. 17.32–17.54), going out to face down Goliath? If we consider him through the New Testament, might he be a young Jesus found among the elders in the temple (Lk. 2.46)? Or the orphan that the Hebrew bible consistently demands be defended (Exod. 22.22, Deut. 24.17, Ps. 10.18, Ps. 82.3, Job 24.3, Isa. 1.17, 23, Jer. 5.28, Zech. 7.10, Mal. 3.5, Sir. 35.17, 2 Esdr. 2.20).

Another frequent subject matter in C215's work are homeless men. This particular portrait is in London, spray painted on metal. A startled man's face stares or glares at the viewer, as though caught by surprise around a corner. It is a close-up of a man's face and the suggestion of a woolen polo-neck jersey or a scarf frames his face in the lower right-hand corner. An angry, vibrant blood-red throws his face forward, just as the visible bolt on this gate enforces his social exclusion. As with the young African boy the focal point here again are the eyes of this man and his right eye is the centre of the composition.

The artist is a master of graphic line work – and that is in evidence here as his fluid lines define the contours of this face, built up through four or five tonal layers, sprayed through a stencil. These contour lines express all the wrinkles, veins and unkempt beard of his weatherbeaten face – overexposed to the elements and other hardships of life. Displaced and dispossessed, he is the holy fool, the clever drunk, a Knight of the Road, the wild man of the careless concrete jungle. His watery cataract-eyes fire a

FIGURE 5   *Untitled by C215, spray paint on metal, London, 2012.*

silent challenge in our direction: 'Who are you to judge me?', he seems to demand. Flecks of paint, splotches of colour and long drips – a favourite technique of street artists – lend a great spontaneity to the piece. Splatters of paint work to imply body fluids, mess, unpredictability, vulnerability. He is Job cursing the day of his birth (Job 3.1). He is Lazarus at the rich man's gate (Lk. 16.20).

Last year, C215 had an exhibition in a chapel attached to a hospital in Paris. In that installation he created what he describes as something like a set of 'Stations of the Cross' – spray painting his distinctive characters onto glass that was then box-mounted and backlit – giving an impression similar to stained-glass windows. Many of the portraits of orphans, including the young African boy and homeless men, featured in these new interpretations on glass. Interestingly, the exhibition was entitled 'Prophétes'.[20] In an interview with C215, he explained: 'a prophet is precisely someone who is seeing what others are not seeing and who is speaking in the name of God about the future but not only about pain but also for the sake of lucidity. That is my intention. I want to use ordinary kids to speak about the future instead of old, ordinary religious symbols. That is a real prophecy, 'cos when you see the face of a kid you have a real idea, a glimpse about the future'.[21] He also went on to explain that he didn't want to use conventional religious symbols because he wants to reach a wider audience – and for his message to be accessible to everybody regardless of their belief. He is influenced by Kandinsky's reflection 'On the Spiritual in Art' and describes himself as searching for 'new icons for the new religion'. He also spoke of his own work in terms of being 'prophetic' and a 'vocation', something he feels compelled to do: 'it is also about craziness somehow ... well, it says in the gospel that faith is a kind of madness, no?'[22]

Ernest Pignon-Ernest

Born in Nice in 1942, Ernest Pignon-Ernest is a Fluxus and Situationist French artist who is well known for his incredible charcoal drawings. He has engaged vociferously with the social justice issues of the past half century, both local to France, such as homelessness in French cities, as well as justice issues further afield including Apartheid and HIV and AIDS in South Africa and the situation in Palestine. This paste-up piece 'Les Cabines' consists of a series of more than ten different charcoal drawings of people, that have been printed up, cut-out and then pasted-up in public telephone booths.[23] All of the people who inhabit these booths are in some kind of deep emotional distress ranging through homelessness, drunkenness, despair and possibly even madness. Edvard Munch's 'Scream' painting comes immediately to mind when viewing more than one of the pieces. Some of the figures are screaming, some press their hands against

---

[20] www.flickr.com/photos/c215/7013736455/ [accessed 6 February 2013].
[21] From a telephone interview I had with C215 on 7 February 2013.
[22] Ibid.
[23] www.pignon-ernest.com [accessed 2 March 2013]. These works were done just before the new millennium, as the mobile phone was usurping the public telephone booth as the means of communication on the move and so it has already lost some of its context, in that sense.

FIGURES 6–7   'Les Cabines' by Ernest Pignon-Ernest, Brest, France, 1997–9.

the glass as if begging for release – as if imprisoned inside the booth. The drawings are so realistic of poor people slouched, shoulders dropped in defeat, huddled in a telephone booth that moving past at night it would be almost impossible at a glance to know that it wasn't a real person. Pignon-Ernest himself has said: 'Places are my essential material'. The urban street is both the setting and the subject of his many ephemeral works. These works placed in telephone booths also capture something of Hopper's urban loneliness: the place of communication, of connection is here the site of solitary disconnection and isolation. The glass of the booth paradoxically hiding the invisible emotional drama happening in the cage of the mind, behind the appearance of accepted normality.

As I understand it, the way these telephone booths worked was that the light would go on when a person entered the booth. This would then illuminate suddenly, for the person who had stepped in, this piece of art and thereby also make a momentary demand of them in terms of their response to both the subject and emotion expressed in the piece. In this sense it challenges the public's attitudes towards not just homelessness and mental health issues but also perhaps a perceived indifference to the accompanying despair. While there is not necessarily a direct or obvious link to either a biblical theme or character in a piece of work like this, its powerful statement about social exclusion and social indifference implies one can read a text through the images, something like this injunction from James, for example: 'For if a person with gold rings and in fine clothes comes into

FIGURES 8–9   *'Soweto' by Ernest Pignon-Ernest, in Durban, South Africa, 2002.*

your assembly, and if a poor person in dirty clothes also comes in, and if you take notice of the one wearing the fine clothes and say, "Have a seat here, please," while to the one who is poor you say, "Stand there," or, "Sit at my feet," have you not made distinctions among yourselves, and become judges with evil thoughts?' (Jas. 2.1–4).

In the top left-hand corner is the famous photograph of Hector Pieterson, a young African schoolboy shot by the police during the Soweto Uprising of 1976. This iconic photograph of the violence that took place under the apartheid government, against its own citizens, is the departure point for Pignon-Ernest's 'South African Piéta'. In much the same pose, an African woman carries an emaciated dying man. This drawing was made in Johannesburg in 2002, the year the Hector Pieterson Memorial Museum was opened in Soweto. The original photo appears like a postage stamp in the top left-hand corner of the new work of art, thereby serving to contextualize this image. The drawing was then replicated and pasted up at chosen sites in Soweto and in the Warwick Triangle area of Durban, KwaZulu-Natal. The Warwick Triangle is an informal trading area, under a concrete flyover bringing traffic in and out of the city centre, flanked by taxi and bus ranks and the Catholic cathedral. The link between the photo and the new 'piéta' image is interesting. The HIV and AIDS epidemic is the scourge of post-apartheid South Africa – a public health and social justice issue that successive governments have hopelessly failed to address in any meaningful way. The staggering statistics of 25 per cent HIV prevalence rates and approximately 800 deaths every day have radically diluted the hopes, energy and potential of the new South Africa. This work commemorates Hector Pieterson while also making a statement about this new oppressor that is HIV and AIDS, on this generation. I have wondered how the people, who looked daily at this image, perceived it and felt about it? A painful image, I imagine, for many because it is documents the daily reality of countless families. Few households have not lost a family member to HIV and AIDS and few children have not seen their mothers, sisters, aunts and grannies caring for a dying loved one. The women of the household are the primary carers, quite literally carrying the burden of care when someone in the household becomes ill. The scene of a woman carrying a sick man to a clinic is familiar. The small image in the top left corner reminding us of the Soweto uprising is surely meant to contextualize this image as saying: This too shall pass, this new oppression, insidious and savage, shall also be overcome. Using a 'scriptural imagination' to read the image, might it be that the artist is here imaging God as an African woman? There is no judgement, no condemnation in this image. However, it is a prophetic word to the global community about the injustice of poverty, 20-year patents on medicines and the lack of access to healthcare that come with that. It is also a challenge to the faith community who are called to tend to the sick. 'Truly I tell you, just as you did it to one of the least of these who are members of my family, you did it to me' (Mt. 25.40). The woman stands in the background, a transient monument to fortitude in the face of despair, silent and brave amidst the broken-hearted. As they bustle about in the cut and thrust of life: commuting, trading, cooking, and cleaning – she is a silent presence who understands what is carried in the heart and mind of those to whom she ministers as memory.

Biblical literacy

In his 2007 book on religious literacy, Stephen Prothero laments the loss of biblical literacy evident among his young undergraduates. He includes a religious literacy test in the book, the same one used on his students to measure their literacy and invites the reader to test their own literacy.[24] While acknowledging that his test was necessarily a simple and 'blunt object' used to illustrate his point, my suggestion is that perhaps the question of biblical literacy needs to be opened out considerably. Perhaps a test like this is asking the wrong questions or working from a concept of literacy that is no longer universally applicable, relevant or desirable? An aspect of Prothero's book that I found problematic was the seeming narrowness of the understanding of literacy. An understanding of literacy must necessarily evolve parallel to the developments in the sources of information available. The digital online environment characterized by an emphasis on the instantly obtainable and visual: the moving image, animated graphics, the seamless merging of trivia and profundity, the soundbite, the vitriolic commentary alongside endless free views of scholarly articles demands an altogether expanded understanding of literacy and a different set of literacy skills to navigate competently.

Prothero's particular subject is Religious and Biblical Studies and this is where he observes the drop in or lack of literacy. However, I meet many university lecturers of various disciplines across the humanities broadly, who similarly, and unprovoked, express concerns about a perceived 'dumbing down' in their own subject: a pervasive 'cut and paste from the internet' approach to research and writing, without any attempt to either disguise the plagiarism or integrate the appropriated information in any meaningful way. Something needs to shift then in response to this and challenge these highly computer-literate students to 'up their game' and integrate the gleaned information in ways appropriate to the technology at their disposal and the new 'information age' in which we operate. The gathering of information is very easy and quick, the real question is how

---

[24] Stephen Prothero, *Religious Literacy: What Every American Needs To Know – and Doesn't*, New York: HarperCollins, 2007, pp. 292–8.

to use it? Anne Haas Dyson has illustrated how music, video games, and movies assist students as they become composers and literate beings. Dyson suggests that students regularly borrow elements from popular culture and transform these materials into a new product. She argued that this vehicle into literacy is largely ignored.[25] In this changing digital environment, are we approaching a point where it is more feasible to ask students to demonstrate their understanding of a biblical text by, for example; designing an app that takes the user/reader on an interactive virtual tour of Paul's journeys – rather than writing an essay about same? Would the ability to integrate the biblical text with both ancient and modern overlapping maps, photographic resources, archaeological data, a soundtrack possibly, and a video/podcast commentary and reflection on the text be a far more appropriately contextual application of the literacy skills and integrated knowledge of the student?

John E. Ingulsrud and Kate Allen in their recent study of literacy development among young manga readers in Japan have stressed that the reading of manga is not done in isolation from other media. They suggest, 'the "kindred" media of anime, video games, light novels, and toys are connected with reading of manga in terms of learning literacy skills, understanding stories, and appreciating characters'.[26] In other words there is a growth in parallel and complementary literacy skills, especially visual and kinesthetic that is happening simultaneously and that draws on other stimuli in the popular culture contextual to their situation in life; toys and games, tv and video, etc. 'Unlike school literacy, popular culture literacies, like manga literacy, are not conceived in terms of "skills" and are not tested.[27] This is not to say, however, that these untested literacy skills are not sophisticated. They have shown precisely that a level of complexity beyond that which is normally tested for in the official school literacy skills tests is to be found among their manga readers. In a not dissimilar study conducted among young students in a very multi-cultural context, in a mid-western American town, Jennifer Urbach elaborating on the overlooked literacy skills of young African-American students notes:

> As our society becomes increasingly multicultural, we can no longer afford to view literacy through a single lens. Literacy is more than a set of skills. It's a dynamic and complex process that is driven by our Discourses – our beliefs, values, and ways of thinking that are associated with our cultural groups. Literacy then is not a set of checklists but a

---

[25] A. H. Dyson cited by Jennifer Urbach, 'Beyond story grammar: Looking at stories through cultural lenses' in *Education and Urban Society* 44 (2012): 392–411 at 395. Originally published online 29 December 2010 and found at http://eus.sagepub.com/content/44/4/392.
[26] John E. Ingulsrud and Kate Allen, *Reading Japan Cool: Patterns of Manga Literacy and Discourse*, Plymouth: Lexington Books, 2010, p. 93.
[27] Ibid., p. 87.

way to express ourselves ... . Looking at story or literacy as if it should fit a specific mold depersonalises the act of literacy. It marginalises individuals as well as the richness that is literacy. It becomes our job to challenge the "politics of representation" and to expand the definition of literacy.[28]

An argument can also be made for Biblical Literacy along these lines. A broader acknowledging of the diverse ways both in which people acquire and express biblical literacy allows for a more nuanced and less dualistic discussion to take place. Biblical literacy, most especially in our postmodern context is about much more than being able to list the ten commandments or twelve apostles. Again as Urbach reminds us, we all 'come to literacy through different paths. These paths are closely connected to our beliefs and values and thus our identities'.[29] As such, our cultural milieu has much to do in shaping our biblical literacy too. In western Europe, at least, that milieu is replete with biblical referents to even the most casual or disinterested observer. From the adorning frieze of sculpted prophets and patriarchs, over the door of the soaring Gothic cathedral, at the heart of almost every city – to the kitsch of wobbley-head 'Buddy Jesus' figures on the dashboard and sloganeering t-shirts; Christian radio, classical music, Victorian graveyards, the turn-of-phrase of talk-show hosts, FaceBook posts, twitter feeds, exhibition posters, TED talks, day-time Christian channels or Easter-time reruns of Mel Gibson's Passion of the Christ on late-night television – the daily possibility of encountering, unintentionally and however briefly, a visual or audio-visual allusion to the biblical text, is extremely high. For most, these allusions are so enduring in the backdrop to their lives, as in architecture for example, as to have become invisible, just part of the 'white-noise' of the environment. Both collectively and individually, we develop strategies to engage with, filter and process all this information and stimuli to suit our capacities, needs, desires and lifestyles. These too are exercises in literacy ... 'an ongoing endeavour fundamental to our very being and to the historical and cultural context in which we live'.[30] Biblical literacy, I argue, is available to whomsoever desires it and is attentive to the ever-present stimuli, operating at various levels of opacity and points of encounter, in the ordinary, everyday environment. One such unexpected and unusual points of encounter is contemporary Street Art.

---

[28] Jennifer Urbach, 'Beyond story grammar: Looking at stories through cultural lenses' in *Education and Urban Society*, 44 (2012): 392–411 at 407. Originally published online 29 December 2010 and found at: http://eus.sagepub.com/content/44/4/392
[29] Ibid., p. 395.
[30] Ibid.

How are these artists expressing their biblical literacy? (Conclusion)

Visual literacy specialist, Yan Ma, pulled together an overview from Postmodern art theorists:

'Contemporary art has become increasingly visible and popular since the mid-1970s. Art is no longer seen as an elitist pursuit, remote from the interest and concerns of the public at large' (Wallis, 1984). Post modern art is a reflection of current political, cultural, and psychological experiences of a society. In terms of its characteristics, Levin (1979) describes it as 'style-free and free-style. Playful and full of doubt, it denies nothing. Tolerant of ambiguity, contradiction, complexity, incoherence, it is eccentrically inclusive. It mimics life, accepts awkwardness and crudity and takes an amateur stance. Structured by time rather than form and concerned with context instead of style, it uses memory, research, confession, fiction-with irony, whimsy, and disbelief'. (Hertz, 1985)[31]

While most of these theorists pre-date this explosion of street-art, their descriptions aptly fit the playful, ambiguous, eccentrically inclusive, amateur stance adopted by postmodern street artists. And the same may be said of their appropriation of the Bible and its themes and motifs. Perhaps one of the comments that most accurately describes what appears to be taking place in the interface between contemporary artists and the Bible comes from Scottish artist David Mach, in reference to his recent work, Precious Light, a monumental reworking of the King James Bible through a series of gargantuan photographic collages.[32] In approaching the Bible, Mach did not set out to illustrate this venerated text but rather to filter it through his contemporary sensibility, seeing its grand narrative themes reflected in our own calamitous world. Recognizable episodes and events including Noah's Ark, the Tower of Babel, plagues and crucifixion are treated in densely detailed photo-collages, with images cut out of thousands of magazines.[33] He is clear that he didn't set out to illustrate the Bible: 'I mean, they're definitely not illustrations for Bible stories. It's me looking at the contemporary world, at what's going on all around me and filtering it through these archetypal themes that are all there in the Bible: plagues, disasters, sacrifice, cruelty, hubris'.[34]

---

[31] Yan Ma, 'Reader response theory: An analysis of a work of chinese postmodern art', Journal of Visual Literacy, 15.1 (1995): 39–72, at 40.

[32] www.davidmach.com/preciouslight/ [accessed 3 March 2013].

[33] David Mach quoted in 'Cross and Passion', an article in The Irish Times, Saturday, 14 July 2012. He was commenting on his exhibition 'Precious Light' at the Galway Arts Festival, also available at: www.irishtimes.com/newspaper/weekend/2012/0714/1224320019105.html [last accessed 27 February 2013].

[34] Ibid.

His reflection speaks volumes about biblical literacy now and how those working in the creative arts approach the Bible through a different lens – namely that of themes and motifs and narratives that parallel, symbolically, our contemporary events and situations. This is not a simplistic viewpoint. True to postmodern impulses it is, paradoxically, not concerned with questions of belief (orthodoxy) and practice (orthopraxy) but rather approaches the biblical text as a historical, mythical, symbolic meta-narrative that has something profound to reveal to contemporary humanity about where we have come from and who we are and where we might want to be going. Faith47 when asked about her use of biblical characters, such as angels replied:

> i greatly admire old religious art. particularly because it served as a vehicle for parables to be told through the visual language. the esoteric nature of old art, including the illustrations one finds in the tarot and alchemical illustrations are truly fascinating as they pull at mankind's struggle on the questions of existence and the search for answers thereof. i like to draw on the feelings from these old paintings, but reinvent them and juxtapose them. i think formalised religion has taken the spirituality out of the existential quest and flattened it, so in a way i like to rethink the way they used art, destroy their power and find a new hidden meaning that is more relevant on an individual spiritual basis and without any 'religious' strings attached.[35]

Artists are appropriating characters, symbols, themes and archetypes from the biblical text as a point of reference that can viably be used as a tool to both interpret, understand and elucidate our present situation. In this sense, they are an important dialogue partner as they are part of the 'hermeneutical cycle' in the popular discourse that informs the biblical literacy of both believers and non-believers alike. Stuart Hall urges us to 'consider the proliferation of sites and places in which the modern artistic impulse is taking place, in which it is encountered and seen'.[36] I suggest Street Art does indeed open up possibilities for 'recovering lost energies in liminal and obscure places'.[37]

'Postmodernity doesn't mean a mere adjustment of modernity. It is a quantum leap into a new world of ideas, values and ethics. Old categories of ethics, race and religion have been reconfigured by post modernity's new way of perceiving the world'.[38] Part of that reconfiguring quantum leap is

---

[35] Faith47 quoted directly from e-mail correspondence, 15 March 2013.
[36] Stuart Hall, 'Museums of Modern Art and the End of History' in G. Tawadros (ed.), *Changing States: Contemporary Arts and Ideas in an Era of Globalisation*, London: inIVA. 2004, pp. 286–91 at 289.
[37] Whybrow, *Art and the City*, p. 16.
[38] Craig Dettweiler and Barry Taylor, *A Matrix of Meanings: Finding God in Popular Culture*, Grand Rapids, MI: Baker Academic, 2003, p. 24.

a shift away from a dualistic worldview characterised by institution-alised, segregated religion towards scientifically-influenced spiritualities of interconnectedness. This is happening alongside a growing awareness and unwillingness to simply ignore the terrible human and environmental consequences wrought by the capitalist-consumerist economic model and the systemic injustices rooted in the policies of many global governing struc-tures. This emerging consciousness critiques the status quo at eye-level, on the street, face to face. The Caravaggisti of our time throw back at us the oldest moral codes of humanity in angry lashings of spray paint across the city walls: 'Cursed be anyone who deprives the alien, the orphan, and the widow of justice'. All the people shall say, 'Amen!' (Deut. 27.19).

Bibliography

Dettweiler, Craig and Barry Taylor, *A Matrix of Meanings, Finding God in Popular Culture*, Grand Rapids, MI: Baker Academic, 2003.

Faith47, *Faith47, On the Run, No.12*, Berlin: From Here to Fame Publishing, 2011.

Hall, Stuart, 'Museums of Modern Art and the End of History', in G. Tawadros (ed.), *Changing States: Contemporary Arts and Ideas in an Era of Globalisation*, London: inIVA, 2004.

Ingulsrud, John E. and Kate Allen, *Reading Japan Cool: Patterns of Manga Literacy and Discourse*, Plymouth: Lexington Books, 2010.

Klein, Naomi, *No Logo*, London: Flamingo, 2001.

Ma, Yan, 'Reader response theory: An analysis of a work of Chinese post modern art', *Journal of Visual Literacy*, 15/1:

Mailer, Norman, *The Faith of Graffiti*, New York: Harper Collins, 1974/2009.

McCormick, Carlo, 'Where Angels Fear to Tread', in Ethel Seno (ed.), *Trespass, A History of Uncommisioned Urban Art*, Cologne: Taschen, 2010.

Meegan, Rua and Lauren Teeling, *Irish Street Art: Stencils, Paste Ups, Murals and Portraits*, Dublin: Visual Feast Productions, 2010, p. 47.

Prothero, Stephen, *Religious Literacy: What Every American Needs To Know – and Doesn't*, New York: HarperCollins, 2007.

Romany, W. G., *Burn After Reading*, Durham: Carpet Bombing Culture, 2012.

The Irish Times, 'Cross and Passion', Saturday, 14 July 2012.

Theissen, Gerd, *The Bible and Contemporary Culture*, trans. David E. Green. Minneapolis: Fortress Press, 2007.

Tickle, Phyllis, *The Great Emergence, How Christianity is Changing and Why*, Grand Rapids, MI: Baker, 2008.

Urbach, Jennifer, 'Beyond story grammar: Looking at stories through cultural lenses', *Education and Urban Society*, 44 (2012): 392–411 at 395. Originally published online 29 December 2010 and found at http://eus.sagepub.com/content/44/4/392

Whybrow, Nicolas, *Art and the City*, London: I. B. Tauris, 2011.

Websites

www.c215.com/ [accessed 6 February 2013].

www.davidmach.com/preciouslight/ [accessed 3 March 2013].

http://davidkrutprojects.com/exhibitions/2012-11-2_faith-47_proj-js [accessed 2 March 2013].

www.faith47.com/inhale/-character/ [accessed 2 March 2013].

www.flickr.com/photos/c215/7013736455/ [accessed 6 February 2013].

www.irishtimes.com/newspaper/weekend/2012/0714/1224320019105.html [accessed 27 February 2013].

www.pignon-ernest.com [accessed 2 March 2013].

www.time.com/time/magazine/article/0,9171,2137420,00.html#ixzz2MaQwYCnU [accessed 4 March 2013].

6

Mary, Mary, Quite Contrary: Eve as Redemptrix in Madonna's 'Girl Gone Wild'

Alan W. Hooker (University of Exeter)

Introduction

This chapter, and the volume in which it appears, revolves around the topic of biblical literacy. In her preface to *A Guide Through the New Testament*, Celia B. Marshall writes, '[b]iblical illiteracy is the norm today'.[1] She argues that high school students have no interest in the Bible, whether in the classroom or Sunday school. Students 'go elsewhere for fun, friendship, and fellowship'.[2] Essentially, for Marshall, it is the older generation who know their Bible better.

This type of knowledge consists of memorizing passages and verses from the biblical texts as well as studying daily devotionals: 'biblical literacy', she notes, 'was part of what it meant to be educated'.[3] This kind of rote learning is based in the 'traditional pedagogies associated with many religious movements' and in fact the idea of rote learning itself goes back to religious foundations.[4] Our current systems of education in the Western world, genealogically linked to religious ideologies, are therefore naturally built around text.

The architecture and layout of many schools still testifies to this textual bias: rows of desks being the primary locus of learning from the

---

[1]Celia B. Marshall, *A Guide Through the New Testament*, Lousiville, KY: Westminster John Knox Press, 1994, p. 9.
[2]Ibid.
[3]Ibid.
[4]Moore, 2010: 212.

all-knowing textbook. Many schools still separate pupils into groups based on their 'ability', where ability here appears to signify how well they do in written examinations. This is not a critique on my part of ability-segregated groups, but a critique of the way in which pupils are segregated as well as of the ultimate nature of classroom learning as primarily textual.

We place blackboards at the front of classrooms and place pupils around it, as if at the feet of a guru. It smacks somewhat of Bentham's panopticon where the blackboard is centralized as the place from which the teacher observes her pupils. The teacher acts more as a scribe for a textbook than as a facilitator for independent learning.

Dale B. Martin in his *Pedagogy of the Bible*, like Celia B. Marshall, discusses his upbringing in a fundamentalist church where biblical literacy was text-centric: 'We knew Bible stories, Bible characters, and memorized many Bible verses [...] We kids — or at least those of us whose parents herded us to church all the time – knew our Bibles'.[5]

In my opinion, the question that should be asked is not about the apparent decline in biblical literacy, but about what we understand by the term 'literacy' itself. In the above quotations, literacy is discussed in terms of text. If this is how we construct the concept, then perhaps it is true that our society as a whole is less 'biblically literate'. But does this statement still hold if we unpack 'literacy'?

The Western world is a post-internet culture which provides us with many new ways to renegotiate the concept of literacy. If culture is 'concerned with the production and exchange of meaning'[6] then the internet itself is one vast repository of it. In 2007, five billion gigabytes of data per month constituted the 'global flow of information' with predictions that in 2013 this figure would increase to 56 billion gigabytes per month.[7] Moreover, 66 per cent of all mobile traffic by 2013 will apparently be video, and the year 2012 saw the first YouTube video, Psy's *Gangnam Style*, reach one billion hits. *Gangnam Style*'s success is due in part to the ability of internet users to upload their own versions of the hit song to YouTube.[8]

Visual images are important in this post-internet culture for 'they are an important means through which social life happens'.[9] The fact that one billion people use the social network site Facebook each month,[10] and Twitter users increased to 500 million in 2012,[11] signifies that there is a need to reimagine the concepts of society, culture, and indeed literacy.

---

[5] Dale B. Martin, *Pedagogy of the Bible: An Analysis and Proposal*, Louisville, KY: Westminster John Knox Press, 2008, p. 1.
[6] Hall, 1997, p. 2.
[7] Miller, 2010.
[8] BBC News, 2012.
[9] Rose, 2007, p. xiii.
[10] Associated Press, 2012.
[11] Semiocast, 2012.

In this paper I use Madonna's 2012 song 'Girl Gone Wild' to demonstrate how we can re-understand the notion of biblical literacy in light of this post-internet boom in image/video sharing. My intention is to analyse the video and note how Madonna uses biblical iconography and tropes in her stated quest to 'stop the lies and hypocrisy of the church'.[12]

Images of Christ, apples, scantily clad men and the Madonna appear in the 'Girl Gone Wild' video and give us adequate reason to suppose that Madonna draws on biblical imagery. Her longstanding and difficult relationship with the Vatican (as discussed below) affords her the opportunity to use her birth name controversially in order to compare herself to the Virgin Mother, the 'second Eve', as she does in one of the shots at the end of the video where Madonna cries tears of blood (a reference to the supposed weeping Marian statues). With all of this in mind, I propose that Madonna pitches herself as Eve, the only female in Eden and 'Girl Gone Wild' (notice the singular), while the men in the video function as representations of Adam.

This framework permits Madonna to challenge the patriarchal hermeneutic of the church and reveal the inadequacy of the masculine trifecta comprising this church, its god, and man ('Adam'). I will read the music video through three of the four segments which comprise her MDNA tour: *transgression*, *masculine/feminine*, and *redemption*. The aim is to demonstrate that in 'Girl Gone Wild' Madonna engages with each of these topics and overturns their traditional Christian understanding, namely that woman is transgressor, man is saviour, masculinity represents order, and redemption is phallocentric.

Thus this chapter is not so much an attempt to write an excursus of the ins and outs of biblical literacy in Western popular culture as much as it is an exercise to demonstrate how biblical literacy can and does function beyond the text.

Reception of Madonna's music

When Madonna did her live performance of 'Live to Tell' in Rome for her 2006 'Confessions' tour, she sang from a large, glittery, mirror-covered cross with a well-fashioned crown of thorns on her head, in what appeared to be a mock of Christ's crucifixion. A spokesperson for the Vatican responded to her performance and called for her excommunicated (Romero, 2010). Spokespeople for Rome's Jewish community and Italy's Muslim World League also both criticized how the song was performed: the first said it was 'disrespectful', the second, 'bad taste'.[13] To make things

---

[12] Madonna, n.d., para. 3.
[13] Associated Press, 2006.

worse, Madonna even invited the Pope to her show – a show which was, according to the Vatican spokesperson, 'a blasphemous challenge to the faith and a profanation of the cross'.[14]

Moreover, in 1990, Madonna's 'Blond Ambition' tour was also criticized by the Roman Catholic group Famiglia Domani who deemed the tour a 'shameful spectacle'.[15] The shameful spectacle in question is probably Madonna's simulation of the masturbatory act to the *Like a Virgin* track which segued into 'Like a Prayer', delivering the audience a wonderful mish-mash of sex and religion.

It might be argued that Madonna's use of religious symbols as entertainment is the reason she attracts the strong disapproval of religious institutions. However, the problem appears to lie more with Madonna's sexuality and the ways in which she uses it during her performances. In the 'Live to Tell' performance especially, I question whether there would have been such a backlash if the person upon the cross were male. Similar portrayals of a female Christ, a Christa, have resulted in comparable religious outcry, most notably in 1984 when Edwina Sandys' sculpture *Christa* was installed in the Episcopal Cathedral of St John the Divine in New York.[16]

Madonna's masturbation in the 'Blond Ambition' tour draws attention to her independent sexuality, free from hegemonic, male masculinity. Even the two men who perform with her wear cone-shaped bras, perhaps to show that her sexuality defines theirs; a stark contrast to Christian organizations run by men informing women how to use their sexuality appropriately.

It is this idea of a powerful female sexuality that I understand Madonna draws on in one of her latest songs and its accompanying music video, 'Girl Gone Wild', from the 2012 *MDNA* album. The video features, as noted above, the Edenic fruit, Christ, the Madonna, and arguably Adam(s) and Eve. These images converge to tell a tale of Eve as a redemptrix, a saviour. The recent 'sex scandals' in which the Roman Catholic Church has been embroiled might be considered part of the lies and hypocrisies Madonna refers to, and if so, Eve's character in 'Girl Gone Wild' presents the church with a new vision of sexuality as a solution.

In 'Girl Gone Wild', we see Madonna eschew the androcentric hermeneutic typically used to read the Eden narrative, a hermeneutic which refuses to challenge the supremacy of the male characters, namely God and Adam. Although the 'Girl Gone Wild' video is full of 'men', Madonna/ Eve takes centre stage and displaces the male privilege given to the Eden account. Indeed, there are, so I argue, no male saviours in 'Girl Gone Wild' – woman must save herself.

---

[14] Romero, 2010.
[15] Braxton, 1990.
[16] Breyer, 2012.

The past, present, and future

Before we dive into the main part of this chapter, it is important to comment briefly on the nature of biblical literacy and its relation to concepts of the past and of memory, both of which bear heavily on how one treats an historical text and the mythos it presents.

Do I believe Madonna studiously pored over Genesis 2–3, delved into commentaries, and consulted exegetes to construct her performance in 'Girl Gone Wild'? It is a possibility, but in my opinion, it is more likely she uses the 'memory' of the text that her tradition, i.e. Roman Catholicism, espouses. Memory here is not understood as a mere recollection of past events which one has experienced, but rather memory in this religio-communal context signifies the investment of a person or group in a specifically propagated ideology or mythos. For example, in the New Testament, when Peter exhorts his audience to 'remember' (*mnēsthēnai*) the words of the prophets (2 Pet. 3.2), he does not refer to his audience's experience of past events then, but to recall of words they have heard through their repetition in a religious context. When they listen, Peter's audience may share in the experience of the prophets; remembrance renegotiates past experience in light of present lives. As 2 Peter 3.2ff. emphasizes, the future and the past are linked and collaborate in remembrance: the past, in which the prophets spoke, and the future, in which the Lord comes, adhere together in the 'now' so that both the past and present are (re)written with the 'now' in mind.

Deuteronomy 5.2–3 may also be cited in which Moses says to the children of Israel: 'Yahweh our God made a covenant with us at Horeb. Not with our ancestors did Yahweh make this covenant, but with us, who are all of us here alive'. Moshe Weinfeld explains these verses as 'an explanatory gloss, which comes to solve a major problem in the theology of Deuteronomy'; that is, how can those Moses now addresses keep the covenant of Sinai if they were not there to experience it, since the 'Exodus generation [...] died out during the forty years of wandering'?[17]

The answer is to make the covenant eternal in what Weinfeld calls the 'blurring of generations'[18]: what was applicable then, is applicable now. The blurring of generations is what allows those of us in religious communities to make sense of our scriptures today. In a negative way, perhaps, this blurring can result in the continued propagation of oppressive ideologies; for example, misogyny, racism and homophobia. Yet there is also something redeemable in it: we can constantly reappropriate the texts and their interpretations. And this is what Madonna has done in 'Girl Gone Wild'.

For the Deuteronomist, to remember Yahweh's actions and to invest in them is to simultaneously create the present, inscribe the past, and envision

---

[17] 1991, 237.
[18] 1991, 238.

the future. The difference between the Roman Catholic Church and Madonna in this context is that they both 'remember' differently.

Paul Connerton distinguishes two types of memory: incorporated and inscribed. The former is memory embodied, while the latter is memory contained on objects, and primarily realized in text.[19] Though the two cannot be absolutely distinguished from one another, we may say that Madonna, through performance, presents memory incorporated, while the Judeo-Christian tradition, broadly, relies heavily on inscribed memory; that is, its scriptures. Rituals are an embodied form of memory, and it seems Madonna through her art gives her viewers new rituals to remember and act.

As a remembrance, Madonna's video is, to borrow from Mieke Bal, a way of 'dealing with the "past today"'.[20] It is a form of 'preposterous history' in which one puts 'what came chronologically first ("pre") as an aftereffect behind ("post") its later recycling'. Peter and Moses, for their communities, deal with the past today, and Madonna too, with her audience, deals with the church's past and its ideologies, which she sees as contaminated by its hypocritical actions in the past and today.

As said above, Madonna's exposé in 'Girl Gone Wild' comes through four areas which form the structure of her 2012 MDNA tour: *transgression*, *prophecy* (which I do not deal with in this chapter), *masculine/feminine*, and *redemption*. In each of these areas Madonna critiques society's inherited understandings and assumptions about the Adam and Eve mythos. Who transgressed? Who will save us? What is man? What is woman? All these questions are embedded, so I would argue, in Madonna's 'Girl Gone Wild' video, and when we examine them against the answers provided by the Christian tradition, we are able to see how Madonna's own biblical literacy functions and to what end.

Transgression

In the MDNA tour, 'Girl Gone Wild' features as the first song in the transgression segment. On stage, the song opens with an entourage of red-robed priests who set in motion a giant censer which swings across the stage. The large thurible employed is a replica of the famous Botafumeiro in Galicia's Santiago de Compostela cathedral. These red-robed priests must be the *tiraboleiros*, who are specifically appointed to set the Botafumeiro in motion at religious festivals and other occasions.

Madonna's use of the 'Botafumeiro' in her performance, especially in front of a large cross which bears the name of the tour (MDNA), could be

---

[19] 1989, pp. 72–3.
[20] 1999, pp. 6–7.

taken as a direct challenge to Roman Catholicism's insistence that it has the ability to define what is and is not a legitimate ritual. Additionally, the MDNA-emblazoned cross is most likely a subversion of the INRI epithet found on crucifixes in Christian art.

The cross no longer bears the male Christ, but (the) Madonna, pure, virginial motherhood, the feminine, and yet at the same time this is a woman who presents herself as someone unafraid of her own sexuality. Perhaps she plays with the Freudian Madonna-whore complex to show the church that it is its own ideologies which force women into these dichotomizing roles: that is, women must either be virtuous or slatternly. I do not see her purpose as one which reinforces this binary, but which deliberately plays the roles up to show that (1) a woman is the one who gets to define who she is, and (2) people cannot be so easily categorized. Madonna has removed a sexless saviour from the cross and put in his place a holistic, sexual person.

To return to the thurible, it is a symbol which relays to the audience that this performance should be read as ritual. To uphold this idea, Madonna makes her entrance via a confessional which descends from the air – it is from this booth where Madonna kneels in prayer that we hear the first words of the 'Girl Gone Wild' lyrics spoken:

Oh my God,
I am heartily sorry for having offended thee,
And I detest all my sins,
Because I dread the loss of heaven,
And the pain of hell,
But most of all because I love thee,
And I want so badly to be good.

In the music video these words are not spoken from a confessional. They are recited by Madonna, standing up, while her eyes look upwards (toward heaven?) A half-naked man in cruciform flashes (up) on screen to accompany the line 'I dread the loss of heaven', while two semi-clad men who take bites from the same apple are shown when the lyric 'and the pain of hell' plays. This interplay of images and lyrics suggests Madonna sees her opening 'confession' in the context of the canonical progression from original sin to crucified and risen saviour, though we should note that although the video runs forward, the images appear in reverse order, i.e. the saviour figure appears first, followed by the two men and the apple. As the video plays, then, Madonna brings us from the present to the past, ultimately to construct a new remembrance of Eden.

The prayer Madonna opens with is an act of contrition usually prayed during the sacrament of penance. Madonna's version however slightly changes the traditional form of the prayer: instead of Madonna's 'but most of all because I love thee', the traditional prayer reads, 'but most of all because they [my sins] offend thee'. This traditional act of contrition ends with the promise not to sin again with the help of Christ, yet Madonna's finishes, 'I want so badly to be good'. We already see here a foreshadowing of the idea that man cannot save women: in refusing to invoke the name of Christ, there is a rejection of his power to save.

The video for 'Girl Gone Wild' is filmed primarily in black and white, and, when coupled with the oxymoronic juxtaposition of 'bad(ly)' and 'good', suggests a critique of the black-and-white world Madonna sees in Roman Catholic hamartiology. The occasional intrusion of colour into the video reveals the illusory nature of the black-and-white setup; there is a reality which lies beneath the imposed worldview. Moreover, the choice to use black-and-white ties in with Madonna's return to the past, for 'after the introduction of color film, choosing to shoot in black-and-white film has certain connotations of "old time footage"'.[21] Indeed, if Madonna's girl gone wild is depicted as Eve, then history is taken back to the beginning, where Phyllis Trible argues female subjugation began, not as a divine given, but as the result of human sin.[22]

Historically, this sin has been considered the woman's action; she is the 'sinner', the one who lost the human race paradise, the first to consume the fruit of the forbidden tree. The early church father Tertullian (in)famously called woman 'the gateway of the Devil' and the destroyer of man, God's image.[23] Later feminist interpretations of the Genesis 2–3 narrative on the other hand emphasize Eve's active status and portray her as a hero, and compare her to Adam, who appears silent, submissive, and passive.[24]

The narrative may also, in my opinion, be read sexually: the use of 'knowledge' (Gen. 3.5, 22) and 'fruit' (Gen. 3.2, 6, 12, 17) gives the story a sexual flavour – the first word connotes sexual intimacy, the second offspring and fertility. When the couple eat the fruit, the first thing they notice, the first piece of knowledge (ידע) they acquire, relates to their nakedness (Gen. 3.7).

The couple do not explicitly have sex until Genesis 4.1, and so I would characterize this account as erotic since sexual language and markers are used in the text without the sexual act itself appearing forthrightly. If eroticism truly is 'assenting to life even in death',[25] and if it really is 'the pleasure of excess',[26] then Adam and Eve fit the bill: Eve saw that the fruit was good, and even though she and Adam knew God's command and the consequence of breaking it, i.e. death (Gen. 3.3), she took from the tree and

[21] Hausken, 2011, p. 98.
[22] 1973, p. 41.
[23] On the Apparel of Women, I, p. i.
[24] Williams, 2001, p. 88.
[25] Bataille, 1962, p. 11.
[26] Tschumi, 1994, p. 71.

her husband Adam also ate. The sexual awakening they experienced as a result brings the erotic, the anticipatory nature of sexuality, into full bloom.

'Girl Gone Wild' is also erotic in the sense that while sex does not occur there is a strong sense of bodily discontinuity, a sense that there is no oneness among the male/female bodies present in the video. Rather there is a sexual anticipation, but unfortunately it can never be realized since Madonna/Woman is treated as a homogenous, monolithic object which serves as the end, the goal, of male sexuality. Woman is a means for men to show and prove their masculinity, but in objectifying her, she is necessarily put out of reach, placed on her own pedestal (see the sequence near the end of the video). As an object out of reach, the men can never actually experience what all discontinuous beings desire: continuity. Since Woman is depersonalized, the men are unable to really experience a personal unifying connection with her.

In Genesis 2.24, man and his wife become one flesh – or in Bataille's terminology experience continuity, and like in Madonna's video, woman is man's helpmeet, created to assist him in the propagation of the human race, or so Thomas Aquinas, that great theologian of the church, says:

> It was necessary for woman to be made, as the Scripture says, as a 'helper' to man; not, indeed, as a helpmate in other works, as some say, since man can be more efficiently helped by another man in other works; but as a helper in the work of generation.[27]

Madonna's video wants to challenge this view of women. In her act of contrition, she asks for no help from a male saviour figure, but instead explains her/Eve's point of view in this whole Eden debacle – this is herstory. Given the historic policing of women's bodies by Christian institutions, notably the Roman Catholic Church, Madonna seeks to reappropriate and re-envision the Eden narrative and to challenge received culture interpretations of the account.

Robert C. Fuller writes that '[c]ultures have as one of their major tasks the regulation of sexuality',[28] and religion usually acts as the medium by which this regulation occurs. The punishment meted out to Eve, as well as later interpretations of this punishment (Thomas Aquinas, Tertullian, for example), have resulted in the heavy regulation of women's bodies as well as the idea that the production of offspring is woman's chief end. Madonna's girl gone wild does not conform to this role – she turns the 'desire' she is meant to direct toward her husband into an ecstatic desire for self-expression: the desire she feels is the desire to sing and dance, to use her body as her own:

---

[27] *Summa Theologica* I, 92, p. i.
[28] 2008, p. 108.

I got that burning hot desire,
And no one can put out my fire [...]
It's got me singing.

Madonna's Eve is a clubgoer: the botanical delights of Eden have been replaced by the dance floor, an arena of creativity and free expression, where movement is not restricted, a place where Madonna can move to her own rhythm and beat. She does not wish to dance to another's song, to accept their choices for her; as she sings, 'DJ play my favourite song / Turn me on ...'.

Northcote describes the club scene as a 'popular venue for rites of passage for many young adults' because it is 'a stage for performative dramas involving negotiation of various social configurations'.[29] Moreover, this developmental stage in the life of a young person is concerned very much with identity construction and experimentation.[30]

Northcote draws our attention to the work of Angela McRobbie,[31] who notes that female clubgoers in particular 'through their dancing style, redefine their feminine identity'.[32] While men may want to dichotomize female identity into Madonna or whore a la Freud, Madonna herself does redefine her own feminine identity through dance. As Northcote writes, 'expressing to onlookers and fellow dancers that one is a free and sensual (even sexual) being can be an essential component of affirming an independent, adult status'.[33]

This recognition by others of one's adult status is important especially in relation to Madonna's video and message. Madonna is no longer a child and thus no longer needs a paternal figure to restrict her actions; the Christ as father figure, for the true liberation of women, must be dispensed of.

The concept of the dance floor as religiously loaded is found in both Faithless' 'God is a DJ' and P!nk's song by the same name, in which she questions what the meaning of Faithless's statement is:

If God is a DJ,
Life is a dance floor,
Love is rhythm,
You are the music.

Like Madonna's Eve who cries, 'I'm about to go astray / My inhibition's gone away / I feel like sinning / You got me in the zone', P!nk calls herself

---

[29] 2006, p. 2.
[30] 2006, p. 3.
[31] 1993.
[32] Northcote, 2006, p. 10.
[33] Northcote, 2006, p. 10.

an 'outcast' searching for a 'new lifestyle', a 'Nirvana', under strobelights, sequins, and sex dreams.

Neither P!nk nor Madonna apologize for their actions, since they do not see any transgression. Madonna comes close when she sings, 'Good girls don't misbehave (misbehave) / but I'm a bad girl anyway'. However, this should not be seen as a confession on Madonna's part but rather an artificial construction of her own person through the rigid sexual ethic of the Roman Catholic Church, by which she would certainly be a 'bad girl'.

In Genesis 3, neither Adam nor Eve 'repent' in the way Madonna does at the beginning of the video, and the line 'I'm a bad girl anyway' appears in the following sequence:

Lyrics	Video
'I know I shouldn't act this way'	Madonna surrounded by men touching and kissing her.
'I know, I know, I know, good girls don't misbehave'	A brief shot of a crudely drawn cross. The camera pans out and Madonna appears chained, and not as uninhibited as one may first have believed from the previous shot. A muscular Christ figure stands akimbo on a rotating platform in the place Madonna made her confession at the beginning of the video.
'But I'm a bad girl anyway'	Once again, Madonna stands in a crowd of men, a small crucifix hangs from her neck. The image fades into the Christ figure again, his head up to heaven, but this time we see his eyes are closed.

By placing the macho and toned Christ into the confessional space, Madonna disempowers the male privilege of Christian interpretation. The finger firmly points at the hypermasculinity (b)latent in tradition. Woman is no longer on trial, and Madonna, when she shows herself chained (by both metal links and the jewellery around her neck), tells her audience that she is not free, but defined by men – her actions and the manner in which she acts have been, she shows, man's domain.

Madonna puts both man and his male God on trial, and in the *Girl Gone Wild* video, the apple, synonymous in Western imagination with sin and temptation, of free will misused, is only ever shown between men. Since 'sin' is defined by a male God in the Bible and the punishments for breaking his laws meted out by male-dominated institutions (the priesthood, the church, etc.), the apple placed by Madonna in her video only between men signifies her rejection of man-made law, not in favour of woman-made law, but in favour of no law.

The muscular Christ in 'Girl Gone Wild' represents an idolization, a divinization, of the male form. As Mary Daly famously wrote, 'If God is male, the male is God'.[34] Madonna shows that masculinity is put on a pedestal to be praised by all – male and female alike. This Christly masculinity is ever more evident in contemporary Christianities. Stephen Sawyer, an artist who has produced pictures of this macho Jesus, says: 'I scarcely think Jesus could have overturned the tables of the money-lenders if he was a wimp'.[35] Reverend Eric Delve further notes the correlation between religion and football, arguing that men take an interest in football because they look for male role models, for action figures, and this has led to the emergence of Jesus the Athlete.

If God is this muscular beefcake, then Adam, made in his image, must also conform to this ideal. The problem with this masculinizing is its close association with violence, domestic abuse, objectification of women, and sexual assault.[36] 'Hypermasculinity', Levy writes, 'is an attempt actively to demonstrate masculinity [exists] in opposition to femininity'.[37]

Since Adam must conform to this hypermasculinity, the way in which Madonna constructs the two men who appear with the apple reveals how she sees their relationship with God. In this regard, I notice the eyes and the mouth play a role in the construction of the Adams. As regards the eyes, one of the men keeps them closed, while the other stares out of the screen directly at the viewer. In this scene, there can be no male gaze, for there is no woman for the male eye to linger over. Instead, there are only two half-clad men – for a heteronormative male this is jarring, but also inviting, for he is forced to consider what Madonna presents. The Adam who looks at us calls us to participate in his transgression; he does what he did in the Garden; that is, deflect responsibility, at least according to Madonna.

The mouth too highlights the sin that man committed: to define the 'other'. As Madonna is the only singer, attention is, through silence, brought to the male mouth, a tool which has been used and is still used to sustain the heteropatriarchy. In the video, the male mouth either bites an apple or kisses Madonna's body, and this links both the apple and the female body. In my opinion, this is a rather ingenious way to reject the 'temptress' model of the woman's presence in the Garden.

In Genesis, Eve does not tempt Adam; he takes the fruit of the tree of his own volition, yet, just like one of the Adams in Madonna's video, shifts

---

[34] 1973, p. 19.
[35] Carey, 2011.
[36] Levy, 2007, p. 326.
[37] Ibid., p. 325.

responsibility, in this case to Eve. The link between apple and female body discussed above exposes the inadequacy of man's objectification, for the woman, like the apple, does not invite its own objectification. Madonna, shown chained throughout, tells the audience that she is subject to man's whim. Later on when she appears unchained she looks at the camera and asks her audience to forgive her, but this is, as the viewer well knows, a disingenuous plea, for she has nothing to apologize for. Her body is hers and the only sin is in the male privilege used to subject women.

Masculine/feminine

In his 2012 Christmas address, Pope Benedict XVI made some controversial statements about gender. Attacking the work of prominent feminist Simone de Beauvoir, the Pope stated that to deny gender as a given element of nature is to play into an obvious falsehood, and that people who subscribe to this idea of gender 'deny their nature'. He understands gender as a product of God's action as recorded, so he believes, in Genesis 2–3.[38]

'[B]eing created by God as male and female', according to Ratzinger, 'pertains to the essence of the human creature'. Those who adhere to an understanding of gender as socially constructed manipulate nature and deny God, since the 'freedom to create oneself' necessarily denies God as creator and consequently 'man [sic] too is stripped of his dignity'.[39] In his speech for the World Day of Peace, Benedict XVI made further references to the supposed duality of men and women; he called his listeners to 'acknowledge and promote the natural structure of marriage' because 'radically different types of union' harm society and destroy the family.[40]

The use of Genesis 2–3 to support the heteronormative concept of marriage has been the mainstay of many Christian traditions and denominations for years. The Catechism of the Catholic Church (§§1604–5) quotes Genesis to affirm that 'man and woman were created for one another'. Such statements inform members of the church *how* their desire should be oriented for the good. It both normalizes heterosexuality and marginalizes a large number of people who may, through choice or culture (or both), be members of the Roman Catholic Church.

In 'Girl Gone Wild', Madonna violates the stark male/female divide through men who 'fuck with gender' and do not fall in line with traditional gender markers. When Madonna sings 'Like a girl gone wild ...', six men are shown dancing, each of them in tights, high heels, and nothing else. During these gender-bending sequences, the image of Madonna chained

---

[38] Benedict XVI, 2012.
[39] Benedict XVI, 2012.
[40] Benedict XVI, 2013.

is interspersed throughout. Furthermore, at the end of the first gender-bending sequence, a crudely drawn cross appears on screen, and at the end of the second sequence, images of the macho Christ fade in and out of the scenes with the chained Madonna. In a way, then, there still appears to be an imposition of rigidity and an aversion to gender fluidity.

The Roman Catholic tradition teaches that Jesus corrected what Adam failed to do, and similarly Mary for what Eve failed to achieve. The Catechism states: 'Christ's whole life is a mystery of recapitulation' (§518). Jesus' purpose then is to restore to humankind what they lost in the Fall. This saviour who accomplishes everything is a saviour who we can never really replicate meaningfully, a problem to which Madonna brings our attention. The Roman Catholic Church has presented a saviour who has been idolized instead of worshipped – this unrealistic portrayal of Christ accomplishes two things: (1) it feminizes men, and (2) it permits and allows the subjugation of women since men feel compelled to regain their lost masculinity in order to reflect their masculine saviour, and they achieve this through exercising power over women.

The ripped Christ figure Madonna uses is problematic since the association it has with athleticism potentially makes the figure a legitimator and advocate of violence.[41] He turns his eyes away from humanity, for he looks up, and yet keeps his eyes closed before God. By fucking with gender, Madonna exposes the problem, but also appropriates the feminized men to sanctify them and reassure us that they are not it. Rather, the problem lies with the phallocentric church, an organization which takes masculinity and maleness as normal, causing femininity and femaleness to be marginalized and seen as 'other' to the male norm. Elizabeth Grosz says that phallocentrism collapses 'representations of the two sexes into a single model, called "human" or "man", but which is in fact only congruent with the masculine'.[42]

Thomas Aquinas, perhaps the most influential theologian of the Catholic Church, wrote of the individual nature of woman: '[she] is defective and misbegotten, for the active force in the male seed tends to the production of a perfect likeness in the masculine sex; while the production of woman comes from defect in the active force'.[43] Again, the male is normative, while the female is an aberration, an imperfection in/of the male seed.

Nonetheless, though femaleness is a flaw, the woman is still portrayed as man's natural counterpart. The Catechism states, '[m]an and woman were made for each other [...] for they are equal as persons [...] and complementary as masculine and feminine' (§372). The equations 'man = masculinity' and 'woman = femininity' contribute further to the sustainance

---

[41] Michael Flood, 2002.
[42] 1990, p. 150.
[43] *Summa Theologica* I, 92, p. i.

of the gender binary since it does not allow femininity in men, or masculinity in women.

To counter this, there is no concept of a solid male/female divide in 'Girl Gone Wild'; it is a rejection of the gender binary affirmed by the Roman Catholic Church. The gender-bending males in 'Girl Gone Wild' are a vanguard against the church's rigidity and ideas of complementarianism. In a sense, they genderfuck to contribute to 'the destabilisation of gender as an analytical category' for through their male embodiment and the female gender markers inscribed on their bodies they subvert 'the possibility of possessing a unified subject position'.[44] Consequently the ability to talk about the genderfucked body is obfuscated and by showing men with traditional markers of femininity, Madonna eschews the idea that men embody masculinity alone and women femininity.

Although 'Girl Gone Wild' was made before Ratzinger's 2012 Christmas message, it may serve as a critique of his attitudes, especially of his condemnation of that famous quotation from Simone de Beauvoir: 'one is not born, but rather becomes, a woman'.

Though silent, the men in Madonna's video are a powerful statement of nonconformity. In the 'MDNA' live tour, the red-robed priests take the place of the gender-bending males, in an effort, so I would argue, to undermine them. Through linking her enemies (and priests are representative of this for they connote denied and repressed sexuality) with symbols of gender fluidity she mocks the church, but also suggests that perhaps Catholic priests themselves do not unwaveringly conform to the church's ideas of gender and sexuality.

Indeed, Madonna's use of genderfuck betrays the camp nature of Roman Catholic ritual, with all its gold, silver, tinkling bells, swinging censers, pretty cups, and men in frocks. The campness of Madonna's *tiraboleiros* indexes the campness of ritual, to make the rituals themselves performances, raising them to the level of entertainment and art. Perhaps this is to contrast what Madonna sees as dead, boring, empty, and outdated with her own concert.

I cannot help but be reminded of Dolores van Cartier's talk with the Reverend Mother in *Sister Act* (1992) in which they discuss each other's view of how a church choir should be run: the Reverend Mother opts for a more conservative method, while Dolores advocates a more wordly way: 'I was thinkin' more like Vegas, you know, get some butts in the seats'. The Reverend Mother views this conceptualization of a church as blasphemy, and perhaps this is what Madonna tries to achieve with her performance (and much to her delight, that's what she gets).

All this genderplay in the video can be applied as a lens to reread the biblical texts to redeem them from the heterosexist grip of the Catholic

---

[44] Reich, 1992, p. 125.

Church. The most obvious application of genderplay comes in Genesis 1, in which God makes humankind 'male and female'. Some Jewish interpretations read here a reference to an androgynous person, later uncoupled as male and female,[45] while Phyllis Trible argues the creature, the *'adham*, is neutral as regards its sexuality.[46]

Madonna's use of the *tiraboleiros* is a return to a pre-two-person humanity, a humanity at one with itself. Although androgyny is in no way genderfucking, it does connote it and implies a breakdown of the gender divide instituted when a male God decided it was not good for man to be alone (Gen. 2.18).

Many readers of the Genesis narratives read in it a hierarchical understanding of man and woman – Phyllis Trible however has said that these readings are not 'altogether accurate and most of them are simply not present in the story itself'.[47] In a way Madonna says this hierarchical interpretation is not in the text either, but that it is a product of the church's history. The pedestalled Christ is what the church has built and in order to justify and sustain this image they have retroactively applied their construction to the beginning; after all, nothing says authority like antiquity.

To return to the video, Madonna further addresses the ideology of complementarianism through the use of mirrored scenes which run throughout. There are four types of mirrored image in 'Girl Gone Wild': (1) Madonna with only her reflection, (2) mirrored images of men in high heels, (3) scenes in which Madonna is with other men on a pedestal, and (4) a man on his own. In this last case, an actual mirror appears in the scene.

The mirror scenes with their inherent duality – image and reflection – provide space to explore the unyielding gender binary. The man on his own in the video, the one in front of a mirror, poses in a similar fashion to the Adam in Michelangelo's *Creation of Adam*. He looks at himself in the mirror, runs a hand over his reflection, perhaps longingly, but becomes agitated and lashes out – through all of this he has his eyes closed.

In Michelangelo's *Creation of Adam*, Adam and God face each other, their fingertips almost touching. God invests Adam with his power and image, yet in contrast, Madonna's own vision of *Creation* has no god; there is no other to look at. The deity of this creature is himself – his own reflection. He does not look for God, for his eyes are closed, he is neither appreciative of, or does he reflect on, God's image in him.

The violence the man displays resonates with a Lacanian construction of the mirror stage during which a child can comprehend its mirror image or see its actions mimicked by another person and 'formulate, however roughly, the propositions "I am that" and "That is me"'.[48] Originally, the

---

[45] Visotzky, 2012, p. 587.
[46] 1978, p. 141.
[47] 1978, p. 73.
[48] Bowie, 1991, pp. 21–2.

child takes the image as his or her ideal self, the Ideal-I, but later 'discovers the contrasting size and inverted movements which destabilize the unity between himself and his image'.[49] The child will spend his or her lifetime resolving the tension between the specular, or inner, 'I', and the outer, or social, 'I'.[50] The child however must pass through this stage and 'must break the charm of his reflected image by accepting the reality of its unreality' in order to successfully form the ego.[51] The confrontation with its own image, however, results in an *aggressive* tension for the child 'because the wholeness of the image threatens the subject with fragmentation' (Evans 1996, 115).

The figure in front of Madonna's mirror though is unwilling to expose himself; he remains a child and will never resolve the tension between his body and its image, yet he still manages to express anger toward the image which he does not see. Madonna shows us a patriarchy both unwilling to see itself and expose itself. This Adam cannot grow for '[i]f he is to make progress towards truth, he must pass beyond the "mirror without radiance which offers him a surface where nothing is reflected"'.[52]

To conclude this section, Madonna uses the cultural symbols of Western depictions of the Garden of Eden to expose the masculine Christ. When Adams become gender-benders and Eve takes control of her own sexuality, then sin has been committed, because these portrayals of masculinity and femininity do not conform to the strict binarism in the Roman Catholic understanding of gender. She reveals that the masculine Christ has caused both men and women to suffer, for men who display femininity are mocked, and women who take control of their own sexuality and are sexual themselves are denigrated. To propagate the idea that these men and women fail to live up to the standard required invites the notion of correction; these gender-bending men can correct themselves through the assertion of strength over women, and women can submit to the headship of men.

Redemption

Salvation is an integral part of Christian doctrine – after all, *extra Ecclesiam nulla salus*. Jesus comes as a saviour to die for the sins of humankind (mankind?) and save them from eternal damnation. The Catholic Church has used this soteriology and Christology to withhold the priesthood from its female members.[53] Since, so the argument goes, Christ was a male/man,

---

[49] McDonald, 1996, p. 73.
[50] McDonald, 1996, p. 73.
[51] Bowie, 1991, p. 23.
[52] Bowie, 1991, p. 23.
[53] Ruether, 1981, p. 45.

women/females are unable to stand *in persona Christi*, unable to represent Christ truly in sacramental offerings.

Theology like this has been called into question by many feminist critics. Rosemary Radford Ruether famously asked 'Can a male saviour save women?',[54] for if women cannot hold the priesthood because they do not adequately respresent Christ, can Christ truly represent women, as a man, in his atoning sacrifice on the cross? She also questions the nature of the Imitation of Christ put forward in the Church's 1976 declaration about women priests in which it is stated that were a woman a priest, 'it would be difficult to see in the minister the image of Christ', for 'there would not be this "natural resemblance" which must exist between Christ and his minister'.

Ruether diligently exposes these 'strange' sentiments as unsound theology. If 'a Negro, a Chinese, or a Dutchman' can represent the image of Christ, even though he was a first-century Jewish man, 'we must assume this imitation of Christ has now been reduced to one essential element, namely, male sex'.[55] In her music video, I believe Madonna engages with this question about whether a male saviour can save women. Moreover, though, she directly questions whether the male saviour presented by the Roman Catholic Church can even save men.

Throughout the video we see scenes in which Madonna appears imposed on a crudely drawn cross and moreover she features herself wearing crucifix jewellery. We see a male body in cruciform position at the beginning of the video while Madonna prays for forgiveness, though ultimately her act of contrition is an empty gesture. Later on, the muscular Christ presented by Madonna is so hypermasculine that we may legitimately ask and wonder how this figure relates to both women and men.

For women this Christ is no saviour. It is a symbol of patriarchal oppression. The star tattooed on Christ's chest in the video may indicate a link with the cult of sports stars and thus, as discussed previously, violence. It is therefore totally justified to ask how exactly this figure can save women? Is a figure used to oppress women systematically able to save them?

Madonna's video and live tour tell us two things: firstly, the Christ figure of *Girl Gone Wild* needs to redeem himself, to open his eyes, and secondly, Woman needs to save herself for she cannot rely on the church for her salvation.

To the already manifold representations of the suffering Christ, Madonna adds her own. Susan Sontag writes that 'the innumerable versions in painting and sculpture of the Passion of Christ ... are surely intended to move and excite, and to instruct and exemplify'.[56] Madonna's Christ however stands

---

[54] 1981, p. 45.
[55] 1981, p. 47.
[56] 2003, p. 36.

with hands on hips; an athlete and a warrior as much as a saviour. This Christ wears a crown of thorns upon his head, a sure sign of suffering and pain, but in him we see none. Just as in Madonna's 'crucifixion' on stage in her *Confessions* tour, the thorny crown is a fashion symbol, used only as a decorative accoutrement.

The message? The church uses the crucifixion and Jesus' pain as tools, and is only superficially concerned with them. Madonna's presentation has resonance with Stephen Moore's interpretation of the Gospels in *God's Gym*. He writes, 'the canonical Gospels may fruitfully be read as bodybuilding manuals, for what all four boil down to is this: no pain, no gain – which also happens to be the supreme gym logion and fundamental syllogism of bodybuilding philosophy'.[57]

Madonna combines the space of the gym with the space of the confessional: she places the hypermasculine Christ in the same space she herself occupied at the beginning of the video. In the live tour this space is a confessional, out of which Madonna breaks forth using a rifle. In contrast, macho Christ does not leave the confessional area. He is stationary, and unable to move. As a reader of the biblical texts, it brings to mind Isaiah 44–6, in which the prophet critiques man-made idols: '[it] does not move from its place ... it cannot deliver [anyone] from distress' (Isa. 46.7). The masculine, chiselled Christ stands there to be admired, not to save anyone. If the masculine Christ cannot save, then neither can his patriarchal church.

Madonna's exit from the confessional in the live tour is done via a weapon, a sign of masculinity. Fiske[58] called the gun symbol a 'penile extender', and Madonna's possession of the phallic symbol here is a reappropriation of the object of her oppression. Gun imagery appears in 'Girl Gone Wild' as well, and throughout the whole 'MDNA' tour.[59] Madonna sings, 'Girls they just wanna have some fun / get fired up like a smoking gun' as her gender-bending dancers mimic guns with their hand gestures (again, they take hold of the phallus which is also used to oppress them since Christ's phallus outlines what the church considers 'man', and it is certainly not them).

Guns also feature at the start of the video, just after Madonna's act of contrition. There is a sequence which combines weaponry with cigarettes, muscular men, and crotch grabbing. These are all signifiers of masculinity, and Madonna herself engages with them all. In the video, then, all actors occupy masculine space; yet Madonna undermines hers by her biological sex, at least in the eyes of the church, and the male dancers in the video undermine the masculinity built up at the beginning of the video through their appropriation of what is traditionally considered women's clothing.

---

[57] Moore, 1996, p. 102.
[58] 1987, p. 210.
[59] *Rolling Stone Music*, 2012.

According to Daniel K. Cortese and Pamela M. Long,[60] the certainty of gender characterizes 'new lad' magazines. They cite Benwell,[61] who writes that certitude of gender is 'an exaggerated emphasis on ... and the preservation of male privilege through the exclusion of the "other," except as an object of desire'.[62]

This statement can be read alongside Ratzinger's previous ones. He, and his church, have faith that God has chosen a definitive gender for each of his earthly children. Furthermore, male privilege is maintained in the church by the vilification of the 'other', in this case, women, who are told that their saviour must needs be male, or, to put it at its most base level, women need maleness to achieve salvation. On the surface, it may not be easy to see how odd this claim is, but Madonna sends it up and draws it to an extreme to show how the concept eventually collapses in on itself. Salvifically, the macho Christ is useless, and so Madonna advocates salvation predicated on self.

The Catholic Church makes women the 'other', objects of desire, by making attraction to women normative for men. Women serve to affirm to men that they are righteous before God because of their sexual attraction. The apparent complementary nature of man and woman means that the correct object of desire for each party is the other.

Naturally, in such a setup the male gaze is significant, for this is the very thing, so Madonna shows us, that the Catholic Church tries to dictate, and, perhaps, to promote. Yet the 'Girl Gone Wild' video does not allow the male gaze to work so easily for the presence of seminaked males disrupts it. Heterosexual men who watch 'Girl Gone Wild' are presented with these figures and they must 'do' something with them. Björn Krondorfer writes, '[t]he male gaze values – when turned toward a woman, it desires; when turned toward a gay man, it often despises'.[63]

Although the viewer cannot ascertain the sexuality of the men in the video, these men are dancers, and as Darcey Callison notes, 'the overwhelming Western notion [is] that men don't dance ... and that men who do dance are gay' (2007, 128). The males on stage in Madonna's 'Girl Gone Wild' then are a sign of homosexuality and femininity for typical heterosexual male viewers. It is interesting to consider the possibility that the anti-woman rhetoric in Christian interpretations of Genesis 2–3 is in part based on the emphatic need for the male gaze to be directed toward the woman. The male audience of the biblical texts must overlook the naked, exposed body of Adam in order for their own masculinity to remain uncompromised.

In the Garden, when Adam shifts the focus to Eve, it may be to hide his own failed masculinity, in God's terms at least. Adam and Eve both

---

[60] 2011.
[61] 2003.
[62] 2011, p. 8.
[63] 2009, p. 117.

suffer under God's rule, for Adam cannot live up to God's headship and so 'blames' Eve to salvage his own masculinity and Eve suffers under patriarchal objectification, turned into the slutty devourer of men.

In this scenario, Eve becomes solely defined by her sexual body – she becomes 'temptress', the one who gave Adam the 'apple'. In 'Girl Gone Wild', a few scenes depict Madonna surrounded by men who touch her and kiss her. It is not difficult to imagine that such a scene could invoke 'slut shaming' from a heterosexual male view; from this patriarchal stance, the woman is to blame for how she treated; after all, 'she asked for it', 'she offered it on a platter'.

As long as patriarchy is able to function like this, it is unfeasible that it should be able to save anyone who does not strictly conform to the gender binary. Moreover, anyone who does not adhere to the 'masculine is normal' model is also further pushed out of the salvific sphere. For this reason, Madonna advocates self-interest where affirmation of one's diversely sexual self is salvation. Essentially, Eve, transgressor under patriarchy, becomes hero under 'Girl Gone Wild'.

Conclusion

While some may say that I have read too much into the video, this chapter remains an exercise in identifying, drawing out, and exegeting the biblical symbolism in 'Girl Gone Wild'. Moreover, it is an attempt to show that biblical literacy can be much more than text (how literacy was understood in Marshall's and Martin's cases). I would say that viewing the video is in itself an act of biblical literacy, since I do not imagine Madonna would be able to make such a video were biblical tropes not so prevalent in our Western and predominantly Christian world.

I believe it is a sign that in the post-internet age biblical literacy is certainly not in decline. The tremendous volume of music, images and videos that pass through the internet every day in all parts of the world totally renegotiates the concept of literacy. As of March 2013, 'Girl Gone Wild' had over 19 million hits on YouTube, and so I think we can be safe in assuming that out of these hits, there will definitely be people who notice the biblical imagery in it. With the internet, these people have the ability to share that information with others, on YouTube or elsewhere, written or otherwise. The internet potentially provides an almost global audience to ideas.

A parallel may be drawn with traditional oral cultures in which knowledge is passed down by word of mouth. In a way, the internet is a global culture, with people sharing stories, information and myths of their own. Through other people, I can become aware of a variety of symbols and the manifold readings it has with manifold people. Other users of

the internet and other technological media help me and others to become literate. We move away from a panoptic classroom, to peer-to-peer learning.
   I become literate because my peer is.

Bibliography

Aquinas, Thomas, *Summa Theologica*, Associated Press, 2006 (Italian criticism of Madonna)
Associated Press 2012 (reference to number of Facebook users)
Mieke Bal 1999
Bataille 1962
BBC News, 2012 (reference to 'Gangnam Style')
Benedict XVI, 2012
Bowie 1991
Braxton 1990
Breyer, 2012
Darcey Callison 2007
Catechism of the Catholic Church (§§1604–5)
Carey 2011
Paul Connerton 1989
Mary Daly 1973
Daniel K. Cortese and Pamela M. Long (Ling?) 2011
Evans 1996
Fiske 1987
Michael Flood 2002
Robert C. Fuller 2008
Elizabeth Grosz 1990
Hall 1997
Hausken 2011
Björn Krondorfer 2009
Levy 2007
Madonna n.d., para. 3
Celia B. Marshall, *A Guide Through the New Testament*, Lousiville, KY: Westminster John Knox Press, 1994,
Dale B. Martin, *Pedagogy of the Bible: An Analysis and Proposal*, Louisville, KY: Westminster John Knox Press, 2008
McDonald 1996
Miller 2010
Stephen Moore 1996
Moore 2010
Northcote, 2006
Reich 1992
Rolling Stone Music, 2012
Romero 2010
Rose 2007
Ruether 1981
Semiocast 2012 (reference to number of Twitter users)

Susan Sontag 2003
Tschumi 1994
Phyllis Trible 1973, 1978
Visotzky 2012
Moshe Weinfeld 1991
Williams 2001

7

Biblical Literacy and
The Simpsons

Robert J. Myles (University of Auckland)

'*God is my favourite fictional character*' – *Homer Simpson*
'*I've done everything the Bible says, even the stuff that contradicts the other stuff*' – *Ned Flanders*

It is hardly necessary to establish the gross popularity of *The Simpsons* franchise which spans not only the television series, but also a movie, comic books, video games, and plenty of extremely profitable merchandise. Its popularity and longevity have made it a part of contemporary mainstream culture. Watching *The Simpsons* has, moreover, become a religious observance in itself, supplementing or replacing traditional church attendance as a televised evening service.[1] For a great proportion of its audience who have little or no religious upbringing – myself included – *The Simpsons* has functioned, in many respects, as a foundation to biblical literacy. Its portrayal of biblical stories and allusions features as a surrogate first encounter with the text, establishing a frame of reference that influences the text's subsequent meaning and significance.[2] As a dominant product of North American culture that has graced television screens worldwide for more than 20 years, the series exports a distinctly Americanized, satirical, and postmodern approach to the Bible and biblical texts. This chapter

---

[1] Jamey Heit, *The Springfield Reformation: The Simpsons, Christianity, and American Culture*, New York: Continuum, 2008, pp. 9–21.
[2] For an exhaustive list of biblical allusions within the series, see: http://www.snpp.com/guides/religion.html#b

focuses on one particular episode, 'Simpsons Bible Stories', to demonstrate what kind of biblical literacy is formed through its selective retelling of several biblical narratives.

A number of contributors to the collected volume *The Simpsons and Philosophy* observe that one of the pertinent benefits of viewing *The Simpsons* is that it can cultivate cultural literacy and inform us about American values.[3] Many consumers of *The Simpsons*, especially those from outside the hyper-religious United States, however, have little if anything to do with the distinctively American institutional structures of Christianity depicted within the show. What, then, are the potential effects of cultural texts like *The Simpsons* if they are to function as a mediator of biblical literacy? And, further, might regular consumption of the television series engender a particular hermeneutical approach to the biblical text? This chapter argues that, given its wide dissemination and entertainment value, the prevalence of biblical afterlives in *The Simpsons* provides a strong foundation upon which to build further biblical literacy. Despite the fact that the show recycles, distorts and parodies its source material, it nevertheless equips viewers with the ability to challenge the authority of the Bible in a secular, pluralistic context.

In what follows, I argue that the kind of biblical literacy formed by *The Simpsons* is influenced by the cultural and political context surrounding the show's production and consumption. Of particular importance is the satirical frame that engages viewers to be more receptive to its critique of the text and interpretive practices in both religious and secular contexts. First, however, it is prudent to establish a working definition of biblical literacy as the concept is utilized in this chapter. From there, we consider the cultural context and satirical comic frame of *The Simpsons*, before focusing on a single episode, 'Simpsons Bible Stories', in which these critical observations can be further developed.

What is biblical literacy?

It is not uncommon to hear the lament (or celebration) of a perceived decline in biblical literacy. Stephen Prothero, for example, argues that although his country the United States is one of the most religious in the world, its population has a shocking grasp of religious literacy. Prothero anchors this rise in religious illiteracy to a lack of formal instruction, observing that, prior to the Second Great Awakening of the nineteenth century and the post-war revival of the 1940s and 1950s, 'basic literacy and religious literacy (at least of the Protestant sort) went hand in hand

---

[3] William Irwin, Mark T. Conard and Aeon J. Skoble (eds), The Simpsons *and Philosophy: The D'oh! of Homer,* Chicago: Open Court, 2001.

– when young people learned to read by learning to read the Bible, and Christian doctrines and stories were part of the mental furniture of virtually all adults'.[4] As Western societies became increasingly secular, and more and more traces of religion were absent from formal educational and public settings, it followed that younger generations became less acquainted with biblical literature and other religious texts and traditions than in previous generations. For Prothero, this amounts to a great cultural loss, for it not only reduces our understanding of different religious traditions, leading to heightened intolerance in our multicultural age,[5] but potentially underrates religion as an important component of American identity and heritage.

But to sidestep for a moment the issue of whether or not biblical literacy is a desirable or even essential quality, we should first ask: is this so-called 'decline' really as bad as some people perceive? In order to answer this question, we need to first address the definition of 'biblical literacy'. For Prothero, religious (or biblical) literacy refers primarily to a narrow understanding of 'knowledge' as consisting of facts about the Bible.[6] For example, the names of the four canonical gospels, that in Exodus Moses leads his people out of Egypt, or that Goliath was a giant slain by David. What Prothero downplays is the associated baggage that comes with this knowledge. Knowledge is always framed by its medium (how it is transmitted) and a cultural, epistemological and institutional context that determines why it is important and/or even true.

Because 'knowledge' does not exist independently of these associations and perceptions, biblical literacy also needs to take account of the ways in which we understand and engage with the text.[7] Recent critical theories of literacy, for instance, suggest that it involves not just knowledge, but

---

[4]Stephen Prothero, *Religious Literacy: What Every American Needs to Know – and Doesn't*, HarperCollins: New York, 2007, p. 11.
[5]See also Robert J. Nash and Penny A. Bishop, *Teaching Adolescents Religious Literacy in a Post-9/11 World*, Charlotte, NC: Information Age, 2010.
[6]A report commissioned by the Bible Literacy Project similarly states that its sample of American teachers defined biblical literacy as 'practical Bible knowledge' consisting of five components: '(a) knowing the book the Bible, (b) being familiar with common Bible stories, (c) being familiar with popular Bible characters, (d) being able to recognize common biblical phrases, and (e) being able to connect that knowledge to references in literature'. Marie Wachlin, *Bible Literacy Report: What do American Teens Need to Know and What Do They Know?*, New York: Bible Literacy Project, 2005, p. 19, cf. http://www.bibleliteracy. org
[7]Indeed, a certain form of biblical literacy based on knowledge comprehension, that of first-hand knowledge of biblical texts through reading, has only become more pronounced over the last few centuries with the rise in literacy rates, given increases in public education, and the not unrelated rise of Protestantism. Hector Avalos reminds us that 'biblical illiteracy has been normative to most of Christian history. For most of the last one-thousand years, many Christians, especially in Catholic traditions, were discouraged from reading the Bible in the vernacular languages'. See Hector Avalos, 'In Praise of Biblical Illiteracy', in *The Bible and Interpretation* (2010), http://www.bibleinterp.com/articles/literate357930.shtml

comprehension and critical thinking in relation to its source material. Society, it is assumed, is in a constant state of conflict and, drawing from cultural studies' interest in matters of class, gender and ethnicity, critical literacy involves focusing on the cultural and ideological assumptions that underwrite texts. This includes addressing the inequitable positioning of speakers and readers within discourses.[8] In other words, literacy also comprises a perspectival component; like all forms of knowledge, biblical literacy is always contextually situated, mediated and conditioned, and, as such, is partial. The knowledge of the Bible one might gain in a church setting, for example, is permeated with assumptions that determine the type of biblical literacy formed: e.g. one with a certain respect for the supposed authority of the text. Knowledge of the Bible gained within a university setting does not necessarily have to adopt these assumptions, and instead may frame the Bible as a significant cultural text, or a text to be scrutinized with historical critical tools, and so on. Afterlives of the Bible in popular culture typically remove the text from canonical control altogether, enabling different meaning and reality effects to emerge.[9] The acquisition of biblical literacy involves certain assumptions about not only the presumed religious authority of the text, but also its political, cultural and ideological function and purpose within wider society.

Given this broader definition of biblical literacy, beyond the simple requisition of facts or knowledge, we can begin to analyse the afterlives of biblical texts within wider culture as potential mediators of biblical literacy. Not only does knowledge of the Bible and its contents filter through to the consumer, albeit in a usually confused and haphazard way, cultural texts like *The Simpsons* posit a particular set of claims about the Bible's political, cultural and ideological function within wider society. As will be discussed below, the biblical literacy formed in *The Simpsons* provides a satirical challenge to the dominance of the Bible and religion within contemporary American political and cultural life. This embodiment of biblical literacy features as a hermeneutical frame and mediates biblical knowledge in a way that often disestablishes, but occasionally undergirds, the text's perceived authority and relevance in contemporary society.

---

[8]See, for example, James Paul Gee, *Social Linguistics and Literacies: Ideology in Discourses* (3rd edn), London: Routledge, 2007. See also Barry Dwyer, 'Religious Literacy: A Useful Concept?', in Maurice Ryan (ed.), *Echo and Silence: Contemporary Issues for Australian Religious Education*, Katoomba: Social Science Press, 2001, pp. 117–25.

[9]For more on this, see George Aichele, *The Control of Biblical Meaning: Canon as Semiotic Mechanism*, Harrisburg: Trinity, 2001, pp. 15–37; George Aichele, *Simulating Jesus: Reality Effects in the Gospels*, London: Equinox, 2011, pp. 18–23.

Biblical literacy and *The Simpsons*

In a previous article on echoes to biblical texts within the cultural medium of television, I suggested that, given the range of biblical literacy that exists today, intertextual linkage is often more creative on the part of interpreters than typically assumed.[10] Popular cultural texts like *The Simpsons* appropriate and reinterpret certain biblical signifiers from widespread cultural knowledge to advance their own artistic and commercial agendas, and not necessarily out of fidelity to or respect for the original text. The gap that exists between the original text and an instance of its afterlife in popular culture, as such, invites readerly engagement and perhaps even creativity – an encounter that can fuel enjoyment for engaged sectors of its audience – fostering audience retention and investment, thus guaranteeing the commercial imperatives of advertising-driven television. If biblical literacy concerns not only knowledge or facts about the Bible and biblical texts, but also the hermeneutical frame in which biblical material is positioned and interpolated to audiences, then *The Simpsons* can be seen to engender an Americanized, satirical, and postmodern literacy of the Bible and biblical texts.

An Americanized bible

First, *The Simpsons* presents us not with 'the Bible', as if such an object has any meaning independent of its context, but a distinctly Americanized Bible. By Americanized I mean that the perspectives depicted are mostly reflective of the North American context in which the show is produced and predominantly consumed.

The show, set in the fictionally generic Springfield, USA, presents a satirical reflection of contemporary life in mainstream America.[11] Jamey Heit explains: 'To understand how *The Simpsons* characterizes Christianity as a part of life in Springfield, one must not forget the obvious. Springfield is not just an abstract secular or amoral town but a town with distinct historical ties to a tradition that has influenced a good portion of American culture'.[12] While the culture it reflects is broad and fragmented, its packaging of religion is situated within a distinctive American (Protestant) perspective;

---

[10] Robert J. Myles, 'Terminating Samson: The Sarah Connor chronicles and the rise of new biblical meaning', *Relegere* 1, 2 (2011): 329–50.

[11] Not only does *The Simpsons* portray a reflection of American life, it also exports this representation around the globe as part of the Hollywood instrument of soft power: America's dominance and influence within the global entertainment industry, of which *The Simpsons* is but a small part, helps to shape perceptions of America and American society, as well as normalize some of its cultural and epistemological values and assumptions.

[12] Heit, *Springfield Reformation*, p. 3.

specifically, a tradition of those who left Europe and settled America in search of religious freedom. As Chris Turner observes, 'The Simpson family attends services at the church every Sunday, as do most of the people they know in Springfield ... That said, the Simpsons are by no means Bible-thumpers. Though religious, they are not particularly pious'.[13] Given this, the religious component of the show does not serve a solely satirical function; rather, it features as a central component of the representation of everyday American life. Not to underrate the influence that fundamentalist forms of Christianity have within the United States, however, friendly neighbour Ned Flanders is characterized as a pious Evangelical Christian who provides a moralizing counterpoint to the Simpson family's lukewarm Christianity (and Homer's occasional infidelity and theological naïveté).[14]

While the Simpson family represents the typical American family, Homer Simpson has often been identified as the Everyman: Valerie Weilunn Chow, for example, suggests that 'Homer embodies *both* the white male head of household *and* the feminized consumer. He is a stock characterization of the "white, male, working-class buffoon ..."'.[15] His views on religion, moreover, carry both the naïveté with which many people adopt the prevailing views of their surrounding culture, as well as the zealous ignorance demonstrated by a significant proportion of North American Christians. In most other so-called secular, Western countries, religion plays a much more subtle role in public and political life.

John Alberti suggests that in many contemporary American cartoons like *The Simpsons*, characters and plot situations aimed at children are 'combined with pop cultural references and an ironic style meant to appeal to the adults watching with (or perhaps instead of) the presumed target audience'.[16] In other words, the show thrives on a blurred distinction between programming aimed at children and adults. This enables the cartoon to open a critical space with which to satirize and critique contemporary cultural forms and practices, and, in addition, religious structures and the interpretation of the Bible as it manifests in the private and public

---

[13] Chris Turner, *Planet Simpson: How a Cartoon Masterpiece Defined a Generation*, Cambridge: Da Capo, 2004, pp. 263–4.

[14] See in particular the episodes: 'Homer the Heretic', 'Home Sweet Homediddly-Dum-Doodily', 'Homer and Ned's Hail Mary Pass' and 'Hurricane Neddy'. See also Gordon Lynch, *Understanding Theology and Popular Culture*, Malden: Blackwell, 2005, pp. 149-60. Homer's religious naïveté is especially apparent in the episode 'Thank God it's Doomsday' in which he predicts the rapture and apocalypse – a parody of the *Left Behind* phenomenon. It should also be noted that although Lisa Simpson attends church with her family she is sometimes cast as a Buddhist and/or New Age spiritual type.

[15] Valerie Weilunn Chow, 'Homer Erectus: Homer Simpson As Everyman ... and Every Woman', in John Alberti (ed.), *Leaving Springfield*: The Simpsons *and the Possibility of Oppositional Culture*, Detroit: Wayne State University Press, 2004, p. 110.

[16] John Alberti (ed.), *Leaving Springfield: The Simpsons and the Possibility of Oppositional Culture*, Detroit: Wayne State University Press, 2003, p. xiv.

life of everyday American society. This leads us into the next category of how the Bible is framed within the show; namely, through satire and parody.

Satirizing the bible

Secondly, *The Simpsons* maintains a cynical perspective on the Bible by utilizing satire to debase its authoritative grip on American cultural and religious life. Satire is typically employed to diagnose a shortcoming or contradiction within society. Corporate capitalism, the Republican Party, education as part of the ideological state apparatus, and religious practices all feature as regular targets of satire on the series. In the DVD commentaries, creator Matt Groening and a number of people who work on the show repeatedly claim a 'very liberal' political bias. Groening also claims to be agnostic, but nonetheless recognizes the important role that religion has in the everyday life of contemporary Americans, including both its positive and harmful effects.

Jonathan Gray argues that *The Simpsons*' use of televisual parody can be used to teach media literacy (understanding the medium, techniques and rhetoric of television). The playful satirizing of advertising and promotional culture within shows like *The Simpsons* and Jon Stewart's *The Daily Show*, he insists, can teach media processes, form and ideology in an entertaining manner, encouraging viewers to reflect more critically upon media messages and structures.[17] I would argue that the satirizing of religion and the Bible within the show also provides a space within which viewers are encouraged to reflect critically on the ways in which the Bible is used and interpreted within contemporary society. Through the satirizing of conventional interpretative practices as they are grounded in wider cultural values and assumptions, *The Simpsons* equips its viewers to challenge the authority of the text in a secular, pluralistic context.

Both Todd V. Lewis and Matthew Henry have independently argued that *The Simpsons* commits to satirizing the pietistic and hypocritical elements of American religious expression, but does not attack the bases of American religious faith. In doing so, the series makes viewers aware of the impact of religion within American public life and society.[18] In considering the representation of the Bible and its presumed authority in *The Simpsons*, Heit

---

[17] Jonathan Gray, 'Television teaching: Parody, *The Simpsons*, and media literacy education', *Critical Studies in Media Communication*, 22, 3 (2005): 223–38.

[18] Todd V. Lewis, 'Religious rhetoric and the comic frame' in *The Simpsons*', *Journal of Media and Religion*, 1, 3 (2002): 153–65; Matthew Henry, '"Gabbin' About God": Religion, Secularity and Satire on The Simpsons', in Timothy M. Dale and Joseph J. Foy (eds), *Homer Simpson Marches on Washington: Dissent Through American Popular Culture*, Lexington: University Press of Kentucky, 2010, pp. 141–66.

similarly observes a repeated disconnect between what the Bible says and how Christians interpret its message. He argues that *The Simpsons* adopts a reformed protestant understanding of the Bible, in which each individual believer is given authority to read and interpret the text as a testament to the salvific work of Jesus Christ as part of God's interaction with the world. But the show repeatedly characterizes Christians in a way that problematizes the task of biblical interpretation. 'While most Christians recognize that the Bible plays an authoritative role in their religion, they also do not understand the salient points, both in a narrative and theological sense'.[19] So, for example, a common strategy is the desire to use the Bible to legitimate one's personal opinions. In the episode 'Secrets of a Successful Marriage', Marge converses with Reverend Lovejoy about her marital issues:

Lovejoy: Marge, get a divorce.
Marge: But, Reverend, isn't divorce a sin?
Lovejoy: [holding up a Bible]; Have you ever read this thing?
    Everything's a sin. Technically we're not allowed to go to the
    bathroom.

Heit explains how Lovejoy's comments insinuate that the Bible's moral authority, presumed within American culture, is problematic.[20] The conversation thus undermines the Bible's ability to address moral issues in contemporary society. This self-reflexive satirizing of the Bible and its presumed moral authority leads us into the third facet of our analysis; namely, the show's grounding in so-called 'postmodern' culture.

A postmodern Bible

Thirdly, *The Simpsons* engenders a postmodern approach to the Bible and biblical texts. Marxist literary critic Terry Eagleton defines postmodernism as:

> a style of thought which is suspicious of classical notions of truth, reason, identity and objectivity, of the idea of universal progress or emancipation, of single frameworks, grand narratives or ultimate grounds of explanation ... it sees the world as contingent, ungrounded, diverse, unstable, indeterminate, a set of disunified cultures or interpretations which breed a degree of scepticism about the objectivity of truth, history and norms, the givenness of natures and the coherence of identities.[21]

---

[19] Heit, *Springfield Reformation*, p. 52.
[20] Ibid., pp. 56–7; cf. Sebastian Moll, 'The Reverend Timothy Lovejoy', *The Bible and Interpretation* (2012), http://www.bibleinterp.com/opeds/mol368022.shtml
[21] Terry Eagleton, *The Illusions of Postmodernism*, Malden: Blackwell, 1996, p. vii.

Many of the aesthetic forms associated with postmodernism are apparent within *The Simpsons*. For example, the show often reveals an ironic and self-reflexive hyper-consciousness about its frame of televisual media. In 'Postmodernism and Television', Jim Collins defines hyper-consciousness as 'a hyper-awareness on the part of the text itself of its cultural status, function, and history, as well as of the conditions of its circulation and reception'.[22] Postmodern television will often recycle, re-articulate and re-package ideas, themes, and discourses that have already been said before, but do so in an ironic and self-reflexive manner. Allusions to the Bible are rarely subtle – the show appeals to well-known biblical stories and texts, in addition to common beliefs about the role and status of the Bible in society, precisely to bolster its own cultural cachet. In recognizing the Bible as an important text within American society, and then by satirizing it, *The Simpsons* demonstrates a hyper-consciousness about the Bible's status and its own controversial agenda.

Part of the appeal of *The Simpsons* is that it often promotes subversive and/or transgressive ideas while simultaneously occupying the space of mainstream culture. This strategy has since been taken up by a number of other television programmes, most notably the animated series *South Park* and *Family Guy* which are, perhaps, more ruthless in their inclusion of oppositional cultural jokes and jibes. Linda Hutcheon suggests that postmodernism works through parody to both legitimate and subvert that which it parodies. The process of simultaneously installing and ironizing features opens potential spaces for critical engagement on the part of the audience.[23] Of course, the dress of counter-culture is regularly subsumed by the dominant narratives within contemporary North American culture. Eagleton, for instance, observes that 'a lot of postmodernism is politically oppositional but economically complicit'.[24] In other words, political opposition is already contained and subsumed within the limits of commodity culture.[25] The same might be said of *The Simpsons*' satirizing

---

[22] Jim Collins, 'Postmodernism and Television', in Robert Allen (ed.), *Channels of Discourse, Reassembled*, London: Routledge, 1992, p. 335.

[23] Linda Hutcheon, *The Politics of Postmodernism* (2nd edn), Abingdon: Routledge, 2002, pp. 93, 101.

[24] Eagleton, *Postmodernism*, p. 132. This is perhaps best illustrated by the fact that *The Simpsons* occasionally contains jokes made at the expense of the Fox network, which broadcasts the show, and Rupert Murdoch, the media mongrel who owns the network.

[25] Postmodernism is also linked to the not unrelated changes affecting global politics and economics of the past 40 years. David Harvey, for example, has argued that the aesthetic and intellectual forms associated with postmodernity came to the fore with the emergence of late capitalism since the 1960s and 1970s. David Harvey, *The Condition of Postmodernity*, Cambridge: Blackwell, 1989. Because commercial television is first and foremost an advertising medium, viewers are positioned as potential consumers. According to Alberti: 'From the perspective of economic structure, television is a product of the corporation as economic entity ... As a result, we can understand the artistic production of television programs as a thoroughly "corporate" activity, with a creative process that takes place within and is directed

of the Bible. While at one level it presents a subversive critique of the text or dominant interpretations of the text, at another level it adds an aura of legitimacy to them. Furthermore, the intended oppositional cultural critique will often fall short, only extending to the point that the show benefits from the controversy it generates without alienating large parts of its audience.

'Simpsons Bible Stories'

Having outlined the hermeneutical frame that mediates the kind of biblical literacy formed through consumption of *The Simpsons*, it is now time to examine the Bible's role within a single episode of the series. Probably the most detailed exploration of biblical texts appears in an episode first aired in 1999 titled 'Simpsons Bible Stories'. The episode contains a number of dream sequences of the Simpson family in which they imagine themselves as participants in well-known biblical stories. Mark I. Pinsky notes that the creator of *The Simpsons*, Matt Groening, joked before this episode aired that 'the reason it was written was that executive producer Mike Scully told him the show hadn't been getting enough angry letters'.[26] Pinsky continues: 'Groening was especially proud of the episode, calling it "our *Prince of Egypt*," although it is anything but DreamWorks' elegant, reverent retelling of Moses and the exodus. Periods and characters from different books of the Bible appear out of chronological order, and events are turned upside down for comic effect'.[27]

Most of the episode takes place during a service at Springfield's protestant church. Reverend Lovejoy reads from the Bible, starting with Genesis, 'the first book of the Bible', but his droning, monotonous voice and the sweltering heat prompts the Simpson family to fall asleep and enter a dream world filled with interpretive, intertextual possibility. While the retelling of well-known biblical stories is framed within its associated institution, a Sunday sermon in church, the Simpson family instead delves into this dream world in order to better connect with the text. The overarching joke, of course, is that the Bible can actually be an entertaining collection of stories, once it is freed from its dominant institutional confines.

Furthermore, the focus on familiar Sunday school stories should not go unnoticed. In many respects the episode functions as a surrogate Sunday

by corporate management structures ... The idea of the artistic text as commodity is not a manifestation of changing modes of production in relation to television; it is instead definitive of the form, as most early television programs did not just sell advertising time within the shows but were in fact produced by the sponsoring corporations'. Alberti, *Leaving Springfield*, pp. xx–xxi.

[26] Mark I. Pinsky, *The Gospel According to* The Simpsons: *The Spiritual Life of the World's Most Animated Family*, Louisville: WJK, 2001, p. 98.

[27] Ibid.

school lesson in the way it similarly initiates viewers into a distorted, moralized, and simplified reading of the original biblical text. The stories are freed from one institutionalized setting with evangelistic agendas and implanted into another setting driven by commercial imperatives and artistic license. As we will observe below, the episode relies heavily on satire to foster audience engagement. A by-product of this, however, is that the episode potentially provides a rudimentary basis upon which to build further biblical literacy.

Homer and Eve

The first dream sequence involves an imaginative retelling of the story of the Garden of Eden in Genesis 2.4–3.24. Marge dreams that she is Eve and Homer is Adam. Ned Flanders features as the anthropomorphized God, speaking from the clouds.

Everything in the garden is idyllic. After being told they can eat anything in the garden except for the fruit from the tree of knowledge, Homer and Marge are tempted by the snake (or 'branch monster' as Homer names him) to sample 'God's private stash'. Unlike the biblical text, Homer/Adam is the first to sin. Soon after, Marge reluctantly joins him noting that 'it is a sin to waste food'. Suddenly God appears in the clouds and Homer implicates Marge, who admits to sampling the forbidden fruit. After Marge is expelled from the garden, Homer attempts to sneak her back in by getting a unicorn to dig a tunnel (the unicorn, named Gary, subsequently dies from exhaustion). Just as Marge re-enters the garden, however, God appears and furiously exclaims: 'This is how you repay me?' On this occasion, both Homer and Marge are expelled permanently into a world of pain and misery.

While this retelling of the Genesis account involves much recycling of its source material, enough remnants of the original story remain to mediate a coherent account of the 'fall' as it has come to encompass dominant interpretations. Heit, for example, observes that:

> [t]he use of the Bible as punishment for some wrongdoing provides yet another example of how *The Simpsons* characterizes the Bible thematically in concert with the Old Testament emphasis on punishment ... *The Simpsons* summarizes the narrow understanding of the Bible that characterizes much of Christianity in American society.[28]

A key difference between the original text and this inception of its afterlife, however, is that Homer eats the fruit because he is tempted not by knowledge, but by gluttony. He does not consume a single apple,

---

[28] Heit, *Springfield Reformation*, p. 63.

but many, leaving behind a pile of apple cores which he quickly sweeps under a bush when God appears. Homer's appetite is frequently used as a trope within the wider series,[29] and ironizes his characterization as the Everyman, especially given the prevalence of fast-food consumerism within contemporary American society.

Another aspect emphasized within this afterlife is a focus on issues of sex and gender. Walter Brueggemann notes that:

> [p]opular tradition concerning fall, 'apples and snakes', is prone to focus this narrative around questions of sex and evil wrought by sex ... But to find in this any focus on sex or any linkage between sex and sin is not faithful to the narrative. Insofar as the text reflects on the relation of the sexes, its concern is with the political dynamics of power, control, and autonomy.[30]

Does not Brueggemann's 'corrective' to the popular imagination, however, betray the text's obvious emphasis on naked bodies and procreation? From the shameful knowledge of bodies that must be covered (3.11), to the intimate post-fall 'knowledge' that Adam has of Eve (4.1), the gaps (not to mention innuendo) within the text invites readerly speculation and creativity.[31] In her book *Admen and Eve*, Katie B. Edwards analyses this portrayal and sexualization of Eve through (postfeminist) contemporary advertising. Edwards argues that Eve has become an icon of female sexual power; the subtext is that this power is achieved through desirable sexuality, which in turn is achieved through consumerism.[32]

Unlike some retellings of the Garden of Eden, though, the cartoon bodies in *The Simpsons* are not overly sexualized. They wear fig leaves over their genitals. Marge's hair, which is usually permed and towers above her head, is, in her role as Eve, let down to (conveniently) cover her breasts. While the cartoon figures avoid risqué sexualization, keeping the episode safely within its broad audience demographic including children, the dialogue relies excessively on sexual inferences and jokes, especially in its portrayal of Homer as a gluttonous chauvinist. This means that the text is retold in a way that conforms to its usual depiction within popular culture: to establish and normalize the male/female binary of gender relations.

---

[29] See, for example, Smith's analysis of Homer's 'forbidden donut' encounter: James A. Smith, 'Outside In: Diabolical Portraits', in Fiona C. Black (ed.), *The Recycled Bible: Autobiography, Culture, and the Space Between*, Atlanta: SBL, 2006, pp. 127–8.

[30] Walter Brueggemann, *Genesis*, Atlanta: John Knox, 1982, p. 42.

[31] Michael Carden, for example, writes that '[t]his story is really a coming of age or puberty story as and is as much about the origins of sex as it is of death'. Michael Carden, 'Genesis', in Deryn Guest et al. (eds), *The Queer Bible Commentary*, London: SCM, 2006, pp. 28–9.

[32] Katie B. Edwards, *Admen and Eve: The Bible in Contemporary Advertising*, Sheffield: Sheffield Phoenix Press, 2012.

Homer's dialogue also conforms to gender stereotypes of men as the dominant and sexually proactive sex and women as passive and reluctant, requiring male persuasion. For example, upon the introduction of Marge/ Eve, Homer remarks: 'Looks like God made you out of my sexiest rib!' From Homer's perspective, Eve is created as a sexual object for his pleasure. After Marge first complains to Homer about him eating the forbidden fruit, he similarly remarks: 'You're pretty uptight for a naked chick. You know what would loosen you up ...? A little fruit'.

This satirizing of Homer's crude chauvinism, however, functions to undermine the means by which the Genesis text is often used, particularly within conservative theological circles, to uphold patriarchal models of heterosexual marriage in the world before the text (usually through code-words like 'complementarianism'). *The Simpsons*' afterlife of this text thus contains subversive elements that attempt to challenge the presumed 'biblical basis' for such models, given that the Bible itself encompasses a variety of sexual and marital relationships, including the practices of polygamy, concubinage, and even the depiction of God as an abusive husband (Hos. 1–3; Ezek. 16; 23). For example, after thanking God for providing him with his 'perfectly crafted mate', Homer continues, 'you're so kind, wise and righteous, I can't believe you don't have a girlfriend', to which God modestly titters. And when God commands Homer not to eat fruit from the forbidden tree, he retorts: 'It would be even easier to avoid that temptation if I had a few extra wives ...'. Homer also expresses a particular fondness for the 'porno bush' within the Garden. This satirizing of lewd sexual banter is effective precisely because it identifies a contradiction between the privileging of heterosexual monogamy in contemporary American society, often grounded in religious rhetoric, and the obverse reality; that is, the pervasive promiscuity of mainstream American culture, particularly as it is reflected in contemporary film and television.

In fact, Heit reasons that because this sequence is Marge's dream, it offers a feminist critique of the traditional Genesis narrative. While the man is primarily responsible for the offence against (a male) God, the woman is forced to take the blame. Homer's selfish behaviour also reflects Marge's frustration with the gender inequality implied within conventional interpretations.[33] In other words, *The Simpsons* demonstrates how the biblical text can be used to uphold unjust gender relations in the world in front of the text. This engenders a critical biblical literacy that, while receptive to the moral posturing of the story, is also able to perceive the text's own cultural limitations. As we will see in the next dream sequence, however, *The Simpsons* only goes so far in its critique of the Bible's moral conundrums.

---

[33] Heit, *Springfield Reformation*, p. 60.

Lisa and Moses

The next dream sequence involves a retelling of the exodus story from the first chapters of the book of Exodus. Within the Jewish tradition, the exodus from Egypt features as one of the major identity-forming events for the Hebrew people, and its influence permeates through much of the rest of the biblical canon. As both a theme and a narrative of liberation, the exodus has featured extensively in contemporary popular culture, from its classic depiction in Cecil B. DeMille's *The Ten Commandments* (1956) through to its inspiration behind Bob Marley's ninth studio album *Exodus* (1976).

Within *The Simpsons* retelling, the exodus loses some of its political edge. Lisa imagines the narrative in terms of her own experience as an elementary school student. The students are the Hebrew people working as slaves for their teachers under the rule of the Pharaoh, Principal Skinner. Bart is an insubordinate slave, and the wimpy nerd Milhouse takes on the role of a reluctant Moses, who requires the encouragement of Lisa to fulfil his mandate as liberator of the Hebrew people.

> Lisa: Moses, we can't keep on living like this. Moses, tell Pharaoh to let your people go!
> Moses/Milhouse: Oh … now they're my people? [sarcastic]

After suffering under the adults for long enough, and with the persistent encouragement of Lisa, Milhouse finally urges the slaves to follow him to freedom. Pursued by Pharaoh's men (the police force led by Chief Wiggum), they escape across the Red Sea in a scene visually reminiscent of its depiction within *The Ten Commandments*.

Lisa's dream pokes fun at some common fallacies when it comes to contemporary biblical interpretation. First, when Principal Skinner comes to discern the slaves' progress, he notices graffiti on his tomb. After asking who is responsible, a burning bush points its flames in the direction of Bart and exclaims in a deep voice, 'Bart did it!' This 'tell-tale' role is obviously quite a contrast to the burning bush's original function in the biblical text. As Heit explains: 'In the Bible, God speaks through the bush to encourage Moses to lead the Israelites out of captivity. Here, however, God plays a significantly different role: God rats out Bart'.[34] Heit sees this change as opening a space into which Lisa is able to cast herself as the inspiration behind Moses' actions (combining both the roles of Aaron and the burning bush).[35] This enables Lisa to project her self-imagined importance

---

[34] Ibid., p. 61.

[35] Furthermore, as mentioned above, popular cultural texts like *The Simpsons* will often appropriate certain biblical signifiers from widespread cultural knowledge with little concern for their original function or purpose. The burning bush makes an appearance solely to solidify the connection with the Exodus story and not because it features as a central impetus of the narrative.

and authority into the text (and also potentially subverts the gendered leadership roles in the biblical tradition). In a blatant example of self-indulgent eisegesis, she cannot but help but see herself as somehow above her peers, and commands the reluctant Moses to act according to the wider parameters of the story.

Secondly, *The Simpsons'* retelling satirizes a number of miraculous occurrences from the original text by providing rationalistic explanations that, while not breaking the laws of nature, exposes a peculiar soft literalism. For example, the plague of frogs (Exod. 7.25–8.11) is caused by Lisa and Milhouse pouring buckets of frogs into the roof of Pharaoh's tent. Similarly, the Red Sea is parted (13.17–14.29) by the combined flushing of toilets, enabling the Hebrew slaves to escape to the other side. Scott M. Langston observes that beginning in the 11th century, the traditional midrashic interpretation of Scripture, which fostered imaginative interpretation of the plagues, was challenged by an emphasis on the text's literal meaning. Some commentators pursued rational explanations; for instance, the plague of boils (Exod. 9.8) was explained as a 'natural miracle' through hot ashes landing on the skin causing boils.[36] *The Simpsons* satirizes this kind of interpretive strategy that effectively allows readers to have their cake and eat it too: the miraculous is permitted, but only insofar as it can be accounted for rationally.

Finally, the dream sequence concludes with an amusing summary of the post-exodus journey for the Hebrew people. In this case, however, *The Simpsons* misses an opportunity for criticism, instead conforming to conventional readings.

> Moses/Milhouse: Well Lisa, we're out of Egypt. So what's next for the Israelites … land of milk and honey?
> Lisa: (reading from a scroll) Hmm well actually it looks like we are in for forty years of wandering the desert.
> Moses/Milhouse: Forty years? But after that, it's clear sailing for the Jews, right?
> Lisa: Uh more or less... Hey! Is that manna?

What this humorous deflection misses, of course, is the subsequent conquest of Canaan, an often forgotten component of the biblical text. This shows that the satirical critique of biblical interpretation only goes so far – a truly subversive retelling would not neglect to mention the problematic glorification of conquest that follows. Perhaps this reflects the inconvenient truth upon which a pivotal aspect of American mythology hinges: while the first European immigrants to the United States employed the biblical

---

[36] Scott M. Langston, *Exodus Through the Centuries*, Blackwell Bible Commentaries, Malden: Blackwell, 2006, p. 95.

imagery of the exodus to theologize their escape from religious persecution, they tended to omit the subsequent conquest of land and the systematic destruction of its indigenous inhabitants. Similarly, *The Simpsons* rarely includes jokes about the United States' support for Israel in the Israel/ Palestinian conflict. What might the ramifications be if they were to depict the Israelites invading Canaan? Would it hit too close to home? Langston notes that those groups who historically have utilized the exodus narrative in their struggle for liberation often place others in bondage once they have achieved their objectives.[37]

Solomon and the pie

The next sequence is the shortest of the episode. Homer dreams that he is King Solomon in the court with the power to administer justice. He is called to settle a dispute between Lenny and Carl, who each claim ownership of a pie. In the original story of Solomon's judgement in 1 Kings 3.16–28, two women claim to be the mother of an infant. Solomon asked for a sword, declaring that the live infant must be cut in two, with each woman receiving half the child. The 'motherly instincts' of the biological mother became apparent as she begged for the child's survival. The judgement is regarded as underscoring Solomon's renowned wisdom.

Within *The Simpsons'* retelling, the baby is replaced by a pie. Homer's judgement is once again guided by his ruthless gluttony: 'The pie shall be cut in two, and each man shall receive ... death. I'll eat the pie'. Such a statement humorously reveals the callous violence that regularly dominates the biblical text and presents a reading of Solomon from the underside by exposing his propensity – irrespective of reputation – for rash, ruthless judgements. Averen E. Ipsen observes that in popular consciousness the meaning of this text is predominantly focused on Solomon's virtuoso display of wisdom and not, say, the occupation of the women, who were prostitutes.[38] *The Simpsons* parody goes one step further by erasing women from the text altogether, replacing them with male characters (Homer's co-workers from the power plant). This enables the object of Homer's desire, the pie, to become foregrounded, thereby emphasizing the satirical effect of Homer's gluttony impeding his ability to make wise, considered judgements.

---

[37] Langston, *Exodus*, p. 147.
[38] Averen E. Ipsen, 'Solomon and the two prostitutes', *The Bible and Critical Theory*, 3, 1 (2007): pp. 2.1–2.2.

Bart and Goliath II

Bart's dream sequence departs the most from the original text upon which it is based. Bart takes on the role of King David and seeks revenge for the death of Methuselah (Abraham Simpson) at the hands of the giant Goliath II, son of Goliath who David slain in 1 Samuel 17. The character of Goliath II, played by schoolyard bully Nelson, does not in fact appear in the Bible. Rather, the creators of *The Simpsons* consciously employ artistic licence to stage an epic battle satirizing comeback/revenge fights in televised wrestling (underscoring that this really is the dream of a ten-year-old boy).

Even while consciously departing from the original text, *The Simpsons* at one point intentionally avoids conflating different narratives. For instance, after cutting Goliath II's hair, the following short dialogue ensues:

> Bart/David: What say you now Goliath? Without your precious hair you no longer possess your fantastic strength.
> Nelson/Goliath II: That's Samson, idiot!

However, the text also identifies the 'tower of Babel' (Gen. 11.1–9), which functions anachronistically as a palace within Jerusalem during the time of David, consequently conflating two distinct biblical texts into one. Pinsky writes that even though the dream is set in 970 BCE, the walled city's appearance seems more like the first century CE.[39] This implies that the producers of *The Simpsons* care little about historical or narrative distinctions; the time of the Bible is constructed as a broad, perhaps mythical, period.

Within this sequence, in particular, the producers utilize well-known characters, events, and themes from the Old Testament, hyper-consciously cashing in on their already prominent status within Western culture. As mentioned above, popular cultural adaptations of biblical texts will often take signifiers that have widespread resonance and accentuate these with little regard for their original context and/or purpose.[40] For example, the connection between Samson and hair is widespread, even though it is not always identified as a container of his strength.[41] After snacking on a whale, Goliath II throws the fish-skeleton out of a window. It lands next to Bart who, noticing a human skeleton inside the fish-skeleton, exclaims 'Jonah!' Again, the text takes a well-known image from the Bible and conflates it with other signifiers. Even if sections of the audience are unfamiliar with the

---

[39] Pinsky, *Gospel According to the Simpsons*, p. 100.

[40] Myles, 'Terminating Samson', 340.

[41] In *The Simpsons*' episode 'Simpson and Delilah', Homer uses a miracle hair growth formula to regrow his hair. As a result, he encounters favour and success among his peers, gaining a promotion at work, only to lose it when the formula runs out and Homer once again goes bald.

Bible, most know to associate the figure of Jonah with a whale, given the pervasiveness of the image across wider popular culture.[42]

After initially defeating Bart/David, Goliath II takes David's crown and becomes king over Jerusalem. David later returns to Jerusalem (specifically the tower of Babel) to fight Goliath, eventually killing him when he falls from the tower onto the ground below. David then proclaims to an assembled crowd that Goliath's reign of terror has ended. But David's moment of redemption is short lived as those in the crowd unexpectedly lament Goliath's passing:

> Dr Hibbert: Goliath was the greatest king we ever had. He built roads, hospitals, libraries.
> Carl: To us, he was Goliath the consensus builder.

This comical exchange pokes fun at the way in which the biblical text often takes sides with those who are unjust and unrighteous, but still retain God's favour. This fosters a more critical perspective on the text: while the Bible is often thought to eschew normative moral standards, it is not above criticism for its own moral failings, particularly when it comes to violence and gender.[43] In a similar vein, the dream sequence ends with Bart/David being arrested for 'megacide'. While placing him under arrest, Chief Wiggum sarcastically ripostes: 'Where's your Messiah now?'

At the conclusion of 'Simpsons Bible Stories', the Simpson family find themselves awake in a deserted church; as they exit the building they appear to have stumbled upon the end of the world. Brimstone is raining from the heavens and the world is ablaze, the four horsemen of the Apocalypse (Rev. 6.1–8) ride across the sky. The Simpsons descend a staircase into a fiery pit. The closing credits roll set to the AC/DC tune 'Highway to Hell'.

Conclusions

In this chapter, I have considered whether the prevalence of biblical afterlives in the long-running television series *The Simpsons* provides a strong foundation upon which to build further biblical literacy. I have also analysed how the show's satirical framing of the Bible and biblical texts is undergirded by its own commercial imperatives and artistic licence.

---

[42] For a discussion of the image of Jonah through culture, see: Yvonne Sherwood, *A Biblical Text and its Afterlives: The Survival of Jonah in Western Culture*, Cambridge: Cambridge University Press, 2000.

[43] Of course, it should be recognized that even heroic biblical characters like David are not always beyond criticism within the biblical text itself (e.g. 2 Sam. 12.1; 24.10).

Near the beginning of the chapter I suggested that definitions of biblical literacy ought to be expanded to encompass not just factual knowledge about the Bible, but also the hermeneutical frame that determines how this knowledge is understood and internalized. For better or worse, cultural texts like *The Simpsons* convey a set of normative claims about the Bible's political, cultural and ideological function, in this case by providing a satirical challenge to its dominance within contemporary North American political and cultural life. In some respects, this is actually an effective means of demonstrating some of the common pitfalls within biblical interpretation. Self-indulgent exegesis, gender stereotypes, and the Bible's propensity for rash violence are frequently critiqued through parody and satire. Viewers are equipped to challenge the moral authority of the Bible in a secular, pluralistic context, and to regard the historical veracity of biblical texts as being of secondary importance. As with any hermeneutical frame, however, there are also limitations to its usefulness in understanding the biblical text. Distinct narratives are regularly conflated, and the criticism of dominant interpretive practices as they relate to injustices in the world before the text does often not go far enough.

If popular cultural afterlives of the Bible present an alternative means of acquiring biblical literacy, then the critical study of its reception becomes all the more important. Given the pervasive influence of biblical afterlives, interpreters cannot help but to internalize these rudimentary engagements with the text, influencing how they subsequently respond to and produce meaning with the original text. Having been removed from its traditional religious context and implanted in a commercial medium, the acquisition of biblical literacy has begun to take new forms, potentially displacing the meaning and reality effects of the original text itself.

Bibliography

Aichele, George, *The Control of Biblical Meaning: Canon as Semiotic Mechanism*, Harrisburg: Trinity, 2001.
—*Simulating Jesus: Reality Effects in the Gospels*. London: Equinox, 2011.
Alberti, John (ed.), *Leaving Springfield: The Simpsons and the Possibility of Oppositional Culture*, Detroit: Wayne State University Press, 2003.
Avalos, Hector, 'In Praise of Biblical Illiteracy', *The Bible and Interpretation* (2010); www.bibleinterp.com/articles/literate357930.shtml
Brueggemann, Walter, *Genesis*, Atlanta: John Knox, 1982.
Carden, Michael, 'Genesis', in Deryn Guest, Robert E. Goss, Mona West and Thomas Bohache (eds), *The Queer Bible Commentary*, London: SCM, 2006, pp. 21–60.
Chow, Valerie Weilunn, 'Homer Erectus: Homer Simpson as Everyman ... And Every Woman', in John Alberti (ed.), *Leaving Springfield: The Simpsons and the Possibility of Oppositional Culture*, Detroit: Wayne State University Press, 2004, pp. 107–36.

Collins, Jim, 'Postmodernism and Television', in Robert Allen (ed.), *Channels of Discourse, Reassembled*, London: Routledge, 1992, pp. 327–53.

Dwyer, Barry, 'Religious Literacy: A Useful Concept?', in Maurice Ryan (ed.), *Echo and Silence: Contemporary Issues for Australian Religious Education*, Katoomba: Social Science Press, 2001, pp. 117–25.

Eagleton, Terry, *The Illusions of Postmodernism*. Malden: Blackwell, 1996.

Edwards, Katie B. *Admen and Eve: The Bible in Contemporary Advertising*, Sheffield: Sheffield Phoenix Press, 2012.

Gee, James Paul, *Social Linguistics and Literacies: Ideology in Discourses* (3rd edn), London: Routledge, 2007.

Gray, Jonathan, 'Television teaching: parody, *The Simpsons*, and media literacy education'. *Critical Studies in Media Communication*, 22/3, 2005: 223–38.

Harvey, David, *The Condition of Postmodernity*, Cambridge: Blackwell, 1989.

Heit, Jamey, *The Springfield Reformation*: The Simpsons, *Christianity, and American Culture*, New York: Continuum, 2008.

Henry, Matthew, '"Gabbin' About God": Religion, Secularity and Satire on *The Simpsons*', in Timothy M. Dale and Joseph J. Foy (eds), *Homer Simpson Marches on Washington: Dissent through American Popular Culture*, Lexington: University Press of Kentucky, 2010, pp. 141–66.

Hutcheon, Linda, *The Politics of Postmodernism* (2nd edn), Abingdon: Routledge, 2002.

Ipsen, Avaren E., 'Solomon and the two prostitutes', *The Bible and Critical Theory*, 3,1 (2007): 2.1–2.12.

Irwin, William, Mark T. Conard and Aeon J. Skoble (eds), The Simpsons *and Philosophy: The D'oh! Of Homer*, Chicago: Open Court, 2001.

Langston, Scott M., *Exodus through the Centuries*, Blackwell Bible Commentaries. Malden: Blackwell, 2006.

Lewis, Todd V., 'Religious rhetoric and the comic frame in *The Simpsons*', *Journal of Media and Religion*, 1, 3 (2002): 153–65.

Lynch, Gordon, *Understanding Theology and Popular Culture*. Malden: Blackwell, 2005.

Moll, Sebastian, 'The Reverend Timothy Lovejoy'. *The Bible and Interpretation* (2012), www.bibleinterp.com/opeds/mol368022.shtml

Myles, Robert J., 'Terminating Samson: The Sarah Connor chronicles and the rise of new biblical meaning', *Relegere*, 1, 2 (2011): 329–50.

Nash, Robert J. and Penny A. Bishop, *Teaching Adolescents Religious Literacy in a Post-9/11 World*, Charlotte, NC: Information Age, 2010.

Pinsky, Mark I., *The Gospel According to* The Simpsons: *The Spiritual Life of the World's Most Animated Family*, Louisville: Westminster John Knox, 2001.

Prothero, Stephen, *Religious Literacy: What Every American Needs to Know – and Doesn't*, HarperCollins: New York, 2007.

Sherwood, Yvonne, *A Biblical Text and its Afterlives: The Survival of Jonah in Western Culture*, Cambridge: Cambridge University Press, 2000.

Smith, James A., 'Outside In: Diabolical Portraits', in Fiona C. Black (ed.), *The Recycled Bible: Autobiography, Culture, and the Space Between*, Atlanta: SBL, 2006, pp. 101–41.

Turner, Chris, *Planet Simpson: How a Cartoon Masterpiece Defined a Generation*, Cambridge: Da Capo, 2004.

Wachlin, Marie, *Bible Literacy Report: What Do American Teens Need to Know and What Do They Know?*, New York: Bible Literacy Project, 2005.

PART THREE

Popular Literacies

8

Lisbeth and Leviticus: Biblical Literacy and *The Girl with the Dragon Tattoo*

Caroline Blyth
(University of Auckland)

The relationship between the Bible and, let's say, secular literature is still a two-way street. And literature can be a kind of magical [device] that leads you to the Bible.[1]

Introduction

It has become a bit of a truism to say that the Bible has had and continues to have an immeasurable influence within popular culture. Over the centuries, biblical traditions, characters and themes have been represented, rewritten, and referenced within a plethora of cultural texts, including those from the genres of literature, poetry, music, theatre, advertising and the visual arts. Despite the perception of its fading religious significance, influence, and sacred authority within an increasingly secular postmodern world and within many individuals' cultural lives and worldviews, the Bible

---

[1]Professor Gerald Bruns, University of Notre Dame, quoted in Marie Wachlin, *Bible Literacy Report II: What University Professors Say Incoming Students Need to Know*, (Front Royal: Bible Literacy Project, 2006), p. 43. Special thanks to Tracy Saunders and Robert Myles for their helpful feedback on this essay.

nevertheless persists as a vivid 'presence' within contemporary popular culture.[2]

Yet, notwithstanding the ubiquitous presence of biblical references within many cultural arenas, there have been growing concerns in recent years raised by teachers, scholars and educationalists that biblical literacy[3] among high school, college and university students is on the wane. These concerns were voiced very clearly in 2009 by Britain's Poet Laureate Andrew Motion, when he opined that a growing lack of knowledge about both the biblical traditions and classic mythology was having a deleterious effect upon the teaching of literature in schools and universities. For Motion, the Bible, like other ancient classical and sacred texts, remains 'an essential piece of cultural luggage', whose words and traditions have had and continue to have great influence, carrying the power 'to connect with deep recurring human truths'. Yet, as biblical study becomes increasingly the preserve of 'only the academies and only parts of the academies', a significant part of many people's cultural legacies, he feared, would ultimately be lost.[4]

Motion's concerns about the Bible as a cultural phenomenon that is increasingly restricted to the dusty corners of the 'academy' are, of course, not new. Almost a decade earlier, biblical scholar Athalya Brenner described the Bible as traditionally 'an elitist object – produced, consumed, transmitted and studied by elites variously defined by religious praxis, age, gender, class, ethnicity, occupation and status'.[5] Subsequently, suggested Brenner, biblical scholars have tended to sustain a 'legacy of secrecy' around it, preserving their own reputation as 'specialists' of these ancient texts and closely guarding its secrets from other interested readers outside the academy of biblical studies.[6] As a biblical scholar, I have doubtlessly been guilty of participating (albeit unwittingly) in this legacy of secrecy myself, to some degree at least; yet, I am also aware, as Brenner herself warns, that ultimately, such a legacy may be self-destructive, serving only

---

[2] Jo Carruthers, 'Literature', in John F. A. Sawyer (ed.), *The Blackwell Companion to the Bible and Culture*, Oxford: Blackwell Publishing, 2006, pp. 253–67 (254).

[3] By 'biblical literacy', I mean some awareness of the individual stories, characters, and genres of literature that can be found within the canons of the Hebrew Bible and Second Testament as well as an appreciation of the potentially multiple meanings and significances that they may convey to different reading communities and contexts. For me, biblical literacy does not need to include any confessional elements, such as a belief in the Bible's sacred authority or its divine origins.

[4] John Bingham, 'Poet Laureate Andrew Motion Calls for All Children to be Taught the Bible', *Telegraph*, 17 February 2009. http://www.telegraph.co.uk/education/educationnews/4678369/Poet-Laureate-Andrew-Motion-calls-for-all-children-to-be-taught-the-Bible.html [accessed 25 January 2013].

[5] Athalya Brenner, 'Introduction', in George Aichele (ed.), *Culture, Entertainment and the Bible*, JSOTSup, 309, Sheffield: Sheffield Academic Press, 2000, pp. 7–12 (11).

[6] Ibid., p. 11.

to preserve biblical studies as some exclusive branch of scholarship that is of interest only to a carefully selected and ever-dwindling few.[7] The question I am left with, then, is this: as a scholar who is engaged in both writing about and teaching biblical literature, what strategies can I adopt in order to throw open the doors of the 'Biblical Scholars Guild' to students and other interested parties, thus allowing them to recognize the biblical texts as a fascinating and significant part of their cultural legacy? Given the declining religious significance afforded to the Bible within the cultural lives and spheres of interest of many young people today, what might I do in order to bring new and exciting possibilities of biblical engagement and interpretation, not only to those students who choose to study the Bible for religious or scholarly reasons, but also to those potentially interested readers from other 'parts of the academy' and, in particular, those outside the 'academy'?

One possible answer to these questions that I am keen to explore is Brenner's own suggestion[8] that the study of the Bible *in conversation with* its representation in popular culture can open new doors of engagement and enjoyment in the study of these fascinating ancient texts and traditions, capturing the reader's imagination and offering 'a creative entry point for deeper dialogue'[9] on the biblical themes and representations that are so pervasive and ubiquitous within contemporary popular culture. Through their various media, cultural texts – such as film, song, advertising, fiction and the visual arts – can serve as accessible and ubiquitous conduits through which individuals might meaningfully engage with the Bible, finding within them elucidations, validations, comments or critiques of the biblical material that they reference. Moreover, and very importantly, contemporary cultural texts can highlight the possibilities of biblical texts being open to multiple readings, rather than being monologic; their cultural representations of the biblical traditions offering a dialogical commentary on these traditions and revealing the multiplicity of meanings that they may carry in different temporal and spatial locations.[10] Intentionally or not, such cultural representations can draw our attention to the biblical text in novel ways, offering new depths, possibilities, tensions, problems and contradictions that may not always be apparent to even the more seasoned and biblically literate reader. In particular, the cultural text may not simply leave the biblical material unchallenged but may instead invite the audience to scrutinize it critically; as Peter Hawkins notes, the relationship between biblical text and cultural text may be 'vexed and stormy; it may involve

---

[7]Ibid.

[8]Ibid., pp. 11–12.

[9]Mark S. M. Scott and Jason Zuidema, 'Religious studies and popular fiction: What does dan brown have to do with the Ivory Tower?', *Journal of Religion and Popular Culture*, 23 (2011): 372–81 (373).

[10]Carruthers, 'Literature', p. 260.

serious repudiation as well as respect'.[11] The various media of popular culture can thus provide the interested reader of the Bible with 'a significant arena of contemporary biblical interpretation'[12] that can invite discussion, dialogue, questions, and challenges – surely valuable ingredients to bring new and accessible ways of knowing to the study of the biblical traditions.

For the remainder of this chapter, I would like to explore the potentialities of this particular 'arena' of biblical interpretation by providing an illustration of the ways in which the study of a contemporary cultural appropriation of biblical material can stimulate new engagements with the biblical material for scholars, students and other interested readers alike. I have chosen as my cultural text the bestselling crime thriller by Swedish journalist and writer Stieg Larsson, *The Girl with the Dragon Tattoo* (hereafter *Dragon Tattoo*). This was the first book in the *Millennium Series* trilogy of novels written by Larsson and was initially published posthumously in Sweden in 2005 under the title, *Män som hatar kvinnor* (*Men Who Hate Women*). Translated into English and released in the United Kingdom and United States in 2008, the *Millennium* trilogy quickly became a global bestseller, selling over 65 million copies by the end of 2011.[13] *Dragon Tattoo* also inspired two movie retellings, the 2009 Swedish version *Män som hatar kvinnor*, directed by Niels Arden Oplev and David Fincher's US adaptation, *The Girl with the Dragon Tattoo*, in 2011. Given the huge popularity and cultural reach that this novel has had on audiences worldwide, it may therefore serve as a valuable example of a popular cultural text that engages with the Bible and that may work effectively as an accessible interpretative tool in the pursuit of biblical literacy.

Before I begin, I am aware that I should perhaps first touch upon the 'thorny territory' of authorial intent.[14] By using *Dragon Tattoo* as the basis for an exploration of biblical meaning, I am not suggesting that Stieg Larsson intended his novel to serve primarily (or even secondarily) as a commentary or critique of the biblical texts it references. Alas, Larsson's death in 2004,

---

[11] Peter S. Hawkins, 'Lost and found: The Bible and its literary afterlives', *Religion and Literature*, 36 (2004): 1–14 (8). See also Carruthers, 'Literature', pp. 256–7; Laura Copier, Jaap Kooijman and Caroline Vander Stichele, 'Close Encounters: The Bible as Pre-Text in Popular Culture', in Philip Culbertson and Elaine M. Wainwright (eds), *The Bible in/and Popular Culture: A Creative Encounter*, Semeia Studies, 65; Atlanta: SBL, 2010, pp. 189–95 (192–3).

[12] Elaine M. Wainwright, 'Introduction', in Culbertson and Wainwright (eds), *The Bible in/and Popular Culture*, pp. 1–9 (3).

[13] The other two volumes in the trilogy are *The Girl Who Played with Fire* and *The Girl Who Kicked the Hornets' Nest*. Sales figures sourced from Genevieve Hassan, 'Hollywood takes on Girl with the Dragon Tattoo', BBC News Online 26 December 2011; www.bbc.co.uk/news/entertainment-arts-16110375 [accessed 30 January 2013].

[14] Lesleigh Cushing Stahlberg, *Sustaining Fictions: Intertextuality, Midrash, Translation, and the Literary Afterlife of the Bible*, Library of Hebrew Bible/Old Testament Studies, 486; New York: T&T Clark, 2008, p. 6.

before the original publication of his novel, meant that there was scant opportunity for him to speak publicly and in depth about his work; his rationale and intentions for including references to biblical traditions in his novel therefore remain unknown. However, as Lesleigh Cushing Stahlberg suggests, one may instead speak about the stance of a cultural text that utilizes biblical material; that is, the semantic and contextual relationship that the cultural text appears to have with the biblical source material.[15] Or, to use the words of J. Hillis Miller, we can consider how biblical texts are 'translated' as they cross the 'border' from their ancient contexts to new locations that inspire 'innumerable other moments of reading'.[16] Are the biblical traditions being parodied, condoned or critiqued within their new cultural location? How might the reader react to them within this location? Do these biblical traditions serve as possible symbols or signifiers for a wider narrative theme or concern within the cultural text?

In the following discussion, I will therefore explore the ways that *Dragon Tattoo* brings the biblical world into the new contemporary location that this novel represents, looking both at the way the biblical material serves as a symbol of meaning within the narrative and, in particular, the potential new meanings and significances that the narrative can likewise bring to this biblical material. In particular, I wish to focus on the possible ways that readers of *Dragon Tattoo* may be invited to make sense of the biblical texts it references in light of one of the primary narrative concerns of the novel; that is, gender violence. How do the allusions to the biblical text serve the seeming aim of the book to confront social systems embedded within patriarchal culture which validate or condone gender inequality and gender violence? Can Larsson's novel act as a hermeneutical lens on the biblical traditions, inviting a cultural and feminist critique of these ancient texts from the reader?

Situating the Levitical laws in *Dragon Tattoo*

Set in modern Sweden, *Dragon Tattoo* combines the two genres of classic locked room mystery and psychological thriller, into which are interwoven occurrences of corporate crime, a missing teenager, and the search for a serial killer. We encounter investigative journalist Mikael Blomquist and his accomplice, computer hacker and private investigator Lisbeth Salander, who have been hired by wealthy businessman Henrik Vanger to look into the decades-old disappearance of his teenage niece Harriet. During the

---

[15] Stahlberg, *Sustaining Fictions*, p. 6.
[16] J. Hillis Miller, 'Border Crossings, Translating Theory: Ruth', in Sanford Budick and Wolfgang Iser (eds), *The Translatability of Cultures: Figurations of the Space Between*, Stanford, CA: Stanford University Press, 1996, pp. 214, 222.

course of their investigation, Mikael and Lisbeth discover that, prior to her disappearance, Harriet had made a connection between the unsolved murders of five women and five verses from the book of Leviticus, the content of each verse seeming to echo the particularly gruesome and ritualized nature of each murder.[17] Using each of these biblical verses as a 'clue',[18] Lisbeth and Mikael eventually discover that the killer was Harriet's own father Gottfried Vanger, assisted in the latter cases by his son, Harriet's brother Martin. Following his father's death, Martin has carried on the 'family tradition' of perpetrating horrific crimes of gender violence, proudly admitting to Mikael that he has since abducted, raped and murdered dozens of women.

How, then, is the reader of *Dragon Tattoo* being invited to make sense of these Levitical laws, particularly given their arrangement within the contours of gender violence that run so strongly throughout this novel? First of all, I would suggest that as a narrative prop, the Bible is presented as somewhat detached from the framework of sexualized aggression in which it is located in *Dragon Tattoo*. It is represented within the novel as an arcane religious text, the sourcebook for elderly, befuddled priests,[19] 'strange sects' and 'religious fanaticism';[20] there is certainly no attempt to identify any explicitly *causal* relationship between the biblical texts and the terrible crimes to which they appear somehow connected. Even in the hands of Harriet, who is noted by other characters to have been a keen reader of the Bible, these biblical references seem to serve as little more than useful 'clues' in her amateur sleuthing to solve a series of bizarre and brutal murders.

Moreover, the novel's protagonists Mikael and Lisbeth consistently describe these murders as stemming from grotesque *mis*interpretations or 'parodies' of the laws, which have been 'pulled out of context' by the killer as the result of his own tangled psyche of psychopathology, misogyny and racial hatred.[21] Both characters note that the murders do not always accurately mirror the biblical laws to which they refer; rather, the killings borrow particular elements of each law, while ignoring or distorting others.[22] According to Mikael, the Levitical theme of these killings is therefore little more than 'some sort of Biblical gibberish that a psychiatrist

---

[17] The Levitical laws listed by Harriet are 1.12; 20.16, 18, 27; 21.9.

[18] Stieg Larsson, *The Girl with the Dragon Tattoo* (trans. Reg Keeland), New York: Vintage Crime, 2009, p. 323. Hereafter, *Dragon Tattoo*.

[19] Ibid. pp. 403–5.

[20] Ibid., p. 316.

[21] Ibid., pp. 379–80, 424.

[22] For example, they both observe that the two women whose deaths are thematically connected to the law prohibiting bestiality (Lev. 20.16) were highly unlikely to have committed this prohibited sexual act. However, the women's close proximity to animals every day (as farmer and pet shop owner) was sufficient for the murderer to associate them topically with this law (ibid., pp. 376–8).

might be able to figure out, something to do with punishment and purification in a figurative sense'.[23] Mikael's uncompromising relegation of the
Levitical allusions to mere 'Biblical gibberish', which is more the purview
of a psychiatrist than a serious reader of the Bible, serves to confirm to
the reader that the biblical texts themselves did not promote the murders,
but rather, their association with these murders is the result of a terrible
misreading by 'an insanely sick sadistic serial killer'.[24] While Lisbeth
disagrees with Mikael about the psychopathology of the killer, she too
seems reluctant to locate the source of these terrible crimes within the pages
of the Levitical text, insisting instead that their origins lie in the ubiquity
of everyday male violence and misogyny; as she says to Mikael, 'It's not an
insane serial killer who read his Bible wrong. It's just a common or garden
bastard who hates women.'[25]

Yet, despite the seeming inclination in *Dragon Tattoo* to downplay any
causal relationship between the Bible and the associated acts of gender
violence that occur within the novel (or at least, to leave this relationship
unspoken), I would suggest that this cultural text may still have a profound
usefulness as an interpretative tool and as a way of knowing the Levitical
laws that it references. Whether intentionally or not, I believe that the
placement of the biblical material within the contours of gender violence
that inscribe this novel offers readers new ways of thinking about these
Levitical laws and invites the opportunity for fresh critical perceptions of
their significance and symbolic meaning, particularly as a body of writing
that has the timeless potential to denote, if not engender, ideologies of
misogyny and marginalization. I will now discuss this in more depth,
arranging my discussion into three interrelated topics: first, the violence
inherent within some of the Levitical laws, secondly, the themes of othering
and marginalization within this law code, and finally, the function of these
laws to preserve and protect the community at the expense of the individual.

Violence and the Levitical laws

One of my first observations on reading *Dragon Tattoo* was that the novel's
inclusion of several Levitical laws within the context of a series of brutal
murders served to accentuate the violence and the horror that is explicit
within these laws but that can at times be overlooked by biblical readers, as
they focus on the law code's seemingly more benign function of maintaining
the purity and holiness of the covenant community.[26] Regardless of the
fact that, as I said above, the novel seems to shy away from identifying a

---

[23] Ibid., p. 473.
[24] Ibid., p. 380.
[25] Ibid., p. 382.
[26] Levictus 20.7–8.

strictly causal relationship between the biblical laws and the killings that are linked to them, the fact that these laws are situated within the narrative environment of lethal aggression can nevertheless serve as an effective means of drawing the reader's attention to the violence that is engrained within them. The terrible cruelty and brutality of the murder victims' deaths is described graphically, sparing no detail; the women are tortured, strangled, burned, and stoned to death as the result of their murderer seeking in his own way to enact these laws. Larsson is uncompromising in his depiction of the gender violence that occurs here, but I was struck by the way that the basis of such punitive violence does lie in the Levitical laws themselves. At their most basic level, some of these laws proscribe certain sexual and social behaviours on pain of expulsion from the community or even death; behaviours including extra-marital sex, same-sex relationships, forms of spiritism and necromancy, sex with a menstruant, incest and bestiality are all identified as sources of impurity to the community of Israel and therefore not to be tolerated.[27] Women and men who do not conform to these priestly purity laws, who seek instead to practise a modicum of sexual or social self-determination, either face the death penalty (by being stoned or burned to death) or are subject to being 'cut off' from the holy community,[28] possibly some form of divine excommunication or even divinely perpetrated murder causing permanent exclusion from the group.

An inherent rule of force therefore forms the foundation of this priestly system of social regulation, the laws functioning unequivocally as an arrangement of threats and punishments, which serve as an 'ever-present instrument of intimidation'[29] to keep in line or, if necessary, to exterminate those who threaten to dismantle the religious, social, and political status quo of the community through their refusal to acquiesce to its divinely sanctioned order. The violence meted out against those who contravene the laws is not treated as extraordinary, but rather as a normal and necessary part of communal existence. We might shrug such laws off as archaic artefacts of an ancient culture, but they deserve our attention as a very troubling and disturbing social reality, not least because some of these laws continue to be regarded as both sacred and influential within certain cultural and religious groups today and have been used and are still used as justification for intolerance and hatred. The Levitical laws are, without doubt, deeply and indelibly tainted with the threat and reality of actual violence and the proscription of social and sexual liberty – *Dragon Tattoo* certainly raised my awareness of this, drawing me into a realization of the horrific *actuality* of the laws' legacies of violence and the lethal potentialities that are embedded within the words of these ancient texts.

---

[27] See, for example, Levictus 18 and 20.

[28] See, for example, Levictus 20:3, 6, 17, 18.

[29] Kate Millett, *Sexual Politics*, London: Virago, 1989, p. 43.

Moreover, the novel's uncompromising and relentless depiction of the sheer ubiquity and customariness of violence in contemporary Swedish society may likewise serve to accentuate the pervasiveness and the normalization of socially sanctioned violence within the Levitical law codes, particularly the ways in which such violence can become so engrained within the structures, spaces, and consciousnesses of a socio-cultural milieu that it is rendered both ordinary and, as a result, almost imperceptible.

Marginalization and otherness in the Levitical laws

Following on from the discussion above, I would also suggest that the biblical allusions in *Dragon Tattoo* can serve to focus the reader's attention on the themes of othering, exclusion and marginality that run as inherent undercurrents throughout these Levitical laws. The five laws mentioned in the novel all prescribe or proscribe certain religious, social and sexual behaviours; they lie within a larger legal code, which reflects a priestly concern for the separation of the clean from the unclean, the holy from the profane, and the centrality of the cult in the maintenance of Israel's systems of purity and atonement. This legal code constructs, typifies and validates specific acts and behaviours that are evaluated by the priestly authors as normative within the sacred boundaries of the divinely sanctioned cosmic order. It does this by effectively problematizing those acts and behaviours that do *not* cohere with such normativities, but that serve instead as metonyms for social disorder and danger – that which is unwelcome and taboo, and which can disrupt the imposed structures, hierarchies and relationships of the idealized holy community.

In other words, through their construction and classification of types and relationships, these Levitical laws regulate what *should be* under the guise of stating what is. By doing so, they effectively construct and maintain boundaries, enabling a clear distinction to be made between those whose compliance with the laws allows them to remain 'insiders' or *bona fide* members of the community and those whose behaviour is defined as unnatural or unacceptable by the law, rendering them 'outsiders' and unworthy of community membership or even unworthy of life.[30] These 'outsiders' thus effectively become representative of the abject body, as defined by Julia Kristeva; symbolic of the exclusion, marginality and vulnerability experienced by those who are regarded as embodying a 'threatening otherness', who 'perturb' established borders, systems and identities of the patriarchal social order, exposing their fragile, breakable, and transitory nature, and who are therefore at risk of becoming a focus

---

[30] Jonathan P. Burnside, 'Strange flesh: sex, semiotics and the construction of deviancy in biblical law', *JSOT* 30 (2006): 387–420 (389).

for antipathy, fear and abuse.[31] The abject body exists in a space outside the boundary that separates the community from danger and extinction – it is a space of impurity not purity, profanity not holiness, and death not life. Consequently, individuals who come to represent the abject must be either re-purified or 'radically excluded'[32] from the community, traditionally by religious means, such as those purity laws and sacrificial systems found within the Levitical material.

In effect then, the Levitical purity laws exemplify attempts by religious priestly authorities to control the community's social, religious and sexual behaviour using a religious mandate that is rooted in ideologies of intolerance to difference, otherness and non-compliance. The fact that, within *Dragon Tattoo*, these priestly laws form the thematic basis for the brutal and ritualistic murder of at least five women can thus draw the reader's attention to their inherent function as a means of ridding the community of abject, undesirable, or harmful elements – those who are deemed to flout the rules and regulations that define proper membership of the community. Within the novel, the 'community' is, of course, not biblical Israel, but the powerful Vanger dynasty, which is symbolically positioned within the borders of the family's own social and spatial locality – the fictional Swedish island of Hedeby. Such a location – a fairly remote island with only the one bridge as a point of entry and exit – serves as a marker in the novel of the extreme sense of exclusivity, elitism and insularity of the Vanger family *vis-à-vis* their wider social context of mainland Sweden.[33] As a micro-community, their self-elected leaders (the family patriarchs) have, over the generations, constructed their own customs, traditions and rules, drawing boundaries of exclusion and defining insiders and outsiders according to their own deeply patriarchal, anti-Semitic and misogynistic heritage. Like the priestly elites who drew up borders of belonging for the holy community of biblical Israel, we get the impression that the Vanger elites have, over the generations, constructed and policed their own metaphorical borders around their deeply insular 'world', symbolically represented by Hedeby island, and have utilized their own particular means of ridding this world of the abject, unwanted 'other'.

Bearing this in mind, we can suggest that Gottfried Vanger appears to have conflated this sense of privilege and insularity that is so deeply entrenched in the Vanger world with the same boundary-drawing and

---

[31] Julia Kristeva, *Powers of Horror: An Essay on Abjection* (trans. Leon S. Roudiez), New York: Columbia University Press, 1982, pp. 4, 95.

[32] Ibid., p. 2.

[33] The detached nature of the Vanger's spatial location on Hedeby is emphasized in the novel by Henrik Vanger, who describes it as being 'cut off from the rest of the world' on an occasion when the bridge was blocked by a traffic accident (*Dragon Tattoo*, pp. 94–5). Special thanks to Robert Myles for drawing my attention to the significance of the various spatial locations within this novel.

intolerance of the 'other' that is intrinsic to the Levitical laws, allowing him to draw upon both traditions to validate and rationalize his brutal murders. He selected his victims either because he judged their behaviour (wrongly, as it happens)[34] as being in breach of particular Levitical laws or because he conceptualized them as necessary sacrifices of expiation, to be offered up as some form of sin offering or cleansing blood sacrifice in a perverse parody of Israel's ritualized system of purification and atonement. Gottfried identified these women, as well as his own daughter Harriet,[35] as in some sense 'different' or 'other', their actions or contexts setting them apart as an 'offence' to his socio-religious order; he classified them as whores, witches, sexual deviants, and therefore as sources of impurity and danger. Not only that, but as Mikael and Lisbeth notice, all the women murdered by Gottfried had Jewish names, another reason for him to regard them as undesirably and intolerably 'other', given some of his relatives' decades-long Nazi sympathies and anti-Semitic hatred.[36] Thus, in the same way that the priestly authorities constructed the Levitical systems of impurity and sacrifice to rid the community of abject, dangerous presences, so too did Gottfried play the priestly function of offering expiation as a means of ridding *his* socio-religious world of the undesirable and defiling elements that he refused to tolerate within its hallowed boundaries, thereby maintaining his place within its 'sacred order'.[37]

Furthermore, while the serial acts of femicide carried out by Gottfried's son Martin and the abuses suffered by Lisbeth's character are not explicitly connected in *Dragon Tattoo* to the Levitical texts, they too nevertheless share some thematic connections with the 'Leviticus murders' that make them a useful study for our contemplation of the biblical material within the novel, particularly *vis-à-vis* the themes of patriarchal power, violence, exclusion and othering that I have suggested permeate these Levitical laws. Like his father Gottfried, Martin's crimes are also given a veneer of religious significance within *Dragon Tattoo*; in this case, his desire to take on the same sacred powers of social inclusion and exclusion as his father through his manipulation of numerous women's lives and deaths. For Martin, the pleasure he takes in abducting, raping and killing women arises from the sense of superhuman supremacy it gives him to have utter domination over another person's existence; or, as he tells Mikael, the 'godlike' feeling he enjoys from 'having absolute control over someone's life and death'.[38] He can achieve this sense of control with impunity because, he admits to Mikael, he chooses women to rape and kill whom he believes no one will

---

[34] This is discussed in more detail below.
[35] Harriet is not one of her father's murder victims; however, we learn late in the novel that he did physically and sexually abuse her (*Dragon Tattoo*, pp. 493-96).
[36] Ibid., pp. 176–8.
[37] Kristeva, *Powers of Horror*, p. 95.
[38] *Dragon Tattoo*, p. 448.

miss – immigrants, foreign prostitutes, drug addicts and 'social outcasts';[39] women who are judged as an abject, worthless, or even impure presence in Swedish society, who disturb the social order, and whose very marginality and otherness in that society therefore renders them easy prey for those men, like Martin, who believe they hold the power to rid their world of the 'other' through some form of sacrificial 'ritual' of repurification.[40]

Once again, then, we can see within the narrative threads of *Dragon Tattoo* certain dominant concerns that echo with the biblical verses from Leviticus, offering the reader a chance to reflect upon the vital connections between violence and marginalization that exist within these biblical traditions. Like the violence sanctioned in some of the Levitical laws, the Vangers' acts of femicide are likewise the product of a dominant patriarchal elite that ultimately uses violence in order to maintain and protect its own privileged social reality.[41] Those in positions of authority, be they biblical priestly lawmakers or affluent and influential Swedish businessmen, have the power to make their own rules; they draw the boundaries that define who 'belongs' and who is the undesirable, disposable 'other'; they marginalize, ostracize, and terrorize those who refuse to conform to these rules and who dare to step outside these boundaries of accepted beliefs and behaviours.[42] Moreover, they legitimate such acts of marginalization and violence by appealing to their own sense of privilege and authority and their desire, like Martin, to exert 'absolute control' over others' lives and deaths.

Such a heady mix of male power and control and the effects that it can have over the vulnerable 'other' is also shown to devastating effect in another strand of the novel, where we see Lisbeth's abuser – her legal guardian Nils Bjurman – relishing the sense of his own state-sanctioned power *vis-à-vis* Lisbeth's legal and social disenfranchisement, which renders her totally vulnerable to the sexual violence he perpetrates against her. Throughout the book, Lisbeth is repeatedly constructed at the very margins of the narrative's social world. Both her appearance and her sexual and social behaviour render her distinctly 'other' within her own cultural milieu of contemporary Sweden, thereby setting her apart as both threateningly 'deviant' *and* terribly susceptible to violence; in other words, she personifies the uncomfortable social presence and reality of the abject. Her pierced and tattooed androgynous body, her choice of clothes, her fierce independence and her willingness to utilize violence when she feels threatened – all of these characteristics flout social and cultural conventions that delineate and

---

39 Ibid., p. 464.
40 Kristeva, *Powers of Horror*, pp. 4, 94–5.
41 Raewyn W. Connell, *Masculinities*, Berkeley: University of California Press, 2005, p. 245; also Jane Caputi, *Goddesses and Monsters: Women, Myth, Power, and Popular Culture*, Madison: University of Wisconsin Press, 2004, p. 121.
42 Connell, *Masculinities*, p. 245.

delimit authorized standards and contours of gender norms.[43] Sexually, she also breaks traditional gender boundaries, eschewing the conventions of heteronormativity and female passivity in favour of initiating and seeking pleasure in an active sex life with both male and female partners. Such choices in her appearance and behaviour set her apart as a 'gender outlaw';[44] by infringing cultural perceptions of femininity, she refuses to 'fit in' to society, preferring instead to remain at its margins.[45] And yet, by doing so, Lisbeth is also aware that, by inhabiting these margins, she renders herself vulnerable to violence and abuse. At one point in the novel, she reflects that as a woman – particularly one who looks and acts the way she does – she has 'zero social status' and is therefore essentially 'legal prey' to rapists and sexual predators; that is, for her, 'the natural order of things'.[46]

Lisbeth's marginality is likewise confirmed to the reader by the revelation that she has been evaluated by corrupt judicial, political, and medical authorities to be legally and mentally incompetent and therefore in need of legal guardianship.[47] As an individual who is denied any semblance of legal agency, Lisbeth appears not only to embody the *failure* of the state to protect her from abuse, one could argue that she also symbolizes the *complicity* of the state in this abuse, by its perpetual inability to recognize her vulnerability and her mistreatment at the hands of those who have had authority over her.[48] At one point in the narrative, her court-appointed guardian Nils Bjurman reminds Lisbeth that, as her state-appointed legal guardian, he enjoys complete control over her life.[49] The fact that he uses this control to assault her sexually and physically adds to our discomfort

---

[43]Catherine G. Valentine, 'Tiny, Tattooed, and Tough as Nails: Representations of Lisbeth Salander's Body', in Carrie Lee Smith and Donna King (eds), *Men Who Hate Women and Women Who Kick Their Asses: Stieg Larsson's Millennium Trilogy in Feminist Perspective*, Nashville, TN: Vanderbilt University Press, 2012, pp. 88–97 (95–6); Kim Surkan, 'The Girl Who Turned the Tables: A Queer Reading of Lisbeth Salander', in Eric Bronson (ed.), *The Girl with the Dragon Tattoo and Philosophy: Everything is Fire*, Hoboken, NJ: John Wiley & Sons, 2011, pp. 33–46.

[44]Misty K. Hook, 'Lisbeth Salander as a Gender Outlaw', in Robin S. Rosenberg and Shannon O'Neill (eds), *The Psychology of the Girl with the Dragon Tattoo*, Dallas: BenBella Books, 2011, pp. 47–64 (53).

[45]Rachel Rodgers and Eric Bui, 'The Body Speaks Louder than Words: What is Lisbeth Salander Saying?' in Rosenberg and O'Neill (eds.), *The Psychology of the Girl with the Dragon Tattoo*, pp. 29–44 (37).

[46]*Dragon Tattoo*, p. 228.

[47]The full extent of the political corruption that underlies Lisbeth's legal status is revealed in the final book of Larsson's *Millennium* Trilogy, *The Girl Who Kicked the Hornets' Nest*.

[48]Patricia Yancey Martin, 'State Complicity in Men's Violence against Women', in Smith and King (eds.), *Men Who Hate Women and Women Who Kick Their Asses*, pp. 39–50 (48).

[49]'No, you're not a child. But I've been appointed your guardian, and as long as I have that role, I am legally and financially responsible for you' (Bjurman's words to Lisbeth, *Dragon Tattoo*, p. 165).

at the ease by which those deemed socially different and legally disenfranchised can be exposed to terrible harm, particularly at the hands of the legal institutions which are intended to protect them.

As I was reading this section of the novel, what struck me was the way in which Lisbeth's lack of legal and social agency and her dependence on a state-sanctioned male guardian seemed to resonate with the legal and social disempowerment of biblical women[50] who are likewise frequently represented in texts as living under the jurisdiction of a male custodian.[51] As Phyllis Trible notes, the Hebrew Bible traditions bear ample testimony that biblical women's bodies 'were not their own'.[52] Indeed, both Lisbeth's experiences as a disenfranchised woman and the fate of the murder victims in *Dragon Tattoo* can invite the reader to reflect upon this theme of female disempowerment within the specific literary context of the Levitical laws. One of the details dwelt upon explicitly in this novel is the fact that the women who were murdered due to their apparent 'violation' of certain purity laws were not themselves guilty of any such violation. For example, consider the case of Sara Witt, whose murder appeared to be an outplaying of the law of Levictus 21.9 – the priest's daughter who must be burned if she profanes herself and her father by 'playing the harlot'. Sara's death is the result of her murderer judging her in some sense to have breached this law, thus becoming a profaning presence within his social world; yet, she was a victim of rape here, not a consenting participant in any sexual act prohibited by this law. How, then, can she really be considered 'guilty' of breaching it and consequently 'deserving' of death?

Similarly, Mari Holmberg, whose murder parodied Levictus 20.18, the law proscribing sexual intercourse during a woman's genital flow, was likewise raped and then murdered – like Sara, she did not actively or consensually engage in a prohibited sexual act and was therefore not complicit in any breach of this law. Indeed, *all* of Gottfried's victims' 'crimes' lay only in the mind of their killer; their 'guilt' was decided by a man whose complex engagement with these biblical texts validated his desire to torture and kill women he considered an undesirable and abject presence. With his deeply misogynistic worldview, rooted as it was in his patriarchal and elitist social context, it is perhaps telling that he felt able to treat these Levitical laws

---

[50] By 'biblical women', I am primarily envisaging those literary female characters whom we imagine occupying the literary world of biblical Israel. However, I also keep in mind those historical women whose lives have come under the influence of the biblical traditions, and, in particular, whose life experiences have been regulated and dominated by the Levitical laws and the priestly ideologies represented therein.

[51] The extent of the control men could exercise over the bodies of women under their authority is amply demonstrated in, for example, the stories of Lot's daughters (Gen. 19.1–11), Abram's wife Sarai (Gen. 12.10–20; 20.1–18), Jepthah's daughter (Judg. 11.29–40), the Levite's wife (Judg. 19–20) and the daughters of Shiloh (Judg. 21).

[52] Phyllis Trible, 'Women in the Old Testament', in *IDBSupp*, pp. 963–6 (964).

as texts which *could* be petitioned to in order to justify hatred, intolerance and the murder of those whom he felt did not 'fit' into his psychological and socio-religious ideations.

This portrayal within the novel of women's subjection to lethal violence for their *non-consensual* involvement in imagined infractions of the Levitical laws may then invite consideration of the agency of *biblical* women in relation to the sacred laws and the potential for these laws to be used against women as an instrument of control, subjugation and violence. Like the victims of Gottfried and Martin, biblical women may likewise have had little if any political or social power to defend themselves against accusations of law breaking; like Martin's victims in particular, their marginalized status within a strongly patriarchal and misogynistic social system would have rendered them horribly vulnerable to abuses of male power. Like Lisbeth, they were essentially denied both agency and voice, existing at the mercy of those androcentric authorities – including the priestly law-making elite – who had the power to control and evaluate their behaviour, judging whether or not it was acceptable. Like *all* the victims of gender abuse within *Dragon Tattoo*, biblical women's right to sexual autonomy was also severely restricted, for they essentially had no legally cognizable right to sexual autonomy.[53] How, then, could those Levitical laws which proscribed certain female sexual behaviours and appeared to assume at least some degree of female sexual agency possibly hope to function justly? Moreover, what repercussions would they have had on the lives of those women who lived under their legislative authority?

For example, consider the law of Levictus 20.18, which prohibits a husband and wife from having sexual intercourse if the woman is experiencing any form of genital discharge. Given our discussion above, did a woman really have any *de facto* ability to deny her husband sexual access in such a scenario? If she had no legally cognizable right to sexual self-determination, what could she do, if, despite her protestations, her husband was to insist that they slept together? For, according to the law, she too would face the serious punishment of being 'cut off' from the community if she participated, however unwillingly, in this sexual act. While some scholars suggest that this law may have been liberating for women, serving to protect them against the unwanted sexual advances of their husbands during times of illness or indisposition,[54] it is difficult to consider as 'liberating' any law that proscribes certain female sexual activities on pain of death, especially when the women affected may have had limited tangible recourse to controlling those activities or preventing them from occurring.

Likewise, we might contemplate Levictus 21.9, which decrees that

---

[53] See Caroline Blyth, *The Narrative of Rape in Genesis 34: Interpreting Dinah's Silence*, Oxford: Oxford University Press, 2010, pp. 111–12.

[54] See, for example, the discussion in Richard M. Davidson, *Flame of Yahweh: Sexuality in the Old Testament*, Peabody, MA: Hendrickson, 2007, pp. 33–4.

a priest's daughter who 'profanes herself by playing the harlot' is to be 'burned with fire'. Who actually decided if a priest's daughter had 'played the harlot'? What does the term 'playing the harlot' actually mean? Going by its usage in another biblical law that deals with an errant wife and daughter (Deut. 22.21), it probably refers here to an act of illicit sexual intercourse (extra-marital or pre-marital), which was not sanctioned by the woman's father or male guardian. Does this law then not merely signify the objectification of the daughter's sexuality as a possession of her father's and thus the law's effective circumscription of her sexual agency and autonomy?[55] What if, like Sara Witt, the priest's daughter had been raped – would she still be considered 'profaned' and thus face the death penalty? What if she was falsely accused of this 'crime' – did she have any recourse to a viable legal defence? Would *her* account of events have been taken seriously, *her* voice given an attentive audience? The law does not tell us, but I am left with Lisbeth's thought ringing in my ears here, that women like her, who were considered to exist beyond the traditional margins of acceptability, had 'zero social status', and, as such, 'the words of other people weighed more heavily than hers'.[56]

These two examples thus draw attention to the fact that the Levitical laws, which attempt to regulate female sexuality, had the potential to legislate very unjustly against biblical women, acting *against* their interests, particularly in light of the biblical convention of female sexual disenfranchisement. They appear instead to grant only *more* male control over an area of women's lives where they had little if any autonomy or agency in the first place. Like the women murdered by Gottfried Vanger in *Dragon Tattoo*, biblical women surely risked being punished for crimes inflicted *against* them, rather than perpetrated *by* them. Like Lisbeth, they were trapped by those socio-legal codes and institutions which both stripped them of power and autonomy and placed them in a position where they were vulnerable to the most terrible abuses by those in whose hands power had been placed. These persistent themes of female powerlessness and vulnerability that permeate *Dragon Tattoo* can thus serve as invitations to readers to look critically at the Levitical traditions referenced therein, asking how such proscriptive laws may have been used or abused in order to cause harm to those living on the margins of society; those whose lack of legal and social agency would have rendered them easy prey to both individuals and institutions occupying positions of authority and power. Like Lisbeth, who viewed the traditional institutions of her own Swedish milieu with such suspicion and distrust because of the ways that they had repeatedly been complicit in her own abuses, perhaps we, as readers of

---

[55] Deborah L. Ellens, *Women in the Sex Texts of Leviticus and Deuteronomy: A Comparative Conceptual Analysis* (Library of Hebrew Bible/Old Testament Studies, 458), New York and London: T&T Clark, 2008, pp. 152–5.
[56] *Dragon Tattoo*, p. 228.

Dragon Tattoo are invited to turn an equally suspicious eye to those institutions and ideologies underpinning the Levitical laws referenced within the narrative, which seem to carry such potentialities of violence and abuse for those women, like Lisbeth, who exist on the margins.

Protecting the community – at the expense of the individual?

The final point I wish to make in this discussion of *Dragon Tattoo* both affirms my view that this novel can offer valuable and alternative insights into the Levitical allusions found therein and, at the same time, reflects upon a critique of the novel that has been raised by a number of its readers. As we have seen thus far, *Dragon Tattoo* overflows with images of abused and violated women, who have suffered at the hands of those in positions of power and authority. And, as discussed in the previous two sections, these images serve as effective critiques of patriarchal power systems and institutions, which can function to render abject and thus instigate violence against those who do not 'fit in' to the community's constructed boundaries of belonging. The novel's references to the Levitical texts within the context of such ubiquitous gender violence also invite this same critique on these biblical laws, gendering the laws and questioning the harmful and marginalizing effects that they may have had upon the biblical women whose lives were regulated by them.

And yet, by the time we reach the end of the novel, certain questions may be raised about the ways that the actions of our two protagonists, Mikael and Lisbeth, could serve to undermine these feminist and cultural critiques of patriarchal power structures within both the biblical texts and contemporary Swedish society. For, at the final reckoning, the novel effectively sweeps under the carpet many of the victims of violence uncovered during the course of the story. At Lisbeth's insistence, details of Gottfried's and Martin's crimes are withheld from the police and instead, Lisbeth charges the Vanger's lawyer, Dirch Frode, with the task of covertly identifying Martin's nameless victims and making some form of financial restitution to their families.[57]

However, by taking such a turn in the narrative, one could argue that *Dragon Tattoo* only ensures the continued voicelessness and marginalization of these murdered female characters, circumventing any official justice or public recognition of the wrongs perpetrated against them. Referred to only in terms of their narrative absence and their violent obliteration, these women's lives and their rights to justice are depreciated to the point of non-existence in the interests of protecting the socio-political

---

[57] Ibid., p. 514.

reputation of the Vanger family and the financial interests of the Vanger Corporation. As Stenport and Alm suggest, *Dragon Tattoo* 'endorses a pragmatic acceptance of a neoliberal world order that is delocalized, dehumanized, and misogynistic'.[58] Ultimately, in the narrative world of this novel, the interests of the dominant group appear to trump those of the individual, particularly when that individual resides at the margins of the group, an object of hatred, fear, othering, and violence.

This critique of *Dragon Tattoo* may, however, provide another valuable source of knowing in our contemplation of the Levitical laws. The victims of both Martin and Gottfried are identified within the patriarchal social world of their killers as ethnically and socially undesirable and, therefore, in need of elimination; when their murders are covered up, they are effectively eliminated from the narrative a second time, becoming 'mere bodies'[59] to be forfeited in the interests of maintaining and protecting the reputation of this same social world. We might suggest, then, that these women once again reflect the fate of those abject bodies defined by the Levitical laws; those whose behaviour, gender, or socio-sexual identity located them in the impure space outside the boundaries of the holy community, and who were therefore regarded as embodying a 'living state of worthlessness' that needed to be excised from the group as a means of protecting its inviolability.[60] As in *Dragon Tattoo*, such an act of excision occurs not once, but twice; both in the Levitical text itself and also within many of its traditions of interpretation, where the fates of those who would have fallen foul to these proscriptive laws are often overshadowed by a more rigorous focus on the righteous necessity of the law to maintain a sense of the sacred order within the Israelite community. Thus, the novel's own narrative silencing of so many unnamed victims of violence may invite us to evaluate critically the prioritization of the community over the individual in the Levitical law code too, and, in particular, to consider the oft-unspoken Levitical reality that a community's own sense of order is often constructed by those situated at its very centre and is maintained only at great cost to those located at its margins.

Conclusions

In her discussion of popular culture as a resource for biblical interpretation,

---

[58] Anna Westerståhl Stenport and Cecilia Overdotter Alm, 'Corporations, crime, and gender construction in Stieg Larson's *The Girl with the Dragon Tattoo*: Exploring twenty-first century neoliberalism in Swedish culture', *Scandinavian Studies*, 81 (2009): 157–78 (158).

[59] Morag Joss, quoted in Barry Forshaw, *The Man Who Left Too Soon: The Biography of Stieg Larsson*, London: John Blake Publishing, 2010, p. 268.

[60] Melissa Wright, *Disposable Women and Other Myths of Global Capitalism*, Boca Raton, FL: CRC Press, 2006, p. 2.

referred to at the start of this chapter, Athalya Brenner asks, 'Do we dare bring popular culture into our classrooms as exegesis, on the same level as our own belaboured efforts?'[61] During *my* own belaboured efforts writing this chapter, Brenner's question was never far from my thoughts and, on reaching this conclusion, I feel compelled to answer with a confident affirmative. If biblical scholars are serious about fostering a continued enthusiasm for the biblical traditions among fellow scholars, students and other interested readers, it is imperative that we do indeed 'dare' bring popular culture into the conversation as a new and infinitely valuable way of knowing these ancient texts. In doing so, we might stand a chance of keeping the Bible alive as the essential piece of our 'cultural luggage' that it unquestionably is. In the pages above, I hope that I have shown glimpses of the potentiality of such a conversation in action, by demonstrating some of the ways that a highly popular cultural text can act as an effective and accessible interpretative lens for the biblical material that it references. As a passionate consumer of both the Bible and popular culture, I believe that cultural texts such as *Dragon Tattoo* can serve as valuable tools to help rescue the Bible from the often inhospitable cloisters of the 'academy', keeping it instead in the public consciousness as a 'book for life'.[62]

Bibliography

Bingham, John, 'Poet Laureate Andrew Motion Calls for All Children to be Taught the Bible', *Telegraph*, 17 February 2009; www.telegraph.co.uk/education/educationnews/4678369/Poet-Laureate-Andrew-Motion-calls-for-all-children-to-be-taught-the-Bible.html [accessed 25 January 2013].

Blyth, Caroline, *The Narrative of Rape in Genesis 34: Interpreting Dinah's Silence*, Oxford: Oxford University Press, 2010.

Brenner, Athalya, 'Introduction', in George Aichele (ed.), *Culture, Entertainment and the Bible* (JSOTSup, 309), Sheffield: Sheffield Academic Press, 2000, pp. 7–12.

Burnside, Jonathan P., 'Strange flesh: Sex, semiotics and the construction of deviancy in biblical law', *JSOT* 30, 2006: 387–420.

Caputi, Susan, *Goddesses and Monsters: Women, Myth, Power, and Popular Culture*, Madison: University of Wisconsin Press, 2004.

Carruthers, Jo, 'Literature', in John F. A. Sawyer (ed.), *The Blackwell Companion to the Bible and Culture*, Oxford: Blackwell Publishing, 2006, pp. 253–67.

Connell, Raewyn W., *Masculinities*, Berkeley: University of California Press, 2005.

Copier, Laura, Jaap Kooijman and Caroline Vander Stichele, 'Close Encounters: The Bible as Pre-Text in Popular Culture', in Philip Culbertson and Elaine

---

[61] Brenner, 'Introduction', pp. 10–11.
[62] Ibid., p. 11.

Wainwright (eds), *The Bible in/and Popular Culture: A Creative Encounter* (Semeia Studies, 65), Atlanta: SBL, 2010, pp. 189–95.

Davidson, Richard M., *Flame of Yahweh: Sexuality in the Old Testament*, Peabody, MA: Hendrickson, 2007.

Ellens, Deborah L., *Women in the Sex Texts of Leviticus and Deuteronomy: A Comparative Conceptual Analysis* (Library of Hebrew Bible/Old Testament Studies, 458), New York and London: T&T Clark, 2008.

Forshaw, Barry, *The Man Who Left Too Soon: The Biography of Stieg Larsson*, London: John Blake Publishing, 2010.

Hassan, Genevieve, 'Hollywood takes on Girl with the Dragon Tattoo', BBC News Online 26 December 2011; www.bbc.co.uk/news/entertainment-arts-16110375 [accessed 30 January 2013].

Hawkins, Peter S., 'Lost and found: The Bible and its literary afterlives', *Religion and Literature*, 36 (2004): 1–14.

Hook, Misty K., 'Lisbeth Salander as a Gender Outlaw', in Robin S. Rosenberg and Shannon O'Neill (eds), *The Psychology of the Girl with the Dragon Tattoo*, Dallas: BenBella Books, 2011, pp. 47–64.

Kristeva, Julia, *Powers of Horror: An Essay on Abjection* (trans. Leon S. Roudiez), New York: Columbia University Press, 1982.

Larsson, Stieg, *The Girl with the Dragon Tattoo* (trans. Reg Keeland), New York: Vintage Crime, 2009.

Martin, Patricia Yancey, 'State Complicity in Men's Violence against Women', in Carrie Lee Smith and Donna King (eds), *Men Who Hate Women and Women Who Kick Their Asses: Stieg Larsson's Millennium Trilogy in Feminist Perspective*, Nashville, TN: Vanderbilt University Press, 2012, pp. 39–50.

Miller, J. Hillis, 'Border Crossings, Translating Theory: Ruth', in Sanford Budick and Wolfgang Iser (eds), *The Translatability of Cultures: Figurations of the Space Between*, Stanford, CA: Stanford University Press, 1996, pp. 207–23.

Millett, Kate, *Sexual Politics*, London: Virago, 1989.

Rodgers, Rachel and Eric Bui, 'The Body Speaks Louder than Words: What is Lisbeth Salander Saying?' in Robin S. Rosenberg and Shannon O'Neill (eds), *The Psychology of the Girl with the Dragon Tattoo*, Dallas: BenBella Books, 2011, pp. 29–44.

Scott, Mark S. M. and Jason Zuidema, 'Religious studies and popular fiction: What does Dan Brown have to do with the Ivory Tower?', *Journal of Religion and Popular Culture*, 23 (2011): 372–81.

Stahlberg, Lesleigh Cushing, *Sustaining Fictions: Intertextuality, Midrash, Translation, and the Literary Afterlife of the Bible*, (Library of Hebrew Bible/ Old Testament Studies, 486), New York: T&T Clark, 2008.

Stenport, Anna Westerståhl and Cecilia Oversdotter Alm, 'Corporations, crime, and gender construction in Stieg Larson's *The Girl with the Dragon Tattoo*: Exploring twenty-first century neoliberalism in Swedish culture', *Scandinavian Studies*, 81 (2009): 157–78.

Surkan, Kim, 'The Girl Who Turned the Tables: A Queer Reading of Lisbeth Salander', in Eric Bronson (ed.), *The Girl with the Dragon Tattoo and Philosophy: Everything is Fire*, Hoboken, NJ: John Wiley & Sons, 2011, pp. 33–46.

Trible, Phyllis, 'Women in the Old Testament', in *IDBSupp*, pp. 963–6.

Valentine, Catherine G., 'Tiny, Tattooed, and Tough as Nails: Representations of

Lisbeth Salander's Body', in Carrie Lee Smith and Donna King (eds), *Men Who Hate Women and Women Who Kick Their Asses: Stieg Larsson's Millennium Trilogy in Feminist Perspective*, Nashville, TN: Vanderbilt University Press, 2012, pp. 88–97.

Wachlin, Marie, *Bible Literacy Report II: What University Professors Say Incoming Students Need to Know*, Front Royal: Bible Literacy Project, 2006.

Wainwright, Elaine M., 'Introduction', in Philip Culbertson and Elaine Wainwright (eds), *The Bible in/and Popular Culture: A Creative Encounter* (Semeia Studies, 65), Atlanta: SBL, 2010, pp. 1–9.

Wright, Melissa, *Disposable Women and Other Myths of Global Capitalism*, Boca Raton: CRC Press, 2006.

9

A Big Room for Poo: Eddie Izzard's Bible and the Literacy of Laughter

Christopher Meredith
(University of Winchester)

What is the meaning of a door in the side: for he says, 'Thou shalt make a door in the side?' [Gen. 6.16]. That door in the side very plainly betokens a human building, which he has becomingly indicated by calling it, 'in the side', by which door all the excrements of dung are cast out ... the Creator, having due regard to the decency of our body, has placed the exit and passage of the different ducts of the body back out of the reach of the sense, in order that while getting rid of the fetid portions of bile, we might not be disgusted by beholding the full appearance of our excrements.

– PHILO, *QUESTIONS AND ANSWERS ON GENESIS*, ON THE ALLEGORICAL POSSIBILITIES OF THE DOOR TO NOAH'S ARK.[1]

I also take large subjects and talk crap about them.

– EDDIE IZZARD[2]

---

[1]Philo, *Questions and Answers on Genesis*, Vol. 3 (trans. Ralph Marcus), Harvard: Harvard University Press, 1961, pp. 77–8.
[2]Eddie Izzard and David Quantick, *Eddie Izzard: Dress to Kill* (2nd edn), London: Virgin Books, 2000 [1998], p. 127.

The first thing that strikes you about 'Glorious', Eddie Izzard's 1997 stand-up tour, is the set. No barstool or cold, solitary spotlight for Izzard. The stage is instead filled with the magnificent wreck of a temple. Corinthian columns crumble into the wings. Faux marble struts bleach under the fresnels. Most of the height of the proscenium is taken up with a ruined basilica roof, a huge broken circle so fractured and skeletal that at first glance one could mistake it for a naked stained glass window.[3] The rents in this dome open out on to deep space, where an enormous apocalyptic sun threatens to engulf the whole structure. Izzard himself – in charming black Cuban heels and a shimmering magenta trouser suit – capers about in the rubble. This is where he chooses to stage his hilarity: at the death of the stable edifice, in the ruins of the ritual sphere. The overall effect is, well, glorious.

For anyone familiar with the tenor of Izzard's performances this shattered and imposing stage space makes an awful lot of sense. Izzard's comedy is larger than life, and his style eschews the fixed or the stable or the orthodox. His routines are always already fractured, sallying forth as flows of ideas, as whimsical meanderings of fantasy interspersed with mimed skits and surreal thought experiments. Rarely scripted (due in part to his dyslexia and in part to his suspicion of the formality of writing),[4] Izzard's comedy is defined by the room he leaves for breaks in proceedings. That is to say, while Izzard's tours are always focused (they are not simply rants), his idiosyncratic additions flow from and then back into his to his pre-prepared material, adding endless variety to a carefully structured routine.[5] As an opening gambit, then, one could make the point that Izzard's comedic praxis very much resembles his 1997 staging. Izzard's delivery shatters the usual fixity of performance, or at least obviates it. The Traditional Joke (capital T, J), in all its formulaic and pseudo-liturgical glory, is subjected to an apocalypse.[6] Izzard capers about in its rubble.

---

[3] Watching and re-watching the footage, I wonder if the stage is designed to make the audience feel as though they are looking directly upwards into the roof of a cathedral. If so, Izzard is in fact imagined to be hovering between the heavens and the earth, like Muhammad's coffin, or like a transvestite Jesus in mid-ascension – or, for that matter, in the middle of his final return.
[4] Izzard and Quantick, *Dress to Kill*, pp. 117, 135.
[5] This aspect of Izzard's work makes quoting him quite difficult, since there is no definitive version of his routines; the official DVD of *Glorious* (Peter Richardson [director], Universal Pictures, released 2004) and the downloadable audio recordings (Ella Communications 1997, released 2003) are clearly different renditions of the act. (Indeed, given the editing, I suspect the audio version is a composite from several live shows rather than the recording of one particular night's antics on stage.) The particular qualities of individual performances seem to govern the published format of the material. Izzard's DVD set uses much more physical; that is, visual, comedy, for example, while in the performances recorded for audio, Izzard seems to *explain* what he is doing far more. For the sake of consistency, and to best showcase what Izzard is talking about, I exclusively quote the audio recordings in this example, downloaded from iTunes in 2005.
[6] Izzard has, in fact, said that if he scripts material he feels like he is simply saying religious prayers; Izzard, *Chain Reaction*, interview with Frank Skinner, first broadcast BBC Radio 3, Wednesday 16 September 2009.

What makes 'Glorious' especially interesting, particularly with this theme of undermined orthodoxy in mind, is the character of the material itself. For while 'Glorious' deals with a range of subjects both ancient and modern (toasters, Helen of Troy, the Swiss Guard, hopscotch), the whole routine is structured around the biblical canon. Izzard's first act uses the Old Testament ('a big fuck-off beard testament') as its comedic spring-board, especially the creation story of Genesis 1–3 and the flood narrative of Genesis 6–9. The second act begins with the New Testament and an account of the birth of Jesus (and the ensuing nativity play that the wise men – who are visiting from the Old Testament – put on for 'baby Jee'). *Glorious* continues with a look at the gospels, the figure of biblical Peter, and the traditions of the Roman Church. Even at the end of the set, when he is brought back on stage to rapturous applause to deliver more, Izzard continues the pattern with a look at the book of Revelation and the trope of Armageddon.[7] Structurally, the show is a Bible transposed into comedy format: Old Testament in the first act, New Testament after intermission and apocalypse as encore.

Izzard's staging of a laughed-at Bible in the rubble of a dying monolith is designed to say something quite explicit about both the Bible and the claims made by religious spaces. But before we even get as far as Izzard's specific treatment of the biblical texts,[8] this basic fact – the structuring of a comedy routine around the Bible – raises some general issues about biblical literacy that we would do well to think about first. After all, according to some scholarly senses of biblical literacy, basing a stand-up act on the Bible would seem to be ill advised. Who is going to get the joke?

Biblical illiteracy: A strange love, or, how I learned to stop worrying …

Biblical literacy is in decline apparently. And in some quarters this fact seems, at times, to represent nothing less than the end of the world as we know it.[9] The problem in the UK was diagnosed by the CBLC, the

---

[7] Begun with those immortal words: 'Armageddon, which is short for Arm-a-geddin-outta-here. It's an Australian saying'.

[8] Incidentally, this religious preoccupation goes beyond this particular routine of Izzard's into other, subsequent tours as well, so we should not be tempted to see the biblical tropes at work in 'Glorious' as an isolated phenomenon.

[9] Numerous news outlets, for example, have decried the so-called decline in biblical knowledge amongst the general public. The following is intended as a representative sample: BBC News. Presbyterian Church (USA). 'Newly Revised Study Encourages Congregation-wide Reading of Bible in its Entirety as Bible Literacy in U.S. Sees Steep Decline', 24 August 2011; 'Declining Biblical Literacy', *Sowhatfaith.com*, 22 January 2012; Hardiman, Clayton, 'Bible Literacy Slipping, Experts Say' *Religious News Service / Associated Press*, 5 October 2009; 'Knowledge

University of Durham's Centre for Biblical Literacy and Communication, based at St John's College, in a national survey undertaken in 2008.[10] The results are summed up in a fairly succinct lament of Philip Davies's, published in *Bible and Interpretation*:

> [A]s few as 10 per cent of people understood the main characters in the Bible and their relevance. Figures such as Abraham and Joseph were unknown; hardly anyone could name even a few of the Ten Commandments. Some 60 per cent were ignorant of the story of the Good Samaritan, and of these not all knew the full story. This despite 60% of those surveyed being in favor of the Church![11]

Hector Avalos, in another article for *Bible and Interpretation*, seems to agree with Davies and CBLC that biblical literacy is poor. Though in his article Avalos is anxious to stress that biblical illiteracy is not a recent phenomenon.[12] Various interested parties have been decrying falling standards in biblical literacy since at least the 1700s, he says, if not for centuries before that. Avalos suggests that the neglected Bible might therefore only exist as part of the self-interested rhetoric of the professorial class, who, having constructed the Bible as a cultural commodity, need to sell it on. In other words, Avalos's (admittedly) brief survey of a long and illustrious history of biblical ignorance indicates that the current concern about biblical literacy may be no more than a storm in a regius professor's teacup. But for Avalos a more important, and attractive, idea is the notion that biblical illiteracy might force the Bible to learn its place. Today, argues Avalos, Moses and Isaiah and Noah must compete 'in a highly diversified global textual market' alongside 'Homer and Pindar and Horace'. The Bible is not a special case, he says, and should not be treated as one. The issue of biblical illiteracy should not be considered a calamity, then, precisely because Biblical scholars must now be content with a smaller piece of what Avalos terms the 'global textual pie'.

There is something of a contradiction amongst Avalos's diminutive tea things, however. Avalos grounds the idea that the Bible must adopt a more modest position in a global textual economy on the sea change that declining biblical literacy represents. Yet he simultaneously argues that biblical

---

of Bible "in Decline"', *BBC*, 12 July 2009. An excellent treatment of these was given in a paper by Iona Hine, 'The Quest for Biblical Literacy: Curricula, Culture and Case Studies', at the Department of Biblical Studies' research seminar, Sheffield University, 5 November 2012. See also her companion article, 'Practicing Biblical Literacy: Case studies from the Sheffield Conference', in *Postscripts: The Journal of Sacred and Contemporary Worlds* (Special Issue: Biblical Literacy & the Curriculum, 2013).

[10] For details see CBLC, *The National Biblical Literacy Survey*, Briefing Sheet #2.
[11] Philip Davies, 'Whose Bible? Anyone's?', *Bible and Interpretation*, July 2009.
[12] Hector Avalos, 'In Praise of Biblical Illiteracy', *Bible and Interpretation*, April 2010.

illiteracy has been exaggerated, or else is nothing new. But either the current situation is socially unremarkable or it represents a profound literary shift of which we must take note. The situation cannot be both. We cannot have our cake, or even our tiny slice of global pie, and eat it. It seems to me that if standards of biblical literacy have long been decried the implication is not that the Bible – that most pervasive and enduring of texts – has always been teetering on the brink of extinction, but rather that the Bible has always been better understood than the loudest and most interested voices would wish everybody else to believe. What is most exercising about Avalos's article is not the claim that the Bible has always been under-read, but the indication *that there have always been people ready to make the accusation that it is being under-read.* If that is so, the current concern for biblical literacy could be tentatively refigured. Allegations of biblical ignorance might not necessarily represent a timely warning about the dangers facing the Bible in the digital age (pitted as it now is against those other über-modern texts: Homer and Pindar!) Instead, we might well consider the fuss over biblical illiteracy to form part of the intellectual class's legitimizing of certain forms of cultural interaction at the expense of other forms.

We could take the CBLC report as an example. When it comes to media, televisual or staged biblical stories, the results are not nearly as depressing as Davies indicates. Fifty-one per cent of respondents said they had seen the blockbuster films such as *Jesus of Nazareth*; 50 per cent said they had seen *The Ten Commandments*; 48 per cent said they had seen either the film or TV versions of *Joseph and his Amazing Technicolor Dream Coat*; 41 per cent had seen *Jesus Christ Superstar*.[13] Despite these quite remarkable ratings the report goes on to demote their significance: 'input from films or TV shows, recorded or live, will tend to provide a one-off, particular input

---

[13] One of the main points in the report that might counter my optimistic reading of the data here is the fact that those people who had seen biblically themed stage shows or television programmes were unable to quote after the fact bits of biblical text that related to these performances. The report uses this point to suggest that encounters with the bible-as-media do not improve biblical literacy on the whole. But it is worth pointing out that this view represents a peculiarly narrow – one might even say backwards – view of biblical literacy in which people are only 'biblically literate' if they can convert biblical references in culture *back* into an abstract theology of chapter and verse. The idea of biblical knowledge enhancing the on-the-spot engagement with a particular cultural product is not valued at all by the report's format. This, surely, ignores one crucial facet of biblical literacy: the ability to see biblical allusions (and the tropes and themes such allusions suggest) within a wide range of extra-canonical literature: when reading poetry, say, or looking at art. One might ask why the ability – and willingness – to quote the Bible at will (and entirely stripped of context) is controlling what counts as legitimate knowledge. To spot biblical allusions in Milton, for example, one does not need to be able to proffer a host of biblical texts unaided, one needs merely to have enough knowledge to respond to particular triggers in the poetry. Not only does the CBLC survey make no attempt to measure these kinds of responses to the biblical literatures at work in Western culture, it actively obscures them, I would suggest, by privileging in its format a certain kind of social and intellectual relationship with the Bible that relies on quiet reflective reading (and regular Sunday morning testing?).

rather than a regular intake of Biblical knowledge'.[14] There are two issues here. First is the rather medical tenor of these comments (do we need a 'regular intake' of Shakespeare? Five sonnets a day?). Second, one cannot help but infer the report's authors intend regular Bible *reading* to be the preferred nostrum for the – what they call 'perilous' – malady of biblical illiteracy.[15] Tellingly, the CBLC are reluctant to endorse 'making the Bible another resource to go to when we decide to watch some entertainment or to Google an answer to a problem'.[16] The Bible is not the Bible when it is entertaining, it seems. Media biblical engagement has the disadvantage, the CBLC goes on to say, of 'disengaging the reader from the text itself'.[17] But why does biblical literacy necessarily equate to the artefact of the Bible? Biblical literacy is about stories, not devotional praxis. It is the supremacy of the Bible's *textuality* in society that seems to be at stake in the CBLC's report, rather than the Bible's value or importance as a cultural driving force, and that seems to affect the way the results have been interpreted. Non-textual bibles are downplayed. As not-written and not-read, they are not counted.

The nature of comedy makes the efficacy of biblical jokes quite perilous in this supposed world of biblical illiteracy, since jokes rely on a particular structural symbiosis between performer and audience. As John Limon points out in his seminal theorizing of stand-up as a literary form, *Stand-up Comedy in Theory*, jokes are peculiarly dependent on audiences' knowledge for their value. All communicative media require an audience to activate them, of course: the billboard, the written text, the stage-play. But, as Limon observes, 'because it is plausible to assert that an audience is wrong about, say, an opera (critics will judge) or a novel (posterity will judge), opera and literature can stake claims to seriousness. To be serious is to despise the audience – to reserve the right of appeal to a higher jurisdiction'.[18] When we come to a stand-up audience, however, laughter is everything. The audience's claiming (or disavowal) of a joke through laughter (or deathly silence) is the only claim the routine can really make on meaning. Audiences are not entirely distinct from comics or their gags, then, since audiences must turn a stand-up's jokes into jokes.[19] As Freud noted, an un-conveyed joke is not, structurally speaking, a joke at all.[20] In order to turn a joke into a joke, the audience must actively engage with

---

[14] CBLC, *The National Biblical Literacy Survey*, pp. 4–5.

[15] Ibid., p. 6.

[16] Ibid., p. 5.

[17] Ibid., pp. 4–5.

[18] John Limon, *Stand-up Comedy in Theory, or, Abjection in America*, Durham: Duke University Press, 2000, p. 12.

[19] Izzard, in fact, sees himself as the 'audience's representative on stage' (Izzard and Quantick, *Dress to Kill*, p. 40).

[20] Sigmund Freud, *The Standard Edition of the Complete Psychological Works of Sigmund Freud* (trans. James Strachey), London: Hogarth Press, 1953–74, p. 431; Limon, *Stand-up Comedy in Theory*, p. 12.

the structure and content of what the comic presents them. Comics, jokes and audiences are not distinct entities but form a kind of performative continuum, where understanding (read: literacy) is the only social currency that matters. Or, as Limon, puts it for us, 'stand-up is all supplement'.[21]

For example, when encountering a mention of Daniel in the lions' den in popular song lyrics – as in Coldplay's 2011 track 'Us Against the World' – one could easily let the biblical reference in the lyric pass by without so much as a thought about the gilt-edged or the leather-bound. Coldplay's song does not cease to function if the audience is untutored in the various plights of biblical Daniel. But when Izzard, in the second act of 'Glorious', refers to God's building of the human body and names the three little bones of the inner ear Shadrach, Meshach and Abednego, he is relying on his audience having a more intimate connection with their copy of Daniel than Coldplay's has with theirs. Without this connection, without a sense of the three names as a cultural unit, and without the sense of Izzard's surreal co-option of them here, the phrase would be daft (very mildly amusing) but not especially funny. But Shadrach, Meshach and Abednego get a laugh – for a full two seconds (which as anyone who has ever stood on a stage will tell you is very respectable).[22] Naturally, it is not possible to argue that each tittering member of Izzard's audience could have given us chapter and verse, but I am not sure the kind of biblical literacy that is often pined for necessarily involves those kinds of rigours anyway (and, if it does, biblical scholars are perhaps being unrealistic when they hope for its proliferation).[23] Needless to say, clipboard-wielding surveyors from the CBLC found the general public less forthcoming about the book of Daniel.[24] Is it possible that analysis of cultural engagement might work as a more effective measure of reading biblical literacy? Izzard's stint at the Hammersmith Apollo drew biblical *recognition* out of the crowd, certainly, so reactionary and contextual responses seem worth exploration.

Izzard's 'Glorious', with its canonical preoccupations, perhaps offers a counterpoint to the notion long whispered about in the tweedy halls of biblical academe that biblical literacy is in general decline. If no one knows the biblical texts, building an entire comedy routine around them and then touring it all around the world would seem to be a rather risky business.

---

[21] Limon, *Stand-up Comedy in Theory*, p. 12.

[22] Limon, indeed, points out that 'two seconds of laughter is respectable; four seconds greets the best joke of a standard *Tonight Show* monologue' – a sobering pair of statistics (ibid., p. 16).

[23] Limon's focus on the audience is methodologically crucial in assessing Izzard's Daniel joke: an individual in the stalls, carried along by the moment, can laugh along with everyone else without necessarily understanding a joke (indeed there is focused research on this phenomenon), but this cannot be asserted for an audience as a whole. It is only audiences, not individuals, that can be analysed as part of stand-up, see ibid., p. 12.

[24] '[W]ith regards to the Old Testament ... 85% could say nothing correct about Daniel in the Lions [sic] Den', *The National Biblical Literacy Survey*, p. 6.

But not only was the biblically preoccupied 'Glorious' a popular and critical hit, the show reached a record-breaking audience. After playing at New York's PS122 for a month, and after a mini-tour of London which saw Izzard play to 56,000 people in four weeks, and after a 27-date UK tour, Izzard added an extra night at the London Arena. There, on December 21, 1997, he played to the largest comedy audience ever convened in the UK at that time.[25] Suffice it to say, everyone seemed to be getting the joke.

In a sense, then, I do not feel an urgent need to make a case for popular, if latent, biblical literacy based on mainstream comedy routines. Laughter at biblical jokes, their ongoing use, re-use and variation, and the vast ticket revenues such texts secure for artists, make that case all on their own. And they do so more spectacularly than I could hope to.[26] Instead, what I want to argue in the rest of this chapter is that comedy-going society is *so* familiar with biblical texts and, moreover, so subconsciously suspicious of this familiarity, that it needs strategies to cope with the disquiet that its own biblical literacy produces within itself. Laughter is, I suggest, one of those strategies. I want to make the case that the biblical texts are not rejected objects in the so-called post-Christendom, so-called 'secular' Western world. Rather, they are sites of social abjection. The abject (a subject to which we shall devote much more attention in due course) is a term Julia Kristeva makes use of to describe those aspects of social life that we are bound into, but which threaten or otherwise impinge upon our identity: shit, spoilt food, dead bodies. In the late twentieth/early twenty-first century, the Bible is the corpus/corpse that audiences like Izzard's are unequally yoked to. The Bible is the recognizable cultural necessity that modern, mainstream society would rather forget about but is irredeemably attached to. The Bible acts within Izzard's routine, then, as a site where association and disassociation meet, as a site of power without authority where claims to meaning break down. This disquiet is part of what makes the Bible funny.[27]

---

[25] http://www.eddieizzard.com/eddie/stand-up/view.php?Id=9 [accessed 20 November 2012].

[26] Izzard, for example, uses Biblical tropes in a number of his tours: *Unrepeatable, Dress to Kill, Circle, The Definite Article, Stripped* (the last of which involves Izzard in front of ten stone tablets with various sacred texts printed on them). Woody Allen and Bill Cosby are perhaps the best known 'traditional' examples of biblical exegesis as comedy, though other additions are being made to the biblical comedy canon all the time – Ricky Gervais's *Animals*, for example, in which Gervais speaks from a pulpit, reading from a Bible as he works through the flood narrative.

[27] That said, pinning down the nature of 'funny' is not especially easy. Recent theorists are at pains to point out the troublesome nature of comedy as a critical concept. For whatever comedy is, its most striking feature is a certain resistance to closed definitions. As Andrew Horton points out, 'like language, and like "texts" in general, the comic is plural, unfinalized, disseminative, dependent on *context* and the intertextuality of creator, text and contemplator' (Andrew Horton, *Comedy/Cinema/Theory*, Berkeley: University of California, 1991, p. 9). Thus we come back to the sentiment of Limon I have already alluded to, that 'the particularities of the relationship of joke teller and audience do not make the joke *seem* more or less funny, they make the joke more or less funny' (*Stand-up Comedy in Theory*, p. 12). But the

In his *Stand-up Comedy in Theory,* Limon analyses American stand-up along these lines. 'A theory of stand-up is a theory of what to do with your abjection'. Of particular relevance is a chapter of Limon's entitled 'Inrage: A Lenny Bruce Joke and the Topography of Stand-up', which assesses the excremental character of a particular Lenny Bruce routine, arguing that the way in which Bruce subverts symbolic (and federal) laws in his comedy is suggestive of the ways in which stand-up works more widely as a cultural operator:

> what is stood up in stand-up comedy is abjection ... [t]o 'stand up' abjection is simultaneously to erect it and miss one's date with it: comedy is a way of avowing and disavowing abjection, as fetishism is a way of avowing and disavowing castration. Fetishism is a way of standing up

---

instability of comic meaning can illuminate as much about the nature of comedy as it obscures. Kirby Olson argues, for instance, that the very problem of defining comedy is a central part of its make-up. 'Comedy is precisely *a certain freedom of definition*' (Kirby Olson), *Comedy After Postmodernism: Rereading Comedy from Edward Lear to Charles Willeford,* Texas: Texas University Press, 2001, p. 6, original emphasis; also see discussions in Andrew Stott, *Comedy,* London: Routledge, 2005, p. 8; Henri Bergson, 'Laughter: An Essay on the Meaning of the Comic', in Wylie Cypher (ed.), *Comedy,* London: Johns Hopkins University Press, 1980, pp. 59–190. The joke is, in other words, a resistance of norm, of set forms, of Symbolic Law. It is always and inevitably a subversion of boundaries. It is not, I think, mere coincidence that in sketching comedy as a violator of social codes, Olson uses the language of dogma to make the point: 'Comedy is an immanent form that does not make us look into the heavens or to God for answers to questions ... Comic theory traces a larger discourse over politics of the body and, within that discourse, between orthodoxy and heresy' (Olson, *Comedy After Postmodernism,* p. 5). Comedy does not look for transcendent answers so much as invoke sacrilege within present realities.

This particular way of understanding comedy – as a pleasing suspension, or displacement, of social law – is, famously, how Mary Douglas frames the term. Douglas argues that jokes emerge from within a social framework against a dominant social order to 'explore alternative social formulations' and to draw attention to lack in the 'realist structurings of experience' (Mary Douglas, *Implicit Meanings: Selected Essays in Anthropology* [2nd edn], New York: Taylor and Francis, 2002/1975, p.108); see also Stott, *Comedy,* p. 11). The joker's role is thus to introduce a different perspective on social consciousness, securing themselves a certain social immunity or liminality: 'The joker's own immunity can be derived philosophically from his apparent access to other reality than that mediated by the relevant structure. Such access is implied in the contrast of forms in which he deals. His jokes expose the inadequacy of realist structurings of experience and so release the pent-up power of the imagination' (Douglas, *Implicit Meanings,* p. 108). Though Freud's sense of the comedic was very different, this sense of the joke as a mechanism that uncovers the shadow side of a particular social formation links Douglas to Freud, at least insofar as they both conceive of jokes as a kind of excremental transaction, a formulation that vents the disguised, repressed possibilities (for Freud, either sexual or aggressive) that societal norms do not leave room for (Freud, *The Standard Edition of the Complete Psychological Works of Sigmund Freud,* pp. 96–8). It is this sense of comedy – triangulated between Douglas, Limon and Freud – that informs my own approach in this piece.

the inevitability of loss: stand-up is a way of standing up the inevitability of return.[28]

As will become clear, my argument is, in a sense, a re-deployment of Limon's approach for Izzard's routine. It seems to me that Izzard, set unharmed in the midst of an apocalypse and with material designed to highlight the inadequacy of religious narrative, is perhaps as archetypal a comic as Douglas and Freud and Limon could ever hope to find: immune and liminal, his excremental jokes expose the inadequacy of a biblical structuring of the universe and in so doing attempt to stand up the inevitability of the return of those narratives. Thus does the Bible provide a centre for the abject quality of Izzard's stand-up form; this abjection, moreover, goes some way to explicating a certain set of contemporary attitudes towards biblical texts.

With all this in mind, I am especially interested in Izzard's rendition of the flood myth of Genesis 6–9, which forms the centrepiece of *Glorious*'s treatment of the Old Testament.

Genesis, with shpeedboats

Izzard's version of Noah's ark follows on directly from his retelling of the creation story of Genesis 1–3. There, Izzard explains that cosmic imperfections (a staple of aetiological myths, even funny ones) are the direct result of God's poor scheduling; in setting himself only seven days to create the cosmos, God finds himself running out of time as the Sabbath deadline looms. This in turn leads to seventh-day cock-ups, parts of the world that are built at the last minute and so not very expertly: Rwanda, the Tower of Pisa, toilets at French camping sites, English football hooligans' sense of humanity, Mrs Thatcher's heart. For Izzard the flood story is, by implication, God's answer to a downward spiral that he himself affected through shoddy workmanship. The flood is, says Izzard, 'the etch-a-sketch end of the world' – God's erasing of his doodle to start again.

The first portion of Izzard's flood, transcribed below, very roughly equates to Genesis 6.9–21 where God determines to destroy the earth with water and to save a representative sample of all the animals, along with Noah and his family, in an ark made to divine specifications. Despite its brevity – this section takes a little under 57 seconds to deliver in real-time – there is quite a lot of ideological complexity going on in the material. Indeed, compressing ideas in such a way that the audience must unpack them for itself is, I would suggest, part of a joke's very form: ingenuity expressed with economy. So, let us begin delving into the density of the section by asking why the routine is funny, or, more specifically, why it

---

[28] Limon, *Stand-up Comedy in Theory*, pp. 4–5.

might have succeeded as humour in its original context. In the following sketch Izzard plays all the characters (each with a different accent to help the audience follow the breakneck pace).[29] And, of course, as is the case in all Izzard's shows, God is James Mason:

> [James Mason]: I will send a flood to wipe out all the bad things. I will save two of everything but everything else goes. And there'll be a lot of umbrellas. You! Noah, stop what you're doing and build me an ark!
> [As Izzard]: And Noah, who was Sean Connery, was [laughter] ...
> [Noah Connery]: I'm working on a shpeedboat at the moment, er [Laughs. mimes sawing], shpeedboat's much farshter, it'll shoot acrosh the water a lot farshter [laugh]. It'll be great photosh for the Bible [big laugh, some applause].
> [James Mason]: No, I appreciate your sense of publicity but er, [pause to allow laughter], I want an ark, with a big room for poo – it's going to be important [big laugh].

The humour here is centred on a series of incongruities. If we look at the 'dialogue', laughter punctuates it pretty much exclusively at its moments of mismatch and anachronism: turning the ancient text *par excellence* into a movie with twentieth-century film stars; Noah Connery's purring speedboat standing in for the ark. The notion of biblical photos gets an enormous laugh, combining as it does primordiality with all the foregoing cinematography to affect a striking contrast. In this last instance, though, the joke is not simply the incongruence of having photos in the primordial age, but of Noah Connery's knowing appeals to a Bible that doubles as a publicity exercise, and the frightening corollary of that thought, that the biblical God is only in the Armageddon business because of the potential for banner headlines. We laugh because the sacred story has been profaned by PR shots, and by a kind of Hollywood sensibility, with its star studded billings, its pap snaps and its status symbols. The strange infiltrations of modern life into the primordial myth are fine examples of that age-old observation on the essential structure of humour, namely that humour relies on one authoritative system being subverted by another less austere one; 'one accepted pattern is confronted by something else', as Mary Douglas puts it.[30] Izzard's sacred text is a Genesis colonized by *Grazia*. That is part of its charm.

So, the structure of Izzard's comedy here is an example of the type of subversive paradigm switching that so much humour is based on, and his

---

[29] Hence its resemblance in transcription to a stage script, which, given the filmic qualities of this particular telling of Genesis 6, is the most fitting format I could find.

[30] Mary Douglas, *Implicit Meanings*, pp. 149–50.

Bible speaks back to the structure of the stage: an austere religious edifice that crumbles in the company of laughter. The following part of the section is oddly paradigmatic in another way. If, for Freud, the joke is always a sexual/excremental transaction,[31] Izzard's shit-centred ark is a particularly poignant offering in that it is a joke that is quite explicitly excremental, and which quite explicitly reverses expectations: the poo room is going to be important.

A big room for poo

The ark's midden is more complicated a symbol than one might expect. First, inherent in the joke is the same kind of incongruity and mismatch that characterizes the humour in the rest of the section: the divine being talks about shit in the most childish of terms, enacting a classic reversal of expectations. Excrement is raised up to the level of a divine concern, and the divine voice condescends to the level of excrement. Moreover, Yahweh talks here not as an adult but as a child.[32] This room is not a politely designated 'toilette', or a washroom, or a more vulgar 'shit-space'. Rather, it is rendered in kiddiewink words; this is 'a big room for poo'.

But the issue of poo in the ark gets a bigger laugh than other parts of this section because the shit subverts the biblical narrative itself. The mention of the ark's poo-room – the only specification of the ark given by Izzard's God, which in *Glorious* takes the place of the lengthy list of cubits in Genesis 6 – calls attention to a fundamental problem implied by (but not voiced by) the biblical narrative. Noah is told to take food with him into the ark (6.21) but there is no account of any of the other practicalities of living aboard ship. Where did Noah, his extended family, and a menagerie of global proportions excrete while shut up in the ark for months on end? Where did they keep it all? Did they dispose of it? How? The question of the urine, and its noxious gases, is even more troubling.

Working within the parameters of the mythology in Genesis 6–8, the biblical Noah – enclosed in a 450 cubits-cubed box of gopher wood (6.14–15) – does not have many options. The door is not a possibility, shut as it is from the outside by Yahweh himself in 7.16 and not touched for a year and ten days until the water subsides (7.11, 8.14). There is a window in the ark, but that is made explicitly to let daylight in (6.16) rather than anything out.[33] Even by biblical mythology's loose narrative standards, this

---

[31] Freud, *The Standard Edition of the Complete Psychological Works of Sigmund Freud*, pp. 96–8; Limon, *Stand-up Comedy in Theory*, p. 14. See discussion above at n. 27.

[32] God is infantilized in most of the early parts of the routine, in fact: ordered about by his clarinet teacher, engrossed in comics in bed, and, here, with his creative prowess compared to a child with an Etch-a-sketch.

[33] Indeed, this aperture in v. 16 is dependant on one's reading of the Hebrew, though the later

aperture is probably not viable as a garbage chute, since Noah appears to be unable to look through the window (8.6–12), let alone able to shovel shit through it. Admittedly, he is able to get a hand out of this opening in 8.9 to pull a bird in, but, again, an opening at arm's length does not necessarily make for a viable toilette of the kind required by a mobile zoo. Noah's excrement, and that of the whole animal kingdom, was shut in with them.[34]

Importantly, and going some way to vindicate Izzard's highlighting of Noah's predicament in the biblical text, older commentators have been similarly bemused (and preoccupied) by the problem of excrement in the ark.[35] In his second homily, for example, Origen maps out the precise functions of each of the Ark's decks, giving over the entire lower portion of the ark to excrements so that 'neither the animals themselves, nor especially the men be plagued by the stench of excrement'. It is perhaps due to the problems of space implied by this particular 'solution' to the issue that Origen, in the Greek text of his second homily, argues that the ark was pyramid-shaped; much more room.[36] By far the most elaborate attempt to map the ark's practicalities came from Alfonso Tostado in the fifteenth century, who posited a complex plumbing system to solve the problem of waste, a 'vent in the habitation of the tame animals and another in that of the wild animals through which dung was conveyed to the sentina'.[37]

In invoking the 'big room for poo', Izzard's retelling raises exactly these same problems. Though, for obvious reasons, he is less interested in creating ingenious ways of letting the text off the hook. Izzard subverts the stability of the biblical paradigm once again, not by imposing anachronism this time but by throwing light on the unsustainable details implied by the narrative itself. It is the tainting of the story with its own mundane implications that creates humour. And, of course, the fact that a grand, famous, religiously significant story is being undermined by the most everyday and

---

details of the story (Noah's antics with the raven and the dove in Ch. 8) rather presume one, regardless of whether or not we slot one into the roof in 6.16.

[34] Noah must, after all, send birds out of this window if he is to discover whether or not the water has receded (8.6–12), and must 'remove the covering' of the ark in 8.13 when, for the first time in the text, he takes a look out of the ark himself.

[35] Unsurprisingly, the comic dimensions of the flood narrative have been explored before. I have mentioned that other comedians use biblical texts already, but comedic accounts in novels abound too – Timothy Findley's, *Not Wanted on the Voyage* (New York: Delacorte Press, 1984), for example, and Jeanette Winterson's *Boating for Beginners* (London: Methuen, 1985). Biblical scholars, as ever, are not far behind; Harold Bloom, Leslie Brisman and, most notably, William Whedbee, all assess the humorous potential of the original text from a scholarly standpoint; David Rosenberg and Harold Bloom, *The Book of J*, New York: Grove Weidenfeld, 1990; Leslie Brisman, *The Voice of Jacob: On the Composition of Genesis*, Bloomington: Indiana University Press, 1990; J. William Whedbee, *The Bible and the Comic Vision*, Minneapolis: Fortress Press, 2002/1998, pp. 49–53.

[36] Origen, *Homilies on Genesis and Exodus* (trans. Ronald E. Heine), Washington: CUA Press, pp. 72–3.

[37] Alfonso Tostado,

puerile of concerns accentuates the effect. Izzard himself says that this
technique underwrites his approach to certain key subjects, namely the
serious, grand or sacred: 'I also take large subjects and talk crap about them
... and then you go on and on and on, giving more and more details about
something that's obviously bullshit. It is better if the idea can resonate ...
Jesus in flipflops was one'.[38] What is funny in Izzard's presentation of the
flood, then, is the idea that Noah, in film star guise, has to live with his
own excrement (and the faeces of quite a lot of other birds, beasts and
insects), unable to get rid of it. What is also at stake here, though, is the
unworkable nature of the story, the fact that the myth implies, or really
demands, a series of everyday details that it cannot sustain. The failure of
the text is comic.

Thus Noah's problem becomes a problem for the biblical narrative itself.
The story as a coherent entity is subverted by its own necessary details,
its indigestible remainders, which it houses within itself and which it can
neither properly assimilate nor entirely reject. Noah must take food on
board with him (6.21), and must live in close quarters with his menagerie
for the duration of the flood. Thus, all the creatures, the extended human
family included, were presumably contributing to a mounting pile of shit. If
Noah has to live with these crappy details the story too, in Izzard's hands,
is subjected to that same set of concerns; forced, that is, into contact with
its own problematic remainders – the bits and pieces that the biblical corpus
cannot ingest. The big room for poo can be made to serve as a synecdoche
for all the unworkable implications that the story implies but which it
cannot assimilate.

After all, this sense of the inescapable waste is not simply limited to
the ark's midden. The idea of the problematic remainder becomes the
controlling theme in the second part of the skit.

> [Izzard]: So he built a whole ark and then he went around the world
>   getting animals, two of everything.
> [Noah Connery]: Right, two ducks ...
> [Izzard]: Ducks going ...
> [Ducks]: We're not coming!
> [Noah Connery]: Well there'sh going to be a huge fuck-off fludd.
> [Ducks]: So!? [Laugh] What's the big problem? We normally swim
>   here; we're going to swim up here [laugh]. What is the big problem?
>   What is all this kerfuffle about?
> [Izzard]: There is a huge hole in the whole flood theory, 'cos it was to
>   wipe out all the animals, you know, I mean there's no point getting
>   two of everything and getting two ducks and then there's loads of
>   ducks swimming around ...

---

[38] Quantick and Izzard, *Dress to Kill*, p. 127.

[Other Ducks]: What are you two up there for? [Big laugh, with
    applause.] What are you doing in that bloody ark?
[Noah's Ducks]: Well, we ... we're special. Errm. I don't know, why are
    we here? Look, Noah ...
[Noah Connery] What'sh the problem?
[Noah's Ducks]: There's a fuck of a lot of ducks here. God?
[James Mason]: Err, yes? [Takes long loud drag of a spliff/cigarette;
    sound of inhalation.] Sorry, I was ... [big laugh], it's my week off.
    Oh, I forgot about ducks. Oh Shit. There's going to be a lot of
    evil ...

Izzard finishes the sentence for him, their voices having now merged
anyway: 'all the evil ducks! There must be a tonne of evil ducks! Ducks
should rule the world now, shouldn't they!? And evil geese and evil swans
[sinister voice, low register]: Quack. Quack. Quack'. Izzard breaks here
into a treatise on the ontological problems of having evil animals; animals,
that is, who need to be wiped out by a corrective flood. How, he asks, can
you have an evil herbivore?

   Izzard's use of fowl in this section seems intended as a knowing counterpoint to the other, more famous, birds of the biblical flood narrative: the
raven and the dove, who each go out from the ark in search of dry land
at the end of ordeal.[39] The raven leaves the ark looking for land and never
returns, while the dove returns to Noah with an olive branch in its beak,
so signalling the receding of the waters (8.11). Here Izzard introduces of a
third bird, the ungainly duck, who would have had no such problems with
the water in the first place. The duck is designed to throw up the issue,
first, of how unconvincing an apocalypse a flood would be from certain
perspectives, and, second, the curious matter of God including animals in
his ethically driven mission for purity on the earth at all.[40] Incidentally, this
last direct criticism of the text, 'what are you two up there for?', gets a huge
laugh, with a smattering of applause, the fury of the laughter spilling over
into percussion, as though laughing were not enough of a response. This
reaction is not simple understanding on the part of the audience, nor is it
merely unbridled laughter; it is approval. In short, the issue of the ducks is
about showing up the problematic remainders in the mechanics of the story,

---

[39] If Izzard is playing with the narrative by means of the birds, he is not the first; indeed, the
biblical flood itself messes around with the Gilgamesh flood story, in which the dove does not
return but the raven does, see Stephanie Dalley (trans.), *Myths from Mesopotamia*, Oxford:
Oxford University Press, 2008 /1989.
[40] Here Izzard takes his cue not from Gilgamesh or Atrahasis, but from Philo's machinations:
Philo of Alexandria, *De animalibus* (trans. Abraham Terian), Chico, CA: Scholars Press, 1981.
For more discussion on Philo's politics of animals see David Clough, 'All God's Creatures:
Reading Genesis on Human and Non-human Animals', in Stephen C. Barton and David
Wilkinson (eds), *Reading Genesis After Darwin*, Oxford: Oxford University Press, 2009, pp.
145–62.

of lampooning the implied details that call the efficacy of the narrative into question, and the audience throws itself behind the idea. At the end of the dialogue, when God exclaims 'Oh, I forgot about ducks. Oh Shit' the 'shit', of course, performs a kind of double service, an exclamation on the one hand, and, on the other, a relabelling of the excrementality of the passage. In narrative terms, ducks are indeed yet more shit in the story insofar as they are an inassimilable trace that has nowhere else to go in the text. Like the menagerie's poo, they are a detail that builds up within the story, posing problems for its coherence.

Noah – Izzard's and the Bible's – is surrounded by waste, or, more specifically, by the troublesome remnants of all the systems that are breaking down around him. Poo is piling up inside the ark, the reminder of decay in the midst of life. Outside the ark, and contrary to virtually every picture of the tale ever sketched, the gopher wood is cutting through waters that are thick, presumably, with the bloated, swollen discoloured corpses of the entire human race – men, women and children (who else are we to presume is opening the umbrellas that James Mason cheerfully mentions at the outset?). These bodies, clinging to the surface of the water like the skin on old milk, represent another kind of waste: the battered remains of the old world order. Meanwhile, under the ark in the high seas, or else quacking about on their surface, are other remnants of the first creation, the wildlife that the flood cannot completely deal with, another sort of shit, another sort of inassimilable remainder. The whole of Noah's cosmos, really, is a big room for poo.

Noah as abject

And so we come back to abjection, literally the state of being sloughed off, which was developed into a complex critical tool by Julia Kristeva in her seminal work *Powers of Horror*. Put simply, for Kristeva, the abject comes to denote the space between subject and object. The abject is the taboo elements of the self, those aspects of our being that disturb or upset social order and convention. Prime examples are filth, dung, urine, vomit, the cadaver, spoilt food. ('When eyes see or the lips touch that skin on the surface of milk – harmless, thin as a sheet of cigarette paper, pitiful as a nail paring – I experience a gagging sensation and, still farther down, spasms in the stomach, the belly'.)[41] The abject is the response, both a fascination and a revulsion, to that which is neither 'I' nor 'not-I', and moreover, which as a result of its grotesque liminality troubles the boundaries that define me.

---

[41] Julia Kristeva, *Powers of Horror: An Essay on Abjection*, New York: Columbia University Press, 1982, pp. 2–3.

The critical significance of Kristeva's sense of the abject is that it confronts a system – be that a communal consensus, or a the notion of the self – with what that system must reject in order to function, but which it can never quite be rid of. The abject is in Kristeva's terms 'death infecting life'. The sight of a corpse or the smell of excrement is the reminder that embedded within social order is a decay that we must survive, a decay on which social order is predicated but which that order cannot fully assimilate.

> No, as in true theatre, without makeup or masks, refuse and corpses *show me* what I permanently thrust aside in order to live. These bodily fluids, this defilement, this shit are what life withstands, hardly and with difficulty, on the part of death. There [at the site of the abject], I am at the border of my condition as a living being. My body extricates itself, as being alive, from that border. Such wastes drop so that I might live, until, from loss to loss, nothing remains in me, and my entire body falls beyond the limit – *cadere*, cadaver. If dung signifies the other side of the border, the place where I am not and which permits me to be, the corpse, the most sickening of wastes, is a border that has encroached upon everything. It is no longer I who expel, 'I' is expelled. The border had become an object … It is death infecting life. Abject. It is something rejected from which one does not part … it is thus not lack of cleanliness or health that causes abjection but what disturbs identity, system, order.[42]

Limon, in his own musings on the interplay of abjection and comedy, simplifies abjection further: 'It may be summarized', he writes, 'as your failure to know what is inside of what'.[43] In other words, abjection is an expulsion that fails to create meaningful distance. Having sloughed off shit, allowed it to drop away from the body – social or personal – we come to a realization, however subtle and unconscious, that we are within a decaying order. We are ourselves liable at any moment to drop away from the order that defines us. The impossible, the absent, becomes recognized as an integral part of the order that rejects it, not reconciled to crap but attached to it only, and purely, through a politics of rejection. Kristeva writes it like so: '[T]hat subject, weary of fruitless attempts to identify with something on the outside, finds the impossible within; when it finds that the impossible constitutes its very being, that it *is* none other than the abject … it is revealed that all its objects are based merely on the inaugural loss that laid the foundations of its own being'.[44]

In the case of Noah's apocalypse, and in the case of Izzard's retelling of Genesis 6–9, this sense of the abject is not too difficult to detect. First, Noah

---

[42] Ibid., p. 3.
[43] Limon, *Stand-up Comedy*, p. 71.
[44] Kristeva, *Powers of Horror*, p. 4.

in his story world must face abjection, and, second, the text itself is subject to it, drowning in its own troublesome narrative remainders, remainders that threaten its own apparent sense of itself. In the ark, biblical Noah is at the border of his condition. Living, and a symbol of the surviving human, he is pressed by death on every side. Death is without the ark, colonizing the bloated corpses of every species, and so to find death within the ark too is overwhelming. Noah's ark is not a box full of life (as it is often construed), but a box that is slowly filling up with the remainder of death. This defilement, this shit is what Noah and every other shipboard life must withstand, hardly and with difficulty on the part of death. Noah's ark must survive the flood; Noah and co. must survive the ark (and somewhat oddly, all the faeces is the dirtiness that God's mission for purity has itself created). Thus the border of Noah's situation has become an object: a big room for poo. His shit is something rejected, but from which he does not part.[45] The flood is something survived, but which defines the fact of Noah's living.

On these terms, the ark's midden becomes a fitting metaphor for the biblical text itself. The very idea of mounting excrement on the ark is as troublesome for the text-as-system as the faeces is for the fictional Noah-as-being. As in all texts, semiotic refuse shows us what the text thrusts aside in order to function. These bodily fluids, the defiling ducks: this shit is what textual meaning withstands, hardly and with difficulty, on the part of incoherence. There, at the site of the interpolated poo room, the text is at the border of its condition as a functioning system. The border has become a metaphorical space of death infecting life, of unassimilable detail infecting the coherence of theological meaning. These difficult details – shit, ducks, and so on – are rejected (read: omitted) by the text, but the text does not part from them, it cannot do without them: all types of animal must board the ark, all must eat, all must survive, but the text cannot fully assimilate these details, it cannot account for the troubling they enact on the system. In Izzard's reading it is no longer Noah who expels, Noah is expelled. No, as in true theatre, stripped of makeup and masks, refuse and ducks *show me* what I permanently thrust aside in order to read.

In a 2009 interview with Frank Skinner for the BBC, Skinner (a professing Catholic) and Izzard (a self-designated 'spiritual atheist') engage in light-hearted debate around the problems and contradictions of religion. In that interview Izzard himself makes the point I have been drawing out of his younger self in 'Glorious', and in fittingly excremental terms. The

---

[45] And if Noah is at the border of his condition, so too is God's first creation: not obliterated, but pressed on every side by the threat of the waters. Noah's ark represents the border of that first creation's condition: a border that has become an object, a remnant of the judged 'shit' of that condemned world order. As a set of women, men and beasts, the ark represents the remainder dropped away from that first civilization. The ark-as-midden is thrust aside by the raging waters but not parted from them, not assimilated into their depth with every other woman, child, man and beast.

abject, he implies, is what must be thrust aside in order for humanity to read coherence in a theological system:

And then: 'God moves in mysterious ways, his wonders to perform', and I think that's a cover-all, that's a good line from the press department [laugh], isn't it? Well, in the end, just stuff happens ... why do we poo and pee? If you didn't have poo and pee, you wouldn't have poo and pee diseases [long, growing laugh]. Stick that in you're Catholicism [massive laugh]![46]

Flood/flush: Disposing of hysterical shit

It follows that the reasons why Izzard might tell biblical stories at all may be more intriguing still, and more intimately involved with the politics of abjection than the retellings themselves. It seems reasonably clear, the murky nature of divining motives notwithstanding, that Izzard invokes the biblical texts in *Glorious* precisely in order to dispose of them, to make them drop away – to turn the biblical corpus into a cadaver that can be thrust aside.

This imperative of Izzard's apparently stems from his longstanding suspicion of authoritative text, and of the Bible in particular. This is most easy to discern in two passages from *Eddie Izzard: Dress to Kill*, a book-length series of interviews put together by David Quantick at about the time of the 'Glorious' tour, in which Izzard speaks around a range of topics including religion and text:

> But there's no humour in religion and there's very little flexibility because the ideas were written down long ago and there is a strong resistance to them being updated ... It was 100 years later before they started writing these gospels. And why do the Apostles have English names?[47]

The problem of English names goes back to one of Izzard's earlier shows, 'Unrepeatable' (1995), where he talks about the oddness of extrapolating ancient names from biblical texts, changing them over time, and then reinserting them back into historical contexts when we think about religious history. The humour comes from the way in which religious ideas become naturalized in society through very everyday means, though, obviously, Izzard does not put it quite so dryly in practice: 'Matthew, Mark, Luke and John? Yes [in received pronunciation] and this our friend Jeremy, that's Sebastian, and ... Kenneth; we're *all* from Galilee'.[48] Does this sentiment link, perhaps, to that first passage of Izzard's flood narrative, where

---

[46] Skinner and Izzard, *Chain Reaction* Broadcast, 12:40–13:09.
[47] Quantick and Izzard, *Dress to Kill*, pp. 129–30
[48] Eddie Izzard, *Unrepeatable* (1994).

anachronism, religion and humour converge? Does the English name link, that is, to the exposing of the religious to the mundane that we get in the ark routine? Possibly. In both cases the anachronisms are put forth in such a way as to undermine abstract religious reverence by means of concrete observation, one paradigm calling time on another. In any case this same sentiment – a suspicion about the formality of writing – becomes more explicitly tied to texts in one of Izzard's later comments in the book, his last in fact:

> So in conclusion, I've just re-read everything that I've said here and I really do talk a lot of crap ... I've noticed that words are much more powerful when written down instead of just spoken. This may seem bloody obvious but I don't write my stand-up – I just talk it. So if you do come across a passage that you think is bollocks, just take it out and wear it as a hat.[49]

There are probably numerous intriguing interpretative possibilities that one could make of Izzard's suggestion that disagreeable texts should be re-appropriated as (testicular?) clothing, particularly given Izzard's own important advocacy of equal clothing rights and his experience as a proud TV. What I want to pick up on here, however, is a more general attitude in Izzard's comments: the idea that the formal power of the written text can, or even *should*, be re-appropriated by speech, and then put to other, more amusing, uses.

This same sense of disposing of texts and their claims to power emerges in parts of 'Glorious', if quite subtly. In the routine's encore, for example, during a section on his love of technology, Izzard advocates the throwing away of instruction manuals ('and the first thing you do if you have techno-joy is you get the instructions and [shouting now] *throw them out the window*!'). It is perhaps not entirely coincidence that a little over two minutes later, when Izzard has moved on to lampooning printers, the Book of Revelation doubles in passing as an instruction manual for the technology. Is the unspoken command the same – 'Throw it out the window!'? Izzard is standing in front of one, of course. The huge window that opens out on to deep space begs to be fed; we could shovel the wafer-thin pages of Revelation through it quite simply, grist to the apocalyptic sun's mill.

Returning to the flood routine, an altogether wetter kind of apocalypse, something similar seems to be in play, and much more obviously. By the end of the section on ducks, the biblical narrative, at least as far as Izzard has configured it, has ceased to be a story at all. The flood has become instead a theory to be debunked ('there is a huge problem with the whole

---

[49] Quantick and Izzard, *Dress to Kill*, p. 135.

flood *theory*'). It is all the foregoing details, problems and anachronisms (shit, ducks, evil geese, a flawed creation, and so forth) that come to be Izzard's primary weapons against the flood-as-theory. Izzard's rendition of the story appears to be an attempt to discard the authority of the text, to demonstrate as many holes in the story as it takes to make it drain away like so much floodwater. The failure of ducks to take over the world, the impossibility of an evil giraffe: these are daft notions, certainly, but Izzard's work is designed to point out that they are no dafter than the biblical material itself, and indicate the failure of that material as explanatory text.

The problem is that in order to discard of the biblical text in this comic way, Izzard and his audience must acknowledge, however tacitly, that the biblical tropes are familiar – they must laugh at them. There is a fascination with the biblical texts, a cultural fluency in them and with their claims to symbolic authority, and this makes the process of Izzard satirizing them humorous. In other words, in successfully mocking the Bible (in getting a laugh), Izzard does not simply degrade the Bible's social standing, but instead demonstrates its continued cultural currency by trading laughs against it. This dynamic is described by Susan Purdie in her book *Comedy: The Mastery of Discourse*, in which Purdie argues that joking is part of the very functioning of language. Laughter, she says, serves to re-inscribe symbolic law precisely by means of violating it:

> Our appreciative response [to a joke] does, of course (as Freud noted), assure the Teller that their joke works and that the often implicit transgression has been transmitted; but this response, and the transgression which it signifies, is itself received back by the Teller in a way that constitutes a further communication. In accepting the 'laugh' as a proper response to the trigger, the Teller confirms the transgressive thought as, nevertheless, constituting part of a meaningful discursive exchange, so that it is held within the bounds of the Law. That is possible because the originally understood intention to joke has produced the 'mistake' as marked; thus the proper rule which the error is agreed to breach is itself stated tacitly between Teller and audience ... this [joke telling] actually constitutes an observance, and not only a breach, of the Symbolic Law.[50]

In short, a joke may be communicative but laughter speaks too. And *what* laughter communicates is that a social law or expectation has been successfully transgressed. As Purdie writes, laughter is 'pleasurable identification with, and also fear of, power that is awarded and withdrawn'.[51] The significance of this is that a successful joke marks the transgression of

---

[50] Susan Purdie, *Comedy: The Mastery of Discourse*, Toronto: University of Toronto Press, 1993, p. 14.
[51] Ibid., p. 70.

social law as precisely that, as a sanctioned breach of convention. Thus jokes do not only overturn symbolic laws, they re-inscribe them too. Laughing at the Bible because of its claims as an exalted text does not lay it low, structurally speaking; laughter reinforces its supposedly exulted status, since we all know we are laughing at a self-conscious inversion of its usual status.

A double process of the kind described by Purdie is at work in Izzard's comedy. The laughed-at-text is at once pushed away by the force of derisive laughter and grounded as a cultural canon by the fact of it. Moreover, in laughing so freely at the quirks of these texts we come face to face with our own knowledge of, our own social reliance on, the text as a cultural canon: Noah and his menagerie, the names Matthew, Mark, Luke and John, the Bible as a pseudo user's guide, and so on. This is why the Bible's comedic outing is funny at all. Audiences, whatever the individual convictions of their members, hold on to the biblical texts by means of debunkings like Izzard's; a satirized Genesis is toured round the Western world for weeks on end; we pay exorbitant sums to download it on iTunes; we stack up the DVDs, we carefully label the elderly VHS. Izzard's audience, millions strong, hangs on to Genesis if only to revel in the process of trying to be rid of it. Derision of the social law re-inscribes it, albeit in sometimes surprising ways.

It might not just be Noah who has shit he cannot shift, then. And it might not just be the narrative of Genesis that is stuck with a mounting pile of implications it can neither be rid or nor fully assimilate. The Bible seems to be functioning within the routine a little like the shit in Noah's ark, or the troublesome Ducks in the biblical story. This is Bible-as-refuse. The failure (perceived or otherwise) of the biblical texts to account for human experience is a precondition of the modern secular subject to whom Izzard seems to address his routine.[52] Izzard and his audience are stuck with a text that exists as the troublesome remainder of a religious order that a modern, rational, 'spiritual atheist' sensitivity does not accept, but which it knows inside out. The Bible-as-refuse thus works in 'Glorious' as an object of fascinating revulsion, as a reminder of the origins of our cultural landscape. The familiarity of the audience with this rejected text is troublesome to a degree, and threatens to undermine certain (so-called) secular sensibilities

---

[52] Not all Izzard's audience can be modern secular subjects of course. Some (presumably) have faith but laugh along anyway, content in the knowledge that the *type* of Bible that Izzard lampoons holds no resemblance to theirs. My point is not whether or not the Bible is rejected (or not) by religious members of the audience laughing at Izzard's jokes, nor is it my argument that the Bible is incapable of coming out of the routine unscathed. Rather the issue is that a particular *mode* of biblical reading is being sent up with which everyone can identify; a particular *mode* of venerated cultural interaction with the Bible cannot come out of the routine unscathed. My point, then, is that Izzard's motivations seem very much geared to manipulating that biblical veneration and our often unspoken fear of it.

and identities (and this certainly seems true for Izzard himself). Like Noah, Izzard's and his audience are stuck with the cultural shit, the corpus turned corpse. The giant temple structure that dwarfs Izzard on stage is in a sense the audience's own 'big room for poo'. Comedy has become a site where that which troubles cultural systemicity and secular identity can be safely housed.

A dreck enflamed

On the face of it, abjection and the undermining of self-identity sound none too funny.[53] The problematic relationship between comedy and abjection stems from Kristeva's own uncertainty of when the abject is humorous and when it is not, and it is on this issue that Limon takes Kristeva to task.

> Discussing Dostoevsky's *The Possessed*, Kristeva asserts that 'Verkhovensky is abject because of his clamming, cunning appeal to ideas that no longer exist, from the moment when Prohibition (call it God) is lacking. Stavrogin is perhaps less so for his immoralism admits of laughter and refusal' (*PH*, 19). This would appear to set up a disjunction: abjection or laughter. Yet when Kristeva goes on to describe the modern world, what she finds is abjection and laughter undivided: 'The worlds of illusions, now dead and buried, have given way to our dreams and deleriums if not to politics or science – the religions of modern times. Lacking illusions, lacking shelter, today's universe is divided between boredom (increasingly anguished at the prospect of losing its resources, through depletion) or (when the spark of the symbolic is maintained and desire to speak explodes) abjection and piercing laughter' (133).[54]

'Laughter would seem to be an ambiguity within a pollution', Limon points out. But while Limon is doubtful that Kristeva has managed to get comedy and the politics of laughter quite right, he stresses that there is a way of reading Kristeva's work that allows us to be more precise about the lines of flight that run between the comedic and the abject.

The issue is the social context for abjection. Abjection is unfunny when the cosmic system that can deal with it is extant but failed, when God and the Law, enervated and atrophied, have themselves fallen away to leave only mounting sin in the world. But when only the *spark* of the symbolic is maintained, when the abject is put into a symbolic order to which we do not

---

[53] Though as Limon goes on to point out the 'presence of signification without meaning seems comic in general' (and the ahistorical, comic Bible reverberates around this sentiment); Limon, *Stand-up Comedy in Theory*, p. 73.

[54] Ibid., p. 74.

really aspire, things are very different. The abject dreck – sin, shit or death –
is enflamed by the faux-symbol, the faux-serious, and becomes funny. The
chief way, Limon suggests, that we slot ourselves into a symbolic frame to
which we do not seriously subscribe is by invoking the trope of the apocalyptic: a world's end where systems falter, and yet are preserved by means
of the telling of their own demise. Limon writes:

> Thus it become clear why laughter, disjoined from abjection generally,
> attaches to it when Kristeva comes to describe modernity: in our century,
> apocalyptic yet godless, abjection is a psychopathology that happens
> to be realistic. When you cannot abject your abjection, according to
> Kristeva, as filth or sin (the God of the Jews and Christians alike being
> dead) – when objectivity lingers in the world only as a measure of abjec-
> tivity – you laugh.[55]

In 'an apocalyptic yet godless age' abjection is dealt with not by means
of the fires that rise from the holy altar, but from the red-hot tendrils that
reach down from the apocalyptic sun, a symbol of a cosmic order but one
that entertains none of God's sobriety or fixity of meaning. An apocalypse is
a beyond, a Freudian state of bliss that waits behind the strictures of social
order – a laugh. In the modern age, and when apocalyptic sensibilities are
in play, abjection can be burnt up in ridicule just as easily as by ritual, then.
Kristeva's confusion of the comedic and the abject can thus be explained,
argues Limon, by seeing the apocalyptic as a necessary context for hilarious
abjection, a context that 'maintains the spark of the symbolic without
revelations … that retains symbolism without meaning – without, that is, a
serious paternal metaphor'.[56]

Not only does Izzard continually invoke a symbolic universe to which
he does not really subscribe, he is surrounded – socially and on stage
– by a peculiarly apocalyptic sensibility. Izzard creates, then, the ideal
environment for burning up social abjection with hilarity. And as we have
seen he seems to be rather good at it, espousing as he goes the kind of
modern outlook that Kristeva describes for us ('The worlds of illusions,
now dead and buried, have given way to our dreams and deliriums if not
to politics or science – the religions of modern times'). But, crucially, Izzard
deals with the mythical shadowy sides of the modern identity in such a way
that the undermining becomes funny. Izzard is an apocalyptic writer of
peculiar clarity, subjecting the biblical texts to their own apocalypse, and
taking our biblical affinities into the abyss along with them.

This brings us back, then, to the issue of biblical literacy and the
particular inadequacies in approach that have seemed to gained ground in

---

[55] Ibid., p. 74.
[56] Ibid.,

some quarters. What Izzard's work shows us is that the main problem with the discourse surrounding biblical illiteracy is not only that it may value the wrong questions, or prioritize particular forms of cultural engagement over other forms, but that it works on the basis of a particular cultural identity that has changed form – the Bible is no longer a social object, but a social abject. In short, many existing discussions on biblical literacy are not *about* biblical literacy, they are about preserving a serious paternal metaphor in the midst of a decentralizing of biblical dissemination. The biblical literature remains in social and cultural circulation, of course, but the metaphor is not as serious as once it was. Nowadays God is James Mason.

Bibliography

Avalos, Hector, 'In Praise of Biblical Illiteracy', *Bible and Interpretation*, April 2010, www.bibleinterp.com/articles/literate357930.shtml

BBC, 'Knowledge of Bible "in Decline"', *BBC*, 12 July 2009, http://news.bbc.co.uk/1/hi/england/wear/8146460.stm

Bergson, Henri, 'Laughter: An Essay on the Meaning of the Comic', in Wylie Cypher (ed.), *Comedy*, London: Johns Hopkins University Press, 1980.

Brisman, Leslie, *The Voice of Jacob: On the Composition of Genesis*, Bloomington: Indiana University Press, 1990.

CBLC, *The National Biblical Literacy Survey*, Briefing Sheet #2; www.dur.ac.uk/resources/cblc/BriefingSheet2.pdf [accessed 2 September 2014].

Clough, David, 'All God's Creatures: Reading Genesis on Human and Non-human Animals', in Stephen C. Barton and David Wilkinson (eds), *Reading Genesis After Darwin*, Oxford: Oxford University Press, 2009.

Dalley,Stephanie (trans.), *Myths from Mesopotamia*, Oxford: Oxford University Press, 2008 [1989].

Davies, Philip, 'Whose Bible? Anyone's?, *Bible and Interpretation*, July 2009, www.bibleinterp.com/opeds/whose.shtml

Douglas, Mary, *Implicit Meanings: Selected Essays in Anthropology* (2nd edn), New York: Taylor and Francis, 2002 [1975].

Findley, Timothy, *Not Wanted on the Voyage*, New York: Delacorte Press, 1984.

Freud, Sigmund, *The Standard Edition of the Complete Psychological Works of Sigmund Freud* (trans. James Strachey), London, Hogarth Press, 1953–74.

Hardiman, Clayton, 'Bible Literacy Slipping, Experts Say', Religious News Service/Associated Press, 5 October 2009; republished at http://home.snu.edu/~hculbert/literacy.htm [accessed 2 September 2014].

Hine, Iona, 'The Quest for Biblical Literacy: Curricula, Culture and Case Studies', paper at the Department of Biblical Studies' research seminar, Sheffield University, November 5, 2012.

—'Practicing Biblical Literacy: Case studies from the Sheffield Conference', in *Postscripts: The Journal of Sacred and Contemporary Worlds* (Special Issue: Biblical Literacy & the Curriculum, 2013).

Horton, Andrew, *Comedy/Cinema/Theory*, Berkeley: University of California, 1991.

Izzard, Eddie and David Quantick, *Eddie Izzard: Dress to Kill* (2nd edn), London: Virgin Books, 2000 [1998.

Kristeva, Julia, *Powers of Horror: An Essay on Abjection*, New York: Columbia University Press, 1982.

Limon, John, *Stand-up Comedy in Theory, or, Abjection in America*, Durham: Duke University Press, 2000.

Olson, Kirby, *Comedy After Postmodernism: Rereading Comedy from Edward Lear to Charles Willeford*, Texas: Texas University Press, 2001.

Origen, *Homilies on Genesis and Exodus* (trans. Ronald E. Heine), Washington: CUA Press.

Philo of Alexandria, *De animalibus* (trans. Abraham Terian), Chico, CA: Scholars Press, 1981.

Presbyterian Church (USA), 'Newly Revised Study Encourages Congregation-wide Reading of Bible in its Entirety as Bible Literacy in U.S. Sees Steep Decline', 24 August 2011; www.pcusa.org/news/2011/8/24/newly-revised-study-encourages-congregation-wide-r/ [accessed 2 September 2014].

Purdie, Susan, *Comedy: The Mastery of Discourse*, Toronto: University of Toronto Press, 1993.

Rosenberg, David and Harold Bloom, *The Book of J*, New York: Grove Weidenfeld, 1990.

Skinner, Frank and Izzard, Eddie, *Chain Reaction* interview, first broadcast BBC Radio 3, September 16, 2009, 18:30, www.bbc.co.uk/programmes/b00mkbyl [accessed 2 September 2014].

Smith, Greg, 'Declining Biblical Literacy' *Sowhatfaith.com*, 22 January 2012 http://sowhatfaith.com/2012/01/22/declining-biblical-literacy [accessed 2 September 2014].

Stott, Andrew, *Comedy*, London: Routledge, 2005.

Whedbee, J. William, *The Bible and the Comic Vision*, Minneapolis: Fortress Press, 2002 [1998].

Winterson, Jeanette, *Boating for Beginners*, London: Methuen, 1985.

INDEX

abject, the 173–4, 194–6, 202–5, 209–11 *see also* marginalization
Absolute Monarchist's Bible, the 24
Adam and Eve mythos, the 122, 126–31, 135, 138–9, 153–5
Admen and Eve (Edwards) 154
Africa 105 *see also* South Africa
agricultural labourers 49–50
AIDS 110
Alive-O series 12–14
Allen, Kate 112
America ix, 147–9, 150–1, 153–4
American Bible Society ix
Americanized Bible 147–9
Angelus bells 4
appropriation 115
Arguments for Socialism (Benn) 36–7
art 114 *see also* Street Art
attainment 53, 61
audiences 87–90, 192–3 *see also* male gaze, the
Augustine, Saint 63
authorial intent 168–9
authority 41
Avalos, Hector 23, 190–1

behaviour 53
    control *see* Levitical laws
Benedict XVI (pope) 131 *see also* Ratzinger, Joseph
Benn, Tony 36–42
    Arguments for Socialism 36–7
Bible, the
    Absolute Monarchist's Bible 24
    Americanized Bible 147–9
    Cultural Bible 29–36, 43
    Gove Bible 32–3, 34, 48
    Hebrew Bible 17

King James Bible *see* King James Bible
    Liberal Bible 24–9, 43
    mass production of 62
    names in 205–6
    Radical Bible 36–43
    translations of 10–11, 49–50, 54
Bible and its Influence, The (BLP) 58–9
Bible in Ireland, The (Ó Fearghail) 8
Bible Literacy Project (BLP) 5–6, 58–9
    Bible and its Influence, The 58–9
Bible Processional Ritual 13–14
Bible Society ix
biblical literacy
    decline of 43, 48–9, 63, 144–5, 166–7, 189–91 *see also* illiteracy
    definitions of ix–x, 5, 113, 144–6, 166n. 3
    Pass it On campaign and ix
Big Other, the 33–4
Bíobla Naofa (Holy Bible) 11
Blair, Tony 25–7, 32–3, 42
BLP (Bible Literacy Project) 5–6, 58–9
blurring of generations 123
Book of Durrow, the 9–10
Book of Kells, the 9
Bottomley, Peter 29
Brenner, Athalya 166, 183
Brueggemann, Walter 154
Bryant, Christopher 42
    Reclaiming the Ground: Christianity and Socialism 42
Bush, George W. 24

'Cabines, Les' (Pignon-Ernest) 107–8
Cameron, David ix, 27–8
capitalism 96
Cathach 8

Catholicism 4–5, 11, 132
    Madonna and 121–2, 125, 133
    salvation and 135–6
CBLC (Centre for Biblical Literacy
    and Communication) 190,
    191–2
Centre for Biblical Literacy and
    Communication (CBLC) 190,
    191–2
Christa (Sandys) 122
civil unrest 96
club scene, the 128
CODEC project 55
Coldplay: 'Us Against the World' 193
comedy 192–3, 194n. 27, 195, 207–10
    see also Izzard, Eddie
Comedy: The Mastery of Discourse
    (Purdie) 207–8
conscience 38–40
Coverdale, Miles 50–2
creation 6
Creation of Adam (Michelangelo)
    134
creative writing 64
critical literacy 145–6
C215 103–7
    'Prophétes' 107
Cultural Bible, the 29–36, 43
cultural literacy 60–2
culture 34, 71–2 see also popular
    culture
    art 114 see also Street Art
    comedy 192–3, 194n. 27, 195 see
        also Izzard, Eddie
    film ix, 86, 191
    internet, and the 120
    literature 57–9, 60–2 see also Girl
        with the Dragon Tattoo, The
    music see Madonna
    television ix, 191 see also Lost;
        Simpsons, The
    theatre 191
    video see Madonna

dance 128, 138
Daniel in the lion's den 38
David and Goliath 159–60
Davies, Philip 23
Dawkins, Richard 31, 32, 57–8

Dress to Kill (Izzard and Quantick)
    205–6
Dyson, Anne Haas 112

education 5–7, 11–20, 29, 56–65, 72
    Jeynes, William and 53
    textual bias and 119–20
Edwards, Katie B.: Admen and Eve
    154
examinations 15–19
excrement 198–204
exodus (from Egypt) 156–8

Faith47 100–3, 115
    'Freedom Charter, The' 99–101
    'Our Lady Poverty' 100
    'People Shall Share In The
        Country's Wealth, The' 102
    'Rest, Leisure and Recreation Shall
        Be the Right of All' 102
Faithless: God is a DJ 128
feminism 136 see also gender; women
film ix, 86
flood, the 196–202, 203–4, 206–7,
    208
France 105, 107–8
Francis, Lesley 53
Freedom Charter, The 100–2
'Freedom Charter, The' (Faith47)
    99–101
Froetschel, Susan 60–1

Gallup polls 55
Gangnam Style (Psy) 120
Garden of Eden, the 153–5
gender 131–9, 154–5, 172 see also
    masculinity; women
Genesis creation story 6
'Girl Gone Wild' (song) (Madonna)
    121, 124–5
Girl Gone Wild (video) (Madonna)
    121, 122–4
    masculine/feminine 131–9
    redemption 135–9
    transgression 124–31
Girl with the Dragon Tattoo, The
    (Larsson) 168–70
    Levitical laws and 170–82
    violence and 171–3, 175–81

'God is a DJ' (Faithless) 128
'God is a DJ' (P!nk) 128–9
God's Gym (Moore) 137
Gove, Michael 32–3, 34, 72
Gove Bible, the 32–3, 34, 48
graffiti *see* Street Art
Gray, Jonathan 149
Great Emergence, The (Tickle) 95–6
Groening, Matt 149, 152
Guémy, Christian *see* C215
Guide Through the New Testament, A (Marshall) 119
Guidelines for Teachers 16–17
gun imagery 137
Gutt, Ernst-August 60

Hallett, Nicky 61
Hebrew Bible 17
Heit, Jamey 149–50, 156
heritage 31, 34
Hirsch, E. D. 60
HIV 110
Holmes, Margaret 'Didi' 38–9
hyper-consciousness 151
hypermasculinity 130, 136, 137

illiteracy 54–5, 71–2 *see also* biblical literacy, decline
Illuminated manuscripts 8–9
immigration 105
incorporated memory 124
individual conscience 38–40
Ingulsrud, John E. 112
inscribed memory 124
internet, the 120–1, 139–40 *see also* technology
Ireland 3–4, 19
    alcohol and 4
    Angelus bells and 4
    Bible use in 7–11
    Catholicism and 4–5, 11
    education and 5–7, 11–20
    monasteries and 8–9
    primary education in 12–14, 19
    secondary education in 14–19
Izzard, Eddie 188, 193, 196, 204–5, 210
    Dress to Kill 205–6
    Glorious tour 188–9, 193–4, 206

names and 205–6
Noah and 196–202, 204, 206–7, 208

Jerome's Vulgate 10
Jeynes, William 52–3, 61

Kennedy, Martin 12
King James Bible, the 30–6, 57, 72 *see also* Precious Light
    as national icon 48
King James Bible Trust, the 30–1
knowable, the 63
knowledge 145–6
Korzybski, Alfred 62–3
Kristeva, Julia 209–10
    Powers of Horror 202–3

Labour Party, the 41–2
Lammy, David 28
Larrson, Steig: *Girl with the Dragon Tattoo, The see Girl with the Dragon Tattoo, The*
Latin 10, 11
Leabhar Breac 10
Levellers, the 36
Levitical laws 170–1
    community protection and 181–2
    marginalization and 173–82
    violence and 171–3, 175–81
Liberal Bible, the 24–9, 43
Like a Prayer (Madonna) 122
Like a Virgin (Madonna) 122
Limon, John 203, 209–10
    Stand-up Comedy in Theory 192, 195–6
literacy 120 *see also* biblical literacy
    cultural literacy 60–2
    media literacy 149
    studies 112–13
literature 57–9, 60–2 see also *Girl with the Dragon Tattoo, The*
Live to Tell (Madonna) 121, 122
Lost 73–5, 86–90
    explicit biblical allusion in 76–80, 87
    fan communities and 87–90
    implicit biblical allusion in 80–7
    literature and 75, 88n. 52

marketing and 85–6
miracles in 84
names in 75–6, 80–2
numbers in 75, 76, 79, 81
philosophy and 76–6
themes of 75, 84

Mach, David 114–15
    Precious Light 114
Madonna 121
    'Girl Gone Wild' (song) 121, 124–5
    Girl Gone Wild (video) 121–39
    gun imagery and 137
    Like a Prayer 122
    Like a Virgin 122
    Live to Tell 121, 122
    sexuality and 122, 125–7, 133,
        134, 135, 139
male gaze, the 130, 138
manga 112
marginalization 173–82
marriage 131, 155
    same–sex 28–9
Marshall, Celia B.: Guide Through the
    New Testament, A 119
Martin, Dale B.: Pedagogy of the Bible
    120
masculinity 129–30, 137, 138–9 see
    also gender
media literacy 149
memory 123–4
Michelangelo: Creation of Adam 134
monasteries 8
Moore, Stephen: God's Gym 137
moral action 50–2
Motion, Andrew 166

names 75–6, 80–2, 205–6
National Catechetical Programme 12
national icons 48
nationalism 29, 32
New Testament, the 10
Noah 196–202, 203–4, 206–7, 208
Northcote 128

Ó Domhnail, Uilliam 10
Ó Fearghail, Fergus: Bible in Ireland,
    The 8
oral literacy 63

Origen 199
Original Sin 40–1
'Our Lady Poverty' (Faith47) 100

paradigm shifts 95–6
Pass it On campaign ix
Patrick, Saint 8
Pedagogy of the Bible (Martin) 120
Pendell, Thomas Roy 54
'People Shall Share In The Country's
    Wealth, The' (Faith47) 102
Perkins, Toby 28
personal Bible reading 53
phallocentrism 132
Phillips, Sarah 56–7
Pignon–Ernest, Ernest 107–11
    'Cabines, Les' 107–8
    'South African Piéta' 110–11
    'Soweto' 109
P!nk: God is a DJ 128–9
political discourse 24
    authority and 41
    Benn, Tony and 36–42
    Blair, Tony and 25–7, 32–3, 42
    Bottomley, Peter and 29
    Bush, George W. and 24
    Cameron, David and 27–8
    Cultural Bible, and 29–36, 43
    Dawkins, Richard and 31, 32
    Gove, Michael and 32–3, 34
    King Kames Bible, and 30–6
    Labour Party, the 41–2
    Lammy, David and 28
    Liberal Bible, and 24–9, 43
    Perkins, Toby and 28
    Radical Bible, and 36–43
    socialism and 36–7, 42
    Thatcher, Margaret and 25, 29–30,
        40–1
popular culture ix, 73, 111–12, 165–8,
    183
    art 114 see also Street Art
    comedy 192–3, 194n. 27, 195 see
        also Izzard, Eddie
    exodus (from Egypt) and 156
    film 86, 191
    internet, and the 120
    literature 57–9, 60–2 see also Girl
        with the Dragon Tattoo, The

music see Madonna
    religious education and 167–8
    television 191 see Lost and
        Simpsons, The
    theatre 191
    video see Madonna
postmodernism 35–6, 114–15, 150–2
Powers of Horror (Kristeva, Julia)
    202–3
Precious Light (Mach, David) 114
printing 62, 96
'Prophétes' (C215) 107
protest 96
Protestantism 11
Prothero, Stephen 111, 144–5
Psalter of St Columba 8
Psy: Gangnam Style 120
Purdie, Susan: Comedy: The Mastery
    of Discourse 207–8

Quantick, David: Dress to Kill
    205–6
Quest of the Historical Jesus, The
    (Schweitzer) 47

Radical Bible, the 36–42
Ratzinger, Joseph 131, 132, 138
Reclaiming the Ground: Christianity
    and Socialism (Bryant) 42
Reformation, the 95–6
religious education 5–7, 11–20, 56–65,
    72 see also education
    Jeynes, William and 53
    popular culture and 167–8
    Prothero, Stephen and 111, 144–5
    rote learning 119
    textual bias and 119–20
'Rest, Leisure and Recreation Shall
    Be the Right of All' (Faith47)
    102
rote learning 119
Ruether, Rosemary Radford 136

same-sex marriage 28–9
Sandys, Edwina: Christa 122
satire 149–50, 151–2, 157
Schweitzer, Albert: Quest of the
    Historical Jesus, The 47
science 62–3

scriptural literacy 52
sexuality
    Levitical laws and 172, 178–80
    Madonna and 122, 125–7, 133,
        134, 135, 139
    Simpsons, The and 154–5
Sheehan, Jonathan 29
Simpsons, The 64, 143, 146–7
    Americanized Bible and 147–9
    postmodernism and 150–2
    satire and 149–50, 151–2, 157
    'Simpsons Bible Stories' (episode)
        152–60
Simpsons and Philosophy, The (Irwin,
    Conard and Skoble) 144
'Simpsons Bible Stories' (episode)
    152–60
sin 126 see also Original Sin
Sister Act (1992) 133
socialism and 36–7, 40
Solomon 158
South Africa 100–3, 109–11
'South African Piéta' (Pignon-Ernest)
    110–11
'Soweto' (Pignon-Ernest) 109
Stand-up Comedy in Theory (Limon)
    192, 195–6
stories 13, 18
Street Art 95, 96–8, 113–16
    C215 103–7
    Faith47 100–3
    Pigeon–Ernest, Ernest 107–11
surveys 5, 54–5, 190–2

technology 96, 111–12 see also
    internet, the
television ix, 191 see also Lost;
    Simpsons, The
texts 119–20, 206 see also literature
textus Receptus 10
Thatcher, Margaret 25, 29–30, 40–1
theatre 191
Thomas Aquinas, Saint 132
Tickle, Phyllis: Great Emergence, The
    95–6
Tighe, Carl 64–5
Towards a Policy on RE in
    Post-Primary Schools 14
translations 10–11, 49–50, 54

Urbach, Jennifer 112
urban living 96 *see also* Street Art
'Us Against the World' (Coldplay) 193

Vatican, the 121–2
violence 110, 132, 158, 170–3, 175–81
visual images 120–1

Weinfeld, Moshe 123
women 110, 125–31, 136–8, 155,
    175–82 *see also* gender;
    marginalization
written texts 206 *see also* literature

Žižek, Slavoj 33–4